KT-367-989

Sport and the Media: Managing the Nexus

Withdrawn

ACCESSION No. T055861

CLASS No. 796.01

Books in the Sport Management Series

Sport Governance
Russell Hoye and Graham Cuskelly

Sport and the Media
Matthew Nicholson

Sport Funding and Finance
Bob Stewart

Managing People in Sport Organizations
Tracy Taylor, Alison J. Doherty and Peter McGraw

Sport and the Media: Managing the Nexus

Matthew Nicholson
Senior Lecturer in Sport Management
School of Sport, Tourism and Hospitality Management
La Trobe University
Victoria, Australia

AMSTERDAM • BOSTON • HEIDELBERG • LONDON • NEW YORK • OXFORD
PARIS • SAN DIEGO • SAN FRANCISCO • SINGAPORE • SYDNEY • TOKYO

ELSEVIER

Linacre House, Jordan Hill, Oxford OX2 8DP, UK
30 Corporate Drive, Suite 400, Burlington, MA 01803, USA

Copyright © 2007

No part of this publication may be reproduced, stored in a retrieval system
or transmitted in any form or by any means electronic, mechanical, photocopying,
recording or otherwise without the prior written permission of the publisher

Permissions may be sought directly from Elsevier's Science & Technology Rights
Department in Oxford, UK: phone (+44) (0) 1865 843830; fax (+44) (0) 1865 853333;
email: permissions@elsevier.com. Alternatively you can submit your request online by
visiting the Elsevier web site at http://elsevier.com/locate/permissions, and selecting
Obtaining permission to use Elsevier material

Notice
No responsibility is assumed by the publisher for any injury and/or damage to persons
or property as a matter of products liability, negligence or otherwise, or from any use or
operation of any methods, products, instructions or ideas contained in the material herein.
Because of rapid advances in the medical sciences, in particular, independent verification
of diagnoses and drug dosages should be made

British Library Cataloguing in Publication Data
A catalogue record for this book is available from the British Library

Library of Congress Control Number:
A catalogue record for this book is available from the Library of Congress

ISBN-10: 0 7506 8109 8
ISBN-13: 978 0 7506 8109 4

For information on all publications visit our web site at
http://books.elsevier.com

Trademarks/Registered Trademarks

All brand names mentioned in this book are protected by their respective trademarks
and are acknowledged

Typeset by Charon Tec Ltd (A Macmillan Company), Chennai, India
www.charontec.com

Transferred to Digital Printing 2009

Working together to grow
libraries in developing countries

www.elsevier.com | www.bookaid.org | www.sabre.org

ELSEVIER   BOOK AID
International   Sabre Foundation

Content

v

Contents

Contents

Series Editor

Dr Russell Hoye is Senior Lecturer in Sport Management, School of Sport, Tourism and Hospitality Management, La Trobe University, Victoria, Australia.

Russell has taught sport management courses since 1993 in Australia at La Trobe University, Griffith University and Victoria University as well the University of Hong Kong and Tsinghua University in China. His main teaching areas are sport management, organizational behaviour, sport policy and sport governance. Russell serves as the Coordinator of Honours and Postgraduate Studies for the School of Sport, Tourism and Hospitality Management at La Trobe University. He is a former Board Member of the Australian and New Zealand Association for Leisure Studies (ANZALS) and a current Board Member of the Sport Management Association of Australia and New Zealand (SMAANZ). He was the Guest Editor for the inaugural special issue of *Sport Management Review* on professional sport in Australia and New Zealand published in 2005.

Russell's areas of expertise include corporate governance, organizational behaviour, volunteer management and public sector reform within the sport industry. He has acted as a consultant for the Australian Sports Commission, Sport and Recreation Victoria and a number of local government and non-profit organizations. His research interests focus on examining how governance is enacted with sport organizations and how volunteers engage with and are managed by sport organizations. He has published articles on these topics in journals such as *Nonprofit Management and Leadership*, *Sport Management Review*, *European Sport Management Quarterly*, *Society and Leisure*, *International Gambling Studies*, *Third Sector Review*, *Sporting Traditions*, *Managing Leisure*, *Football Studies*, *Annals of Leisure Research* and the *Australian Journal on Volunteering*.

Sport Management Series Preface

Many millions of people around the globe are employed in sport organizations in areas as diverse as event management, broadcasting, venue management, marketing, professional sport and coaching as well as in allied industries such as sporting equipment manufacturing, sporting footwear and apparel, and retail. At the elite level, sport has moved from being an amateur pastime to a significant industry. The growth and professionalization of sport has driven changes in the consumption and production of sport and in the management of sporting organizations at all levels of sport. Managing sport organizations at the start of the twenty-first century involves the application of techniques and strategies evident in the majority of modern business, government and non-profit organizations.

The *Sport Management Series* provides a superb range of texts for the common subjects in sport business and management courses. They provide essential resources for academics, students and managers, and are international in scope. Supported by excellent case studies, useful study questions, further reading lists, lists of websites and supplementary online materials such as case study questions and PowerPoint slides, the series represents a consistent, planned and targeted approach which:

- provides a high-quality, accessible and affordable portfolio of titles which match management development needs through various stages;
- prioritizes the publication of texts where there are current gaps in the market, or where current provision is unsatisfactory;
- develops a portfolio of both practical and stimulating texts in all areas of sport management.

The *Sport Management Series* is the first of its kind, and as such is recognized as being of consistent high quality and will quickly become the series of first choice for academics, students and managers.

Preface

We live in a world immersed in sport media, yet it has become so much part of our daily lives that it often goes unnoticed. Sport media has become an important part of the ways in which people and nations construct individual and collective identities, as well as understand their place in the world, yet it is often left unquestioned. This book was borne out of a desire to write a text for students that provided a detailed examination of sport and the media, as well as provided them with the skills to engage in sport media management. It is hoped that through reading the book the world of sport media will not only be noticed, but understood, and that questions will not only be asked, but answered.

The book has primarily been written for first and second year university students studying sport management and sport studies courses. It is particularly suited to students studying sport management within business-focused courses, as well as students studying human movement or physical education courses who require a more detailed understanding of the skills required to manage the media in a variety of sport contexts. The book is divided into four parts. The first part sets the foundations, the second explores the contexts of the nexus, the third examines the skills of sport media management, while the fourth part provides an analysis of possible futures.

To assist students, teachers, instructors, tutors and lecturers, all chapters include a set of objectives, an overview of core principles and practices, and a set of review questions or suggested exercises. In many chapters the intention of the review questions and exercises is to encourage students to become actively involved. For example, Chapter 9 that deals with media communications asks the students to acquire a media release from a sport organization, evaluate it and then write their own. It is hoped that through these processes students will begin testing their knowledge and skills. In addition to the objectives, overviews and review questions, Chapters 2 through 12 each contain two cases that help illustrate the key concepts or provide jumping off points for further discussion.

I would like to thank Fran Ford, Associate Editor at Elsevier Butterworth-Heinemann, for her support and encouragement from the book's conception through to its publication and Dr Russell Hoye, Series Editor, for his valuable comments and unwavering attention to detail, not to mention his friendship. My thanks also go to Associate Professor Aaron Smith for his insightful comments and feedback on drafts of the book and to Associate Professor Bob Stewart, who many years ago encouraged me to teach sport and the media. Over the years my students have allowed me the opportunity to test my ideas and teaching methods and indulge a passion for sport and the media. I deeply appreciate their input and inspiration. I would also like to thank my friends at Graaf, for their friendship, support and a place to clear my head. Finally, my thanks go to my family and to Leverne and Indigo in particular. Without their support, patience and love this book simply wouldn't have been possible.

**PART
ONE**

Sport Media
Foundations

1

Sport and the media: a defining relationship

Overview

This chapter provides an overview of the nexus between the sport and media industries, and outlines why sport and the media is an important field of study. It also defines sport, the media and the sport media nexus. The study of sport and the media is placed within a management context in order to explain its relevance to students of sport management, as well as sport managers and administrators in professional settings. This chapter also discusses the core drivers and major features of the sport media nexus in order to context-ualize the material in subsequent chapters. Finally, this chapter provides an outline of the structure of the book.

After completing this chapter the reader should be able to:

■ Identify the core features of the sport media nexus.
■ Explain the core features of the sport media nexus and what underpins the relationship between the sport and media industries.
■ Understand the environment in which sport media is produced and consumed.
■ Identify and explain the impact of each core driver of the sport media nexus.

Defining sport and the media

Prior to discussing the sport media nexus in detail, it is important to clarify what is meant by the terms sport and media. Although sport seems a superficially simple concept, it can be difficult for players, policy makers, managers, marketers and media alike to define. Depending on the context, sport might be interpreted in different ways, which will in turn influence whether and how it is mediated. Sport is best understood as having three core dimensions (Guttmann, 1978). First, it has a physical dimension. Second, it is competitive. Third and finally, it must be structured and rule bound. These dimensions might appear self-evident, but are worth noting because mediated sport is almost exclusively highly structured, highly competitive and very physical. In fact, sports such as football, which emphasize, if not exaggerate sport's tripartite definition, tend to dominate media coverage generally and television coverage in particular. On the other hand, sport that has low or non-existent levels of competition, structure and physicality are typically not attractive media products.

Figure 1.1 graphically represents a sport typology, which illustrates different types of sport (Stewart, Nicholson, Smith & Westerbeek, 2004). Spontaneous sport includes 'pick-up' sport that occurs by chance, which is often formalized as recreational sport. Recreational sport also includes extreme sport activities, as well as informal exercise. Exercise sport typically occurs in formalized settings, such an aerobics class or a gym workout. These first three categories, represented at the bottom and sides of Figure 1.1 are minor components of the sport media nexus. By contrast, competitive sport, which includes competitions below the elite level, receives media coverage and uses it to increase participation and financial capacity. This category includes sport played by amateurs at the community level through to high level school and University (college) sport. The final category, elite sport, is a major player in the sport media nexus. It comprises professional and semi-professional competitions and major events, from state and national championships through to the Olympic Games and FIFA (Federation Internationale de Football Association) World Cup.

The final two categories of competitive and elite sport can be segmented further to demonstrate various tiers of activity, which are graphically represented in Figure 1.2. Figure 1.2 illustrates that competitive and elite sport cover the spectrum from local community level sport through to major global events. However, the diagram should not be interpreted as a hierarchical model of media interest or influence, as national leagues are often the most valuable sport media properties in the world.

Definitions of media are likely to make people think of vastly different and distinct occupations, people, organizations, texts and artefacts. The word media has come to mean a variety of things, in a similar fashion to sport, but in far greater complexity and breadth. According to Briggs and Burke (2005) ancient Greeks and Romans considered the study of oral and written

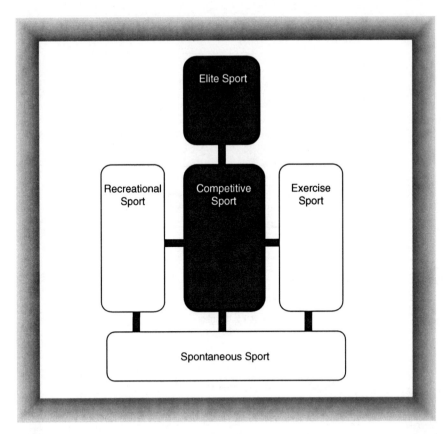

Figure 1.1 Sport Typology (Adapted from Stewart, Nicholson, Smith & Westerbeek, 2004)

communication important, as did scholars during the Middle Ages and the Renaissance. It was not until the 1920s, however, that people referred to the concept of 'the media'.

In contemporary usage the term media typically applies to two separate yet related elements. First, media refers to the means of mass communication, such as television, radio, newspapers or the Internet. The various forms of communication and its types are illustrated in Figure 1.3. Importantly, within one form, such as television, there are many different types, such as commercial, public, independent and community. Furthermore, these types also have various levels. For example, a commercial media organization might own national television networks through to local stations that service a city or town. Second, media refers to those people employed within an organization such as a television station or newspaper, such as journalists and editors.

It is important to note that these two definitions span a variety of meanings that are context specific. In reference to broadcasting regulation the media might be interpreted as the entire industry, which in turn might be national or global. In a discussion focusing on mergers and acquisitions, media might refer to a transnational corporation such as the Walt Disney Company. If the

BISHOP BURTON COLLEGE

Figure 1.2 Elite and Competitive Sport Levels

issue relates to the sale of broadcast rights, media might refer to different forms such as pay television, free-to-air television or the Internet. Referring to the way in which a telecast of a game uses metaphors of war, the media might refer to the commentators. Finally, if the issue relates to the reporting of a scandal or crisis, media might refer to the specific article or broadcast in which it was first announced.

The nexus

The word nexus has its etymological roots in Latin and is a derivation of the word *nectere*, which means to bind. In essence a nexus is a connection, bond

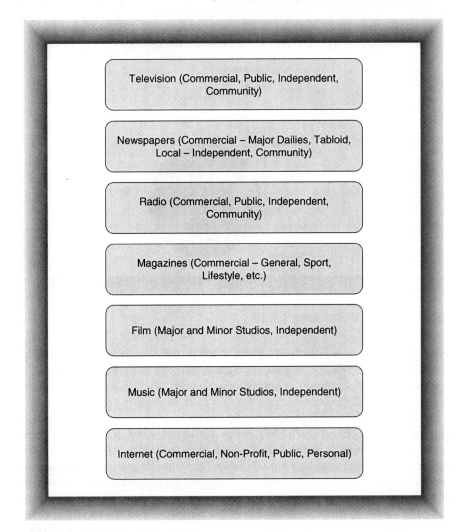

Television (Commercial, Public, Independent, Community)

Newspapers (Commercial – Major Dailies, Tabloid, Local – Independent, Community)

Radio (Commercial, Public, Independent, Community)

Magazines (Commercial – General, Sport, Lifestyle, etc.)

Film (Major and Minor Studios, Independent)

Music (Major and Minor Studios, Independent)

Internet (Commercial, Non-Profit, Public, Personal)

Figure 1.3 Media Forms and Types

or tie between two or more things. The use of the word nexus in the subtitle of this book is deliberate. It is meant to signal that sport and the media are not two separate industries that have been juxtaposed coincidently. Rather, their evolution, particularly throughout the twentieth century, has resulted in them being inextricably bound together. Furthermore, the word nexus can refer to the core or centre. In this respect the use of the word nexus is meant to illustrate that the relationship between sport and the media is at the core of contemporary sport. Whether in reference to the way in which children are socialized through sport, the power of player associations and unions, or the use of talent identification programmes to foster elite development, the relationship between sport and the media is likely to reside at the very centre of the issue or problem. Thus, the sport media nexus refers to the relationship between sport and the media industry generally, the relationship between

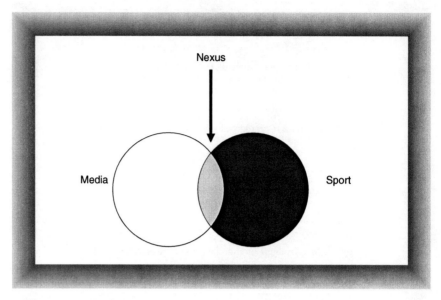

Figure 1.4 Sport Media Nexus I

sport and specific media institutions such as television, the relationship between sport and media employees such as journalists and finally, the ways in which sport is presented in specific media texts, such as a radio broadcast or newspaper article.

Figure 1.4 represents the sport media nexus in its most basic form. In this diagram, the sport and media industries are represented as two equal partners and the nexus is the point at which they intersect. Although simple, Figure 1.4 also illustrates that not all of sport is part of the nexus. Rather, a proportion of sport is mediated. Similarly, not all media is sport related. However, this diagram does not represent the reality of much elite, professional and competitive sport, nor does it represent the importance of the media in daily sport consumption. In this respect the nexus is more accurately represented in Figure 1.5. Elite and professional sport is enveloped by the media. In this case sport might accurately be described as media sport, because without the nexus or bond between the two, the product would not exist. Consumers of sport must necessarily consume a mediated product. As the sport media nexus develops, the amount of sport consumed by the media increases (the circles in Figure 1.4 move closer together), as does the commercial importance of sport to the media (the black circle in Figure 1.5 grows larger).

Sport media saturation

Every 4 years the world stops to watch football teams compete for a trophy called the World Cup. A cumulative total of 28,800 million people throughout 213 countries watched the 2002 tournament in Korea and Japan. The

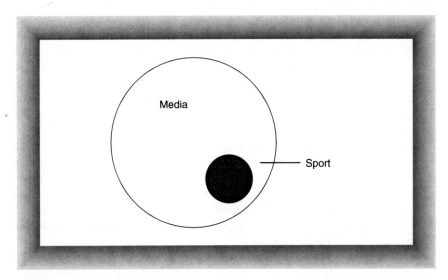

Figure 1.5 Sport Media Nexus II

world also tunes in on a 4-year cycle to watch athletes strive to go higher, faster and stronger at the summer and winter Olympic Games, with approximately 36 and 20 million respective cumulative viewing hours of television coverage available internationally. These mega-events compete for the attention of media consumers with yearlong sport circuits, such as Formula One Racing, the Professional Golfers' Association (PGA) European Tour and the Sony Ericsson Women's Tennis Association (WTA) Tour. The Formula One Racing circuit alone was watched in 2005 by a global audience in excess of 800 million people. These events and circuits, in turn, compete with national sport competitions that take place over the course of a season, with games played between one and four times per week. In the United States of America the nation stops every year for the Super Bowl, the championship game of the National Football League, when families and friends gather around television sets for what equates to a secular holiday. In 2006, the television audience was large enough for the television broadcaster to command US $2.5 million for each 30-second block of advertising time.

It is clear from the examples above that there are large numbers of people watching sport on television, that there is a significant amount of sport broadcast on television and that televised sport is a primary vehicle for advertising. However, it is not only the major sport events and leagues that are broadcast by television, and television is not the only media form that is saturated by sport. In fact, from even a cursory examination of the media available in a single city or nation, it is readily apparent that sport has a significant presence across all media forms. Moreover, the media coverage of sport saturates daily life (Rowe, 1999), a phenomenon clearly illustrated by the way in which News Corporation sees itself in the following annual report excerpt:

> Virtually every minute of the day, in every time zone on the planet, people are watching, reading and interacting with our products. We're reaching

people from the moment they wake up until they fall asleep. We give them their morning weather and traffic reports through our television outlets around the world. We enlighten and entertain them with such newspapers as *The New York Post* and *The Times* as they have breakfast, or take the train to work. We update their stock prices and give them the world's biggest news stories every day through such news channels as FOX or Sky News. When they shop for groceries after work, they use our SmartSource coupons to cut their family's food bill. And when they get home in the evening, we're there to entertain them with compelling first-run entertainment on FOX or the day's biggest game on our broadcast, satellite and cable networks. Or the best movies from Twentieth Century Fox Film if they want to see a first run movie. Before going to bed, we give them the latest news, and then they can crawl into bed with one of our best-selling novels from HarperCollins (News Corporation, 1999; cited in Law, Harvey & Kemp, 2002).

The relationship between sport and the media has become the defining commercial and cultural connection for both industries at the beginning of the twenty-first century. The media has transformed sport from an amateur pursuit into a hyper-commercialized industry, while sport has delivered massive audiences and advertising revenues to the media. The coverage of sport on television in particular has created a product to be consumed by audiences, sold by clubs and leagues, bought and sold by media organizations and manipulated by advertisers.

Throughout the latter half of the twentieth century and into the twenty-first, the relationship between the media and sport industries intensified, to the point that they have become so entwined it is difficult to determine where one ends and the other begins. In an attempt to identify this process, as well as inform public and academic discourse, authors have combined the words sport and media in a variety of permutations. The common theme has been the creation of a new word or phrase that is representative of the nexus between these two commercial industries. In 1980s and 1990s, the sport/media complex and the media/sport production complex were both used to frame academic analyses of sport and the media (Jhally, 1984, 1989; Maguire, 1993; Maguire, 1999). At the end of the twentieth century an edited collection was published with the title *MediaSport* (Wenner, 1998). Whether the words are juxtaposed, jammed together to create a new word or separated by 'and the', it is clear that there is an imperative to characterize the process by which 'sports, and the discourses that surround them' became, as Boyd (1997:ix) suggested, 'one of the master narratives of twentieth-century culture'.

The importance of this master narrative has been enhanced by the growing globalization of media corporations and the use of sport to consolidate established markets and exploit new ones, as well as the ways in which mediated sport is used to construct individual and collective identities. The extent to which this master narrative has become an assumed part of global, cultural, commercial and personal discourses is illustrated by Rowe's (1999:8) assertion that 'a trained capacity to decode sports texts and to detect the forms of ideological deployment of sport in the media is, irrespective of cultural taste, a crucial skill', and 'an important aspect of a fully realized cultural citizen-ship'. In other words, the mediation of sport has become so pervasive that in order to live within the cultural and social world you must necessarily be able to understand the sport media nexus.

Managing the nexus

Over the course of the twentieth-century sport was transformed from a typ-ically ad hoc unregulated amateur activity to one driven by professional standards and accountability at all levels. This transformation has resulted in the proliferation of and demand for sport management training in related areas such as human resource management, financial management, event management and organizational behaviour. The broad transformation from amateur to professional and the need for professional sport management, par-ticularly at the elite or major league level, is directly related to the extent and breadth of the sport media nexus. Whereas sport organizations were once guarded and cautious about the role of the media and the impact that broad-casting might have on live attendance, they are now engaged in a media part-nership that delivers a majority of revenue through broadcast rights and associated sponsorships. The corollary of the importance and significance of the nexus is that it requires management. This notion is compounded by the competitiveness of the media industry generally and the sport media indus-try more specifically. An examination of a major daily newspaper will reveal that national, state and local governments, entertainers from television, film and music, business corporations, tourism destinations, not to mention sport stars, teams and leagues are some of the people and institutions vying for media coverage. Media space, despite the proliferation of types and forms, is limited. As such it is a valuable commodity because it can generate awareness and revenue, as well as confer status, prestige and credibility.

Without athletes sport cannot exist. Hence, player management has expanded exponentially in professional and elite sport since the 1960s in par-ticular. Player welfare programmes have been developed, as have talent identification schemes, elite pathways, player associations and unions. In other words, the importance of players and athletes to the sport enterprise has been matched by administrative and management systems designed to protect and enhance sport as a product. It is too much to say that without the media sport cannot exist. In this respect, those who play the game are more important than those who watch or report on it. However, it is clear that pro-fessional sport in particular would cease to exist in its current form without the media. Thus, like the development of player management, the manage-ment of the media also requires systems and strategies to ensure the success of sport organizations.

Sport teams are not only competing against other teams for coverage, but against other sports, against other leisure options and against a myriad of other newsworthy events and announcements. This competitive environment

11

cannot be left to chance, whereby a sport team or league conducts its business in the hope that it will receive media coverage. Rather, like other aspects of the sport business, where individuals, teams and leagues seek to obtain a competitive advantage, media coverage is enhanced by effective planning and management.

The media coverage that a sport receives is directly proportional to the amount of revenue that individuals and organizations are able to generate from its broadcast or reporting. A large organization, such as the National Football League in the United States of America is able to generate massive revenues through broadcast rights fees because of the audiences it is able to deliver to media organizations. It is also able to generate revenue through commercial sponsorship, which is proportional to the amount of media coverage. Throughout the last quarter of the twentieth century and the early part of the twenty-first professional sport in particular has become dependent on the media. It is clear that in order to be successful in the competitive arena of professional sport, a team, league or event must not only have official media partners, but must also be able to attract general media coverage that illustrates a broad interest or awareness among the population. In order to remain successful, teams, leagues and events must manage their ongoing relationship with the media, while teams, leagues and events that are not as successful as they would like to be must develop systems and apply strategies to either begin the relationship or enhance it. This book is designed to provide prospective and practising sport managers with the knowledge and skills to engage in effective sport media management and successfully navigate the sport media nexus.

What is driving the sport media nexus?

The relationship between sport and the media is defined by change. Neither sport nor the media are static industries and their relationship has enhanced both the rate of change and the fluidity of each at the beginning of the twenty-first century. The following discussion identifies a series of drivers that influence sport, the media and the relationship between the two: technology, commercialization, convergence and globalization. These drivers provide the context for much that follows in subsequent chapters.

Technology

Technological change has been a key driver in the relationships between the media and all aspects of society, not to mention the nexus between sport and the media. In simple terms, the transition from newspapers to radio, to television and then to the Internet illustrates a rapid development in communication technology. In turn this development has had an impact on access for consumers, as well as power and influence for owners and operators.

As a result of technological change, in a relatively short period of human history, a transformation has occurred. People who were previously limited to information that related to their local surrounds now have access to information on a global scale. The currency of this information was previously bound or constrained by the lack of technological development. Whereas information might have taken days or weeks to reach its audience, through advances in mobile technology in particular, this information is now effectively immediate. These developments within the context of the evolution of the sport media nexus will be addressed in more detail in the following chapter.

Commercialization

The relationship between sport and the media is not predicated on benevolence or generosity. The media does not report on sport as a function of public service, nor does sport provide the media with access merely to increase public awareness. Rather, the sport media nexus is driven by commercial forces.

Since the late 1960s sport has become a commercial vehicle for media organizations, sponsors and advertisers. As a result, professional sports in particular have become increasingly wealthy, as well as dominant. Professional athletes and teams are often referred to as products, properties, commodities or businesses. Professional football teams in Europe such as Manchester United in England, Real Madrid in Spain and AC Milan in Italy are estimated to have annual revenues of between US $250 million and US $1,250 million. By any measure these are significant businesses. Importantly, their wealth has been driven by the media. Where their revenue was once derived primarily from match or gate receipts, they are now dependent on broadcast rights or commercial sponsorship that is directly proportional to the amount of media coverage they generate. Professional sport is now a commodity that can be bought and sold by the media, as well as a vehicle through which other businesses can promote and sell their products. This 'hyper-commercialism' is discussed throughout the chapters in Part II.

Convergence

Convergence has become a buzzword in media studies and to a lesser extent within sport media studies (Turner & Cunningham, 2002). Convergence refers to a multitude of drivers in the sport media landscape.

First, convergence refers to technological change, whereby the means of delivery are becoming integrated. For example, where a household might previously have had an antenna to receive a television signal, a telephone to place and receive calls, and a radio to receive transmissions, these might now be available through a single cable, which also delivers pay television and Internet access.

Second, convergence refers to the phenomenon of increasing cross-media ownership. For example, a newspaper or television station might previously have been owned independently of any other media interests. In the late nineteenth century and early twentieth century it was usual for a newspaper to be a family business. At the start of the twenty-first century this is the exception rather than the norm. It is now far more likely that a single media organization will have commercial interests in television, print media, film and Internet. In short, this means that media organizations are able to promote a single product, such as a sport team or league, across multiple media forms for commercial advantage.

Third, convergence refers to the increasing national and global domination of large media organizations, otherwise known as media conglomerates or transnational media corporations. The rise of media organizations such as News Corporation, Walt Disney Company and Bertelsmann has resulted in an increasing lack of diversity. Rather than a variety of small media organizations, the global media landscape is dominated by massive media organizations that continue to acquire smaller organizations, increasing both their reach and economies of scale. Furthermore, it is increasingly likely that these conglomerates will have mutual commercial interests, which further increases the industry's complexity and lack of diversity.

Fourth and finally, convergence refers to the ownership of content and the means of distribution. For example, in the United States of America, many sport teams are owned by media organizations. In these cases the commercial interests of previously independent entities have converged.

Globalization

It could be argued that globalization is the most important driver of the sport media nexus, however, it is more useful to view technological change, commercialization and convergence as drivers that have all led to the increasing globalization of media and sport media. Without advances in technology and increases in access to information, globalization would not have occurred to the extent that it has. The commercial imperative behind the sport media relationship has driven sports and media organizations to find and then reach new markets, often on the other side of the world, while the rise of media conglomerates has facilitated, not hindered globalization. It should be noted that there are other important factors that have had an impact on globalization, such as economic trade, labour migration and the ease of international travel. However, the media remains the most important driver of globalization in the world today. The media is both an essential feature of daily life and the most tangible indicator of globalization.

At one level globalization has driven and accelerated changes in the relationship between sport and the media, while at another level sport and its media partners have played an important role in the globalizing process. Sports like cricket and rugby union created World Cups to determine a world champion in the sport every 4 years, despite the fact that only a handful of nations are proficient at an international level. World championships such as these are the direct result of the global appeal of sport, as well as the increasing amounts of revenue available to sports through broadcast rights agreements. On the other hand, sport has been used as a conduit of globalization. The popularity and appeal of the FIFA World Cup and the Olympic Games are examples of the impact of sport and sport media in the globalizing process.

The structure of the book

This book is divided into four parts. The first part, of which the current chapter forms the first half, consists of two chapters that are designed to introduce the reader to the concepts that underpin the sport media nexus and examine its evolution. The premise of the book's second chapter is that an understanding of the history and development of the sport media nexus is essential to participating in the contemporary sport media management landscape. In other words, without a clear sense of the ways in which the relationship between sport and the media evolved, it is difficult to understand its current status and contexts.

The second part of the book, sport media landscapes, is a detailed examination of the sport media nexus. The chapters in this part are intended to provide a comprehensive examination of the way in which the sport and media industries interact. More specifically, the chapters provide: an overview of the sport and media industries; an examination of the way in which broadcast rights are bought and sold and how sport and media organizations leverage sponsorship and advertising revenue from the media coverage of sport; an analysis of sport media regulation and government intervention in both industries; a thematic examination of sport media texts and finally an investigation of the production of sport media texts from an institutional perspective that will provide the basis for some of the information contained in Part III of the book.

The third part of the book, sport media strategies, is a detailed examination of the key strategies used to manage media communications and interactions within the sporting context. The chapters in this part are not designed for those people who produce media, as there are numerous textbooks that examine the role, functions and skills of journalists, editors and associated media professionals. Rather, the chapters in this part are designed to develop the knowledge and skills of those people who will be engaged in managing the media, communication and public relations activities of sport organizations, which include clubs, leagues, associations and event organizers. The sport media strategies part contains five chapters that examine specific components of sport media management. First, the process by which sport media managers plan for media coverage and what strategies they use to promote their organization. Second, media communications such as media releases, fact sheets and media guides. Third, media interactions such as media conferences and interviews. Fourth, the management of elite athletes in a celebrity culture. Fifth and finally, managing crises and scandals to ensure the reputation of the organization is maintained. Upon completing this part of the book the reader should be able to apply skills, strategies and techniques to the planning, acquisition and management of media coverage within a variety of sport organizations.

The fourth and final part of the book contains a solitary chapter that examines the future of sport media. This chapter is intended to introduce the reader to a variety of trends and scenarios that might influence the sport media nexus throughout the next one to two decades. It is expected that the reader will be able to relate these trends and scenarios back to the knowledge and skills gained during the preceding chapters and be able to contextualize the role of sport media management professionals in the future.

Summary

This chapter has introduced the concepts of sport and the media, as well as the nexus between them. Importantly, it has highlighted that we live in a world that is saturated by sport media, the result of a defining cultural and commercial relationship between these two massive industries. The extent of these commercial and cultural connections is such that the sport media nexus demands management, a theme that will be reinforced throughout the following chapters. The chapter also contained discussion of a series of key sport media drivers – technological change, commercialism, convergence and globalization – each of these drivers or contexts inform the evolution of the sport media nexus, as well as its continued development. Finally, the chapter concluded with an outline of the structure of the book and the chapters that follow. Review questions and exercises are listed below to assist with confirming your knowledge of the core concepts and principles introduced in this chapter.

Review questions and exercises

1. What are the key features of sport?
2. Should card games and similar activities be considered sport, and does media coverage of the World Poker Tour indicate that only two of the three sport dimensions are required for media coverage?
3. What is media?
4. List the media you interact with on a daily basis. To what extent is your day saturated by media in general and sport media more specifically?
5. What sustains the sport media nexus?
6. Why does the sport media nexus require management?

7. What is the most important driver of the sport media nexus? Why?
8. Compare a major daily newspaper from today with one from the 1950s. Is the sport being reported local, global or international? Are there any differences?
9. Identify the most popular newspapers, television stations and magazines where you live and find out who owns them. Is there any convergence?
10. Choose a professional sport or league and find out what percentage of the revenue is directly or indirectly related to media coverage.

2 Media games: the evolution of the nexus

Overview

This chapter examines the evolution of the sport media nexus, including developments in newspaper, radio, television and the Internet. In particular, it explores the way in which each industry uses the other as a commercial stimulus, particularly in the United States of America and Great Britain. This chapter provides an historical perspective on the sport media nexus in order that contemporary practices and relationships are able to be contextualized and understood more completely.

After completing this chapter the reader should be able to:

- Describe the evolution of the sport media nexus.
- Identify the way in which each of the key media forms influenced the development of sport and used sport to popularize itself.
- Generalize about the types of sport coverage provided by each media form throughout the history of the sport media nexus.
- Contextualize the contemporary sport media nexus by referring to its evolution and history.

Introduction

As the previous chapter illustrated, the contemporary world we inhabit is saturated with media sport, where both commercial industries engage in symbiotic relationship of mutual benefit. McChesney (1989) suggested that this concept of symbiosis is not only a way of interpreting the present, but is also an ideal lens through which we might view the history of the relationship between sport and the media. In writing specifically about the sport media nexus in the United States of America, McChesney (1989:49) argued that 'virtually every surge in the popularity of sport has been accompanied by a dramatic increase in the coverage provided sport by the media'. Furthermore, he also argued that this symbiotic relationship is not one of chance, but rather is defined by the way both institutions have operated as commercial entities. In other words, the history of the sport media nexus is characterized by organizations driven together in search of greater profits, audiences and resources.

The impact of sport news on the popularity and profitability of new media forms has only been equalled by the transformation that sport has undergone, as a result of its interplay with the media. If it was possible in the 1890s to construct or conceive of an image of sport without reference to the media, by the 1990s the task was impossible. It is now as if 'one is literally unthinkable without the other' (Rowe, 1999). Sport and the media have been fused together at a number of levels. On the one hand the media's involvement in sport has created the context for sport's increased commercialization and globalization, and on the other it has supplied a myriad of vehicles to mediate the game and its immediate aftermath. The media has also been an instrument to foster and promote phatic discourse, or 'sports chatter' (Eco, 1986). It is clear that an understanding of the evolution of the complex relationship between sport and the media is an essential component of any analysis of sport media's contemporary structure and practices.

The beginning?

The dominance of television in the media coverage of sport often leads to the false conclusion that the sport media relationship began in the middle of the twentieth century with the advent of television. In fact, the sport media nexus has a much longer and more complex history, which began at the end of the eighteenth century with the establishment and then development throughout the nineteenth century of a sporting magazine industry in Great Britain and the United States of America in particular (McChesney, 1989; Boyle & Haynes, 2000). The commercial opportunities of gambling most notably influenced the development of these magazines, which generally focused on sports such as horse racing and boxing and the publication of results. Often the way in which sports were covered in high-circulation magazines had a significant bearing on their popularity. For example, in America William Porter attempted to popularize the game of cricket in the 1840s in his *Spirit of the Times* periodical,

19

which had a circulation of 100,000, but by the 1850s had turned his attention to baseball. The *New York Clipper*, a new sporting weekly in the 1850s, soon took over from the *Times* in popularizing the sport of baseball, and employed a full-time sportswriter (McChesney, 1989). Today the sport of cricket is almost non-existent in America, while baseball became its national game. In Great Britain the sporting press began to contribute to the widespread dissemination and organization of sport from the 1820s and 1830s in particular (Harvey, 2004). From 1824 *Bell's Weekly Messenger* employed expert writers for particular sports and provided extensive and detailed coverage of boxing. The sporting press during the middle of the eighteenth century in Great Britain and America in particular were important in creating an audience for sport, impelling it toward a commercial outlook and operation.

Throughout the 1830s and 1840s the newspaper industry generated its income through the combination of advertising space sales and circulation. This commercial emphasis laid the foundation for the exploitation of sport as a form of entertainment that could generate both sales and advertising revenue. Sport was covered by newspapers throughout the middle of the nineteenth century and Boyle and Haynes (2000) have noted that the establishment of regular fixtures and seasonal events greatly contributed to the steady flow of news for the sporting press.

In 1883 Joseph Pulitzer purchased the *New York World*, an American metropolitan daily newspaper with a circulation of approximately fifteen thousand and immediately set about creating the modern mass-circulation newspaper. He lowered the cost of the paper, changed its layout and look, developed its editorial and news gathering functions, refined a sensationalist approach to news, sold advertising space on the basis of circulation and was the first to use headlines in a concerted effort to capture the attention and stimulate the curiosity of audiences. By 1892, the *New York World* had increased its circulation to 2 million readers and it was clear that Pulitzer had set a new standard for the newspaper business (Schudson, 1978; Hughes, 1981).

The *New York World*, according to Oriard (1993), was also a pioneer in sports coverage throughout the 1880s and early 1890s. One of Pulitzer's first initiatives as publisher was to establish a sports department, with its own sporting editor. The subsequent increase in the amount of space devoted to sport was a significant factor in the increased circulation of the *New York World*. By the end of the nineteenth century, most newspapers had their own sport editor, while in 1895 Pulitzer's competitor William Randolph Hearst introduced the first sport section in the *New York Journal* (McChesney, 1989). The late nineteenth century and early twentieth century was a boom time for the print media coverage of sport across the world, and many instances this coverage helped to popularize and nationalize variety of sports. By the 1920s, newspaper sport sections and considerable attention to sport were features of most American major daily newspapers.

The sport media nexus throughout the print media era was characterized by localized coverage and a slow growth in sport's popularity. Newspapers and magazines used sport to increase sales and advertising revenue, while sport used the media to increase attendances and subsequent revenue. During the print media era both sport and the media enjoyed a relationship of mutual benefit, through which they were able to increase their audiences. They did this through associating their respective 'products', rather than engaging in an overtly commercial relationship.

Radio waves

In 1893 Hungarian inventors Theodore Puskas and Nikola Tesla offered subscribers in Budapest what has been described as the world's first broadcasting system, a Telefon Hirmondo service (Briggs & Burke, 2005). The service, which had over 5,000 subscribers by the end of the century, offered a daily schedule of items including sport news. In 1897 Italian Guglielmo Marconi established the Wireless Telegraph and Signal Company, but it was not until the 1920s that radio was introduced and established itself as a mass medium around the world. From the start, sporting events on radio were popular in most countries (Briggs & Burke, 2005) and sport was used to popularize the new medium. Unlike daily and weekly newspaper reporting, however, early radio coverage of sport was limited to sporadic events, such as the baseball World Series in America.

In Great Britain the British Broadcasting Corporation (BBC) developed the range and scope of sport broadcasting on radio throughout the 1920s, 1930s and 1940s. By 1930 broadcasts of cricket test matches, Wimbledon, the Football Association Cup Final, the Grand National and the Derby were annual, with trained commentators and established commentary conventions (Whannel, 1992). These events were nationally significant and radio helped to increase their popularity and appeal (Boyle & Haynes, 2000). In 1934 the Australian Broadcasting Corporation's description of play of the cricket series between England and Australia coincided with large increases in the sale of radio sets, and marked a break from routine programming. In the same year the Ford Motor Company paid $100,000 to sponsor the World Series on the National Broadcasting Company (NBC) and Columbia Broadcasting System (CBS) in America, which illustrated the popularity of radio sport programming and the increasing connection between sport, money and the media (McChesney, 1989). In 1948 the BBC introduced the 'Sports Report', which attracted more than 12 million listeners in the late 1940s and early 1950s, and included reports from towns throughout Great Britain and in some cases from other countries (Boyle & Haynes, 2000).

Radio's immediacy and its ability to broadcast to large audiences was a challenge to newspapers, if not a threat to their livelihood. Newspapers relied on being able to provide accounts of games and matches and in the late nineteenth and early twentieth centuries newspaper reporting of sport was extremely colourful and detailed. Newspaper reporting was the next best thing to attending the event, but radio brought sport consumers a step closer to the action, in the same way that television brought them even closer in the 1950s and 1960s in particular. The introduction of radio and then television meant that newspaper reporting changed from typically factual reporting to

21

BISHOP BURTON COLLEGE

include a greater emphasis on opinion and analysis. Similarly, the introduction and then development of television presented a challenge to radio, although in many cases the companies and corporations involved in broadcasting radio became major players in television.

Radio altered the sport media nexus by regionalizing and in some cases nationalizing the audience for sport. Where newspapers were limited to previewing and reviewing games and matches, radio created immediacy and enabled live coverage. Through radio, geographically distant audiences were able to consume sport at the same time. This was different from newspaper consumption, which was distinctly personal and idiosyncratic. The notion of a simultaneous audience was enhanced by the broadcast of events that were of national importance. Both radio and sport enjoyed an association that provided increased audiences and financial returns, however, like the era dominated by print media, the relationship was one of mutual benefit rather than overtly commercial.

Small screen, big impact

According to Whannel (1992), in Great Britain television was second behind radio as the popular broadcast medium throughout the 1930s and 1940s, although outside broadcasts of events such as the 1948 Olympic Games provided a publicity and sales stimulus (Case 1). It was not until the 1950s that television began to establish itself as the primary broadcast medium. In 1950 only 9% of American homes and approximately 5% of British homes contained television sets, yet by 1965 the figures had increased massively to 93% and approximately 80% respectively (Chandler, 1988). This increase in the ownership of television sets was both a factor and a result of the increase in sport programming. The 1960s in America were a period in which there were massive battles between the major television networks for the rights to broadcast football in particular. One of the key results of these battles was the merger of the National Football League (NFL) and American Football Leagues, while the national passion for the sport was entrenched with the establishment of 'Monday Night Football' on the American Broadcasting Company (ABC).

Case 1   From 12 to 25,000?: Media at the Olympic Games

Media coverage of the first modern Olympic Games in Athens in 1896 was limited to newspaper and magazine reports, with 12 journalists covering the event. Print media remained the dominant form until the 1930s, although selected cinematic broadcasts were evident during the early twentieth century and limited radio broadcasting occurred at both the 1928 and 1932 Games. There was significant radio broadcasting in 1936 at the Berlin Olympics, with a complex short wave system reaching

40 countries. The 1936 Games were also the first to be televised, with 'tele-viewing' rooms set up with a cathode-ray large screen projection receiver, although this was limited to the Berlin area and was of variable quality. The 1940 and 1944 Games were both cancelled as a result of the Second World War and by the time they resumed in 1948 in London regular tele-vision broadcasting was available in both the Unites States of America and Britain. Although radio remained the dominant broadcast medium for international audiences, 64 hours of Olympic television broadcasting was available to approximately 500,000 people who lived within 50 miles of London.

In 1952 broadcast rights negotiations were held for the first time and almost 2,000 media passes were distributed to journalists, while the Melbourne Olympics in 1956 can be considered the first time where broadcast rights negotiations broke down. The organizing committee for the 1956 Games demanded approximately half a million dollars for the US broadcast rights, but were refused on the basis that it was a news event and should therefore be free. The dispute was not resolved and international audiences had to rely on radio broadcasts. In 1958 televi-sion broadcasts rights were incorporated into the Olympic charter, with the Olympic organizing committee selling the rights with the approval of the International Olympic Committee (IOC) and sharing in the accu-mulated revenues.

The 1960 Rome Olympics were televised live for the first time to 18 European countries in close proximity using terrestrial technology, with delayed coverage to the United States of America, Canada and Japan, but only 1 out of every 400 dollars required to stage the Games was recovered from the sale of rights. In 1964 satellite technology was used to relay trans-missions overseas, increasing both the availability of the Games and its worth to international broadcasters. The 1968 Games in Mexico City were the first to be broadcast in colour, within excess of 4,000 personnel regis-tered at the media centre. In 1972 Olympic broadcasting took another quantum leap with the Japanese broadcaster NHK providing the generic feed for the Sapporo Games so that international broadcasters could select what events would appeal to their audiences. There were also indications that the amount of money paid by American broadcasters was determin-ing programming, as the basketball final at the Summer Games was played at 11.30 p.m. to maximize audiences in the United States of America. In 1976 there were approximately 8,500 journalists, editors and camera oper-ators in Montreal to report on the Games for print and broadcast media. Television revenue in 1980, by contrast to its relatively meagre contribution in 1960, contributed 1 in every 15 dollars required to stage the Games.

The Los Angeles Olympics in 1984 are considered to mark a strategic shift in the organization of the Games, as the organizing committee focused on television rights and sponsorship revenue in order to stage an economically successful event. In 1984 approximately 10,000 media attended the Games, whereas in Seoul in 1988 more than 16,000 media reported on the Games. It was clear that the number of media required to report on the Games was growing at a rate matched only by the increases in broadcast rights fees. Many of the events at the Korean Games were staged in the morning to ensure events were available live in American prime time, a further indication that ensuring the Games' profitability meant ensuring the greatest possible television audience. In 1992 the NBC in the United States of America experimented with offering some of the Olympics on pay-per-view cable television, but since then the IOC has been firmly committed to ensuring that Olympics Games reach the widest possible audience.

There were in excess of 21,000 media personnel at the 2004 Athens Olympic Games, with media outnumbering athletes at a ratio of two to one. At the 2006 winter Olympic Games in Torino, Italy, there were approximately 2,600 athletes, but by contrast there were approximately 10,000 media personnel, which equates to four media representatives for every athlete competing at the twentieth winter Olympic Games. The modern Olympic Games began with 12 journalists covering the events, whereas the 2008 Beijing Games and 2012 London Games are likely to attract 25,000 media representatives from all over the world, an increase that indicates that from humble beginnings the Olympics have grown into one of the largest and most complex media events in the world.

Sources: McCoy (1997), Verdier (1996), Slater (1998), www.olympic.org.

The 1970s were a boom period for American professional sport leagues. Baseball, basketball, ice hockey, college football and college basketball all secured network broadcast contracts, while the annual number of hours of sport broadcast on television increased from 787 to 1,356 throughout the decade (McChesney, 1989). In 1977 NFL commissioner Pete Rozelle negotiated a 4-year US $656 million broadcast rights deal, which was proportional to the advertising revenue networks were able to achieve, as well as intense competition to secure the rights to premium sport leagues and events (Rader, 1984). Similarly, Boyle and Haynes (2000) have claimed that the 1970s and 1980s were 'golden years' for sport broadcasting in Britain, with the BBC and ITV providing extensive sport coverage. In 1985 Britons were able to enjoy the first live telecast of a league soccer match, which is relatively late given the developments in the sport media relationship and the rights fees being paid in America. According to Barnett (1990), ABC's approach to sport broadcasting in America in the 1970s and 1980s, where sport represented entertainment value, influenced sport programming around the world. Contemporary sport broadcasting is evidence of the connection between sport and entertainment, with dramatic introductions, detailed analysis of off- and on-field activities, instant and slow motion replays and interviews before, during and after games. The half-time show at the NFL Super Bowl and the opening ceremony of the Olympic Games are entertainment exemplars.

Televised sport was so popular in America in the 1970s and broadcast rights deals were lucrative enough that sport leagues were created to capitalize on potential audiences and revenue. The American Basketball Association (ABA) was one celebrated example that began in 1967 with the hope of prospering with television revenue and support, but had to disband in the 1976 in a takeover by the National Basketball Association (NBA). As an indication of the magnitude of American sport broadcasting then and now, the new league took four of the remaining ABA teams and the two teams that were not selected were compensated. John Y. Brown, owner of the Kentucky Fried Chicken fast food chain and the Kentucky Colonels accepted a US $3 million buyout. The owners of the Spirits of St. Louis, Ozzie and Dan Silna, however, agreed to a perpetual share in the broadcasting rights fees paid to the NBA. In each broadcast rights deal since the takeover, they have been paid a share for not being part of the league. Since the ABA folded the Silna brothers and their lawyer Donald Schupak have shared in an estimated US $170 million (Rovell, 2002). In the 1970s their share was worth approximately US $500,000 annually, while by 2006 its value had increased to US $24 million per year.

As previously noted, the relationship between sport and television has been viewed by many as the central component of the sport media nexus. This view has been shaped by three central themes: globalization; commodification; and modification. First, television globalized sport. Events such as the Olympic Games and the FIFA World Cup have become global spectacles, while national sports have crossed boundaries that were previously impenetrable (Barnett, 1995). While national events such as the Tour De France cycling race are celebrated through its television coverage, Barnett has noted that indigenous sports such as cricket in the West Indies have been threatened by the transmission and popularity of American sports such as basketball. This tension between global appeal and local traditions is as prevalent today as it was when television was introduced.

Second, through broadcast rights and sponsorship revenues, television has transformed sport from an amateur pursuit into a highly commercialized activity. It is important to note, however, that in many respects this is a relatively recent phenomenon. Prior to television and then throughout the early years of television into the 1960s sport was a commercial enterprise, but the vast majority of revenue was derived from gate receipts and memberships. For example, only 2 years after the end of the Second World War in 1947, Americans were spending approximately US $250 million on entry to sporting events annually, which increased to US $650 million by 1965 (Chandler, 1988). By contrast, in 1962 the NFL in America signed a national broadcast rights deal worth US $4.7 million annually. In Europe, the annual broadcast rights fees for premier football leagues did not reach the equivalent of US $5 million until the 1980s. In the last quarter of the twentieth century, however, broadcast rights fees and sponsorship revenue increased exponentially, to the point that for many sport organizations they now represent the majority of overall revenue. Prior to television, sports and athletes were commodities to be bought and sold. But, the availability of television and the capacity for sport organizations, advertisers and sponsors to capitalize on the mass television market resulted in the process being refined and expanded, to the point that television is now viewed as the key agent in the selling, buying and re-selling of sport.

Third, the revenues that sport organizations have earned from the television coverage of sport have resulted in sports being modified to suit the needs of broadcasters and appeal to mediated rather than live audiences. These modifications have varied, depending on the sport, the country and the commercial and cultural contexts. Football as it is played in Europe and South America has largely remained unchanged, with 45-minute halves uninterrupted by advertising. By contrast, football codes in America and Australia have created special breaks or elongated natural stoppages to provide more time for advertising messages during television coverage. For example, in 1958 the NFL commissioner permitted the use of television time-outs, specifically designed to facilitate advertising and increase associated revenues (McChesney, 1989). In Great Britain the half-time break was extended from 10 to 15 minutes in the 1980s in order to provide advertisers with more time to promote their products (Barnett, 1995). At the other end of the spectrum new events, such as the X-Games in America, and new versions of old sports, such as Twenty20 cricket, have been created primarily as television products. Television networks have also played an influential role in determining the scheduling of events, which in the worst cases has resulted in athletes playing or competing at inappropriate times. Football games played in the middle of the night, or the Olympic marathon being scheduled in the heat of the day to enable its broadcast in prime time in large commercial markets are two such examples (see Case 1).

Case 2   Cricket's entertainment revolution

In 1977 Australian media magnate Kerry Packer contracted 35 of the world's best cricketers to play for him, rather than the controlling bodies of world and Australian cricket. The challenge to the status quo was such that many commentators at the time considered it to be the end of cricket, rather than the beginning of an era in which cricket would become increasingly more commercial and popular. The World Series Cricket (WSC) competition that Packer created consisted of traditional test matches, as well as one-day games. These one-day games were played at night under lights, white balls were used instead of the traditional red, coloured clothing was worn instead of the traditional all-white and rules were introduced to make the play more exciting for spectators.

Unlike other sports that have a single format, the game of cricket has a number of variations at the international level. The oldest version is 'test' cricket, which consists of 5 days of play in daylight, with approximately 6 hours of play each day, depending on weather conditions. In one-day cricket, which began in England in the early 1960s, teams are each allowed an innings of 50 overs (six balls are bowled per over) and games are often played under lights in the late afternoon and early evening. In the twenty-first century another form of cricket has developed, Twenty 20, where teams are allowed only twenty overs each. Although the equipment and number of players is the same in each of the three variations of cricket, there are differences in rules, ostensibly to make the two shorter versions of the game more attractive to spectators.

Source: Stewart (1995).

Pay television

Although technically not a new medium, the development of pay television (this term will be used throughout the book to denote television content that a viewer pays for, rather than receives via free-to-air television) has had distinct implications for the sport media nexus. The introduction of pay television created the opportunity for spectators to pay to watch sport without attending a live event. Prior to the introduction of pay television, spectators were able to attend the event and pay the sport organization directly, or watch the event on free-to-air television. The requirement to pay to watch a sporting event on television has entrenched the notion that sport is a product to be bought and sold. As an example, in 2006 the Commonwealth Games were held in Melbourne, Australia and sport watchers were able to view a selection of events on free-to-air television. On pay television a service was available through Fox, whereby for AUD $49.95 a viewer was able to access seven separate channels, with over 1,100 hours of coverage, including 650 hours of live coverage. A viewer could switch between sports, depending on their interests or the closeness of the contest, or watch a channel dedicated to the best performances and moments of the games. Throughout the history of televised sport, sport organizations have been concerned by the relationship between mediated and live attendance. The ability to access 650 hours of coverage, which is not possible through a single free-to-air channel or by attending the event changes the relationship further.

At the beginning of the twenty-first century the impact of pay television is yet to be fully realized. Pay television is an accepted component of the sport media nexus in North America and Europe in particular, where sport consumption and disposable incomes are high, but has limited penetration throughout the rest of the world. In North America and Europe the introduction and entrenchment of pay television has altered the consumption of sport media. Whereas viewers were once able to consume televised sport through free-to-air channels and programs, they are now being required to pay to access the product. In each of the previous nexus developments (print media, radio and television) a return on investment was achieved by media organizations through advertising revenue. Newspapers, radio stations and television stations were paid to access the audiences generated by sport programmes. Pay television has created a direct commercial relationship between the media organization and the consumer.

Internet

The Internet is a significant competitor to traditional sport media and in the context of the evolution of the nexus it is important to discuss six key themes. First, like radio and television before it, the Internet is a medium that provides consumers with immediacy. If a consumer wants to access the results of a match underway, or one that has been completed, the Internet is often the quickest option. As the immediacy of radio and television caused newspapers to change the way they covered sport, the Internet has exacerbated the trend, so that hard copy newspapers now provide even more analysis and opinion and rely less on acting as a record of events, although many still provide this function. Partly as a result of the challenge of the Internet to traditional media forms, almost all major daily newspapers now have an online version, which includes analysis and opinion, but also provides breaking sport news and results.

Second, the Internet provides greater access to a greater variety of sport than any other media form. Although consumers are able to watch multiple sports via developments in split screen technology and by changing channels to receive different sport news and telecasts, the Internet's depth and breadth of sport coverage is unrivalled. An Internet user is able to access information about almost any sport in the world at any time of the day. Developments in technology will in all likelihood allow a majority of consumers to watch these sports in the future. As examples, FIFA provided Australian Internet users with highlights of 2006 World Cup matches on the Internet within an hour of the end of the television broadcast, while surfing fans have access to live web casts of all world tour events.

Third, the Internet is global. Newspapers and radio are necessarily local, regional or national in their content and audience, while television has had an important role in globalizing sport. However, beyond the coverage of global events such as the FIFA World Cup and the Olympic Games, free-to-air television coverage in particular still exhibits a parochial nationalism. Pay television is more global, however, even this is dominated by American professional sport and European football and motor sport. The Internet is a truly global medium in that it allows users to follow a sport on the other side of the world and this has led to trend of most sport organizations developing websites to provide greater exposure and stimulate interest. The progression from local to global and from newspaper to the Internet is represented in Figure 2.1. Larger sport organizations are also capitalizing on the global nature of the Internet by providing a range of language options for their websites. The Houston Rockets (of the American National Basketball Association) have a Chinese version of the website because of the popularity of Yao Ming, while the FIFA 2006 World Cup website provided by Yahoo was available in English, German, French, Italian, Spanish, Portuguese, Korean, Japanese and Chinese.

Fourth, the Internet is personal. Although this seems to contradict the previous feature of the global medium, the Internet has allowed consumers to personalize their sport preferences and experiences. Whereas television is dominated by sports that are able to attract a mass audience, the Internet allows consumers to not only choose from a greater range of sport options, but also to become members of sport communities that cross cultural and geographic boundaries. In particular, the Internet has enabled sport fans to 'talk' and share experiences in virtual online communities, as well as participate in fantasy leagues. By contrast, analogue television does not allow for any audience interaction, while radio and newspapers have included limited audience interaction in the form of talk-back callers and letters to the editor respectively.

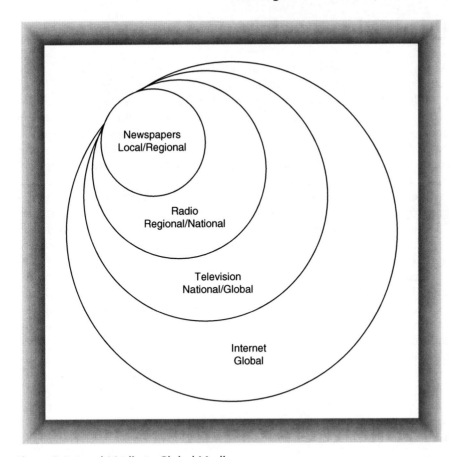

Figure 2.1 Local Media to Global Media

Fifth, the Internet provides sport organizations, advertisers and sponsors with direct access to consumers. While television, radio and newspapers are able to sell advertising space and time, it is rare for consumers to be able to interact with or purchase products while they are accessing sport media. By contrast, consumers of Internet sport media are able to click through to sponsor or advertiser websites and products. In the example referred to previously, the live web casts of world surfing events are hosted on the websites of sponsors such as Rip Curl and Billabong. In general, consumers are able to access sport information and telecasts through the website of a league or team and purchase merchandise and tickets to games at the same time.

Sixth and finally, the Internet is a converged medium. In other words, the Internet has the capacity to provide consumers with the products or services offered by newspaper, radio and television. Text based information and photographs provide a basis for many websites, like newspapers, while websites are also able to stream radio broadcasts and some sport organizations offer these to fans at a cost. As previously noted, websites are also able to stream live action in the same way that television does, although advances in technology will be required so that the quality can be matched.

Digital television

At the end of the twentieth century television broadcasting evolved again with the introduction of digital television in France and the United Kingdom, through Canalsatellite and SkyDigital respectively (Griffiths, 2003). In many respects, the impacts of digital television, like the Internet and to some extent pay television are not yet clear. Digital television has been largely confined to Europe, but it is clear that the technology provides many advantages that will be utilized in media and sport media programming. Digital technology provides more bandwidth, allows more channels, enables video on demand, allows interactive entertainment such as games and gambling and provides more sophisticated pay-per-view capacities (Griffiths, 2003). Through the use a TiVo device, digital television watchers are also able to access programs whenever they want, rather than being bound by a television schedule. Furthermore, digital television enables consumers to make purchases through their remote control, as well as access the Internet and send and receive emails (Griffiths, 2003). How digital television changes the sport media nexus is unclear, but given its range of new features it is likely to shift the emphasis towards the consumer and away from the traditional television model of advertising revenue supported by mass audiences.

Mobile technologies

Although also relatively new, communication technologies such as third generation mobile phones are already beginning to have an impact on the sport media nexus. The Walt Disney Company refers to mobile phones as the 'third screen', following television and the Internet (Walt Disney Company, 2005). Through ESPN's digital centre, it claims to have created a 'technological interface in which producers of television, Internet, radio and wireless content work literally or virtually side by side to produce sports content that is delivered in ways that were unimaginable just a few years ago' (Walt Disney Company, 2005). However, this media relies on other media, such as television and the Internet for content and format. In other words, these technologies have not yet evolved into a separate media form that presents or represents sport in new or radically different ways. Rather, these communication technologies are able to access Internet websites or receive live coverage or highlight packages from television broadcasters. In this respect, these technologies are enabling a greater personalization of sport media coverage in the sense that it is available on demand, when and wherever the consumer wants to access it. As a result, media and sport organizations, as well as advertisers and sponsors will also have greater access to consumers, a theme that will be discussed further in an analysis of the commercial dimensions of the sport media nexus in Chapter 4.

Conclusion

The sport media nexus has been steadily evolving since the eighteenth century. It is clear from the information contained in this chapter, which is necessarily brief and selective, that sport has been irrevocably changed through its relationship with the media. However, it is important to note that the sport media nexus continues to evolve and does not end with the maturity of the Internet, or the entrenchment of pay television. Rather, the evolution of sport media continues, a theme that will be taken up in the final chapter of this book that examines possible sport media futures. Furthermore, the evolution discussed in this chapter is uneven. For America and Europe the evolution of the sport media nexus has been comparatively rapid, yet in other countries some of the phases described in this chapter have yet to be experienced. For example, despite massive audiences and recent developments, the sport media nexus in China and India is still in its relative infancy, while many of the world's poorer countries have sporadic access to television and the Internet.

Summary

This chapter has examined the history and evolution of the sport media nexus. In particular, it has examined the impact that various media forms, such as television and the Internet have had on sport. It is clear from the information and discussion presented in this chapter that sport has influenced the development of the media, while the media has transformed sport, particularly at the elite and professional levels. Review questions and exercises are listed below to assist with confirming your knowledge of the core concepts and principles introduced in this chapter.

Review questions and exercises

1. When did the relationship between sport and the media begin?
2. How did sport contribute to the creation of the modern mass-circulation newspaper?
3. Were the early days of radio broadcasting characterized by regular or sporadic sport coverage?
4. How did radio and then television change the focus of newspaper sport reporting?
5. What are the three major themes that can be used to describe the relationship between sport and television?

6. Identify any examples within your country that illustrate the tension between global appeal and local traditions in sport broadcasting.
7. Beyond those identified in the chapter, identify three to five examples of the modification of sport or sport scheduling as a result of the mediation of sport.
8. In what decade did broadcast rights fees markedly increase in your country? Why?
9. Will pay television increase or decrease live sport attendance in the future? Why?
10. Which of the six key themes or features referred to in the discussion about the connection between sport and the Internet will be most important in its future development? Why?

Sport Media
Landscapes

3

Global players: the sport and media industries

Overview

This chapter examines the sport and media industries at a global level. Specifically, it explores the major players of the media industry and the structure and extent of their business operations. The major sport players are also examined, such as the major football organizations and leagues, major events and sport circuits. An examination of the media and sport industries reveals the role of both in creating the sport media nexus.

After completing this chapter the reader should be able to:

■ Contextualize the sport media nexus within a broader knowledge of the media and sport industries.
■ Identify the key players in each of the media and sport industries in order to explain their place in the sport media nexus.
■ Understand the interactions between media organizations and the way in which sport is used as a conduit for these linkages and commercial relationships.

Introduction

Viewed in isolation, the media and sport industries are two massive commercial systems. But, as the first two chapters illustrated, these systems are increasingly difficult, if not impossible, to disentangle. At a macro level their spheres of influence include the processes of globalization, the flow of trade and the ways in which nations seek status on the international stage. At the micro level their influence might include the ways in which we choose a particular product to quench our thirst or communicate with friends. The media 'mediates' our day-to-day experiences and actions, as we watch, read and download on a daily basis. Our knowledge of the world around us, either at a local or global level, is dependent on the media. Similarly, we learn, adopt and reject a variety of values and behaviours through our participation in and spectatorship of sport. Viewed together, sport and the media are a powerful combination.

It is likely that a cursory examination of the ways in which sport and the media interact will reveal a jumble of images, messages, replays and action shots and as a result it will be difficult to determine the major players: those media and sport organizations that have influence at national and global levels. In order to understand the sport media nexus more completely it is necessary to dig down beyond the pastiche of sport celebrity, sponsor's products and mega events to examine how the sport and media industries operate as a series of organizations. In terms of the media this means examining the major players in various locations across the globe, although necessarily only a sample is possible because of the diversity and size of the industry. In terms of sport this means examining those sports and organizations that dominate the media landscape; those sports and global events that capture the lion's share of audience attention.

Entertainment and profit driven

It has often been noted that the media perform three essential functions: information, education and entertainment (Briggs & Burke, 2005). Sometimes education is substituted with interpretation (Coakley, 2003), but there is general agreement that information and entertainment are the most prominent functions of any media form or outlet. It is typically a relatively simple exercise to distinguish what the role the media is playing at a particular time in a particular context, although for some events the categories can easily become blurred. For example, at times when a disaster causes suffering and loss of human life, such as a flood or an act of terrorism, the media are providing a service by disseminating information. However, it is also clear that the media often structures these events as entertainment to be consumed by an audience.

In the case of sport these distinctions are usually far clearer and a significant majority of all sport media is entertainment driven.

As the previous chapter demonstrated, as the sport media nexus has deepened and become more complex, sport leagues and clubs have sought to make their sport more entertaining in order to appeal to the media and consumers alike. This appeal is required by both the sport and media industries to drive profits. The next chapter will examine the commercial dimension of the sport media nexus in more depth, but in order to contextualize a discussion about the two industries and their connections it is important to recognize that a commercial imperative is at the heart of the nexus. This profit motive is the basis for the growth in both industries, the way in which the nexus has developed and the size and influence of the major players in the current market.

Key media players

There are several key media players at a global level. Because of the importance and value of sport, these companies are also key sport media players. Table 3.1 shows the five largest media companies in the world based on 2005 sales and profits, current assets and market value. These companies are based in either the USA or Europe, but have global reach through subsidiary companies and by on-selling sport programming content.

It is important to note, however, that designated media companies are not the only companies to have media or sport media interests. For example, General Electric, the world's second largest company with a market value of US $348,450 million, has controlling interests in National Broadcasting Corporation (NBC) Universal, a company created in 2004 as a result of a commercial partnership between NBC and Vivendi Universal Entertainment. NBC Universal is one of the four major television networks in America, serves more than 230 affiliated stations and delivered 8.4% of General Electric's consolidated revenue in 2004. According to General Electric's 2004 annual report, the company's 'operations include investment and programming activities in cable television, principally through USA Network, Bravo, CNBC, SCI FI

Table 3.1 World's Largest Media Companies (2006 – all figures in US $ million)

Company	Sales	Profits	Assets	Market Value
TW-AOL	43,650	2,910	122,480	79,370
Walt Disney Company	32,130	2,700	53,670	54,820
News Corporation	24,500	2,770	55,440	54,890
Comcast	22,260	930	103,150	57,380
Vivendi Universal	29,070	1,020	58,720	35,000

Source: www.forbes.com

Channel, MSNBC, CNBC Europe, CNBC Asia Pacific and entertainment channels across Europe and Latin America' (General Electric, 2004:17). Through NBC Universal, General Electric acquired the rights to broadcast the 2006, 2008, 2010 and 2012 Olympic Games.

Time Warner AOL

Like many of the world's largest media companies, Time Warner AOL (TW-AOL) has diverse business interests across the media sector. TW-AOL's 2004 annual report divides the company into five distinct corporate segments: publishing, networks, filmed entertainment, AOL and cable, represented in Figure 3.1. In 2004 revenue was fairly evenly distributed among the five, with filmed entertainment slightly higher and publishing lower. TW-AOL achieves global distribution through all five segments, of which sport features most prominently in networks, cable and publishing. TW-AOL has a network of more than 130 magazines worldwide and in America, the largest single market, one in two people read a TW-AOL magazine every month (TW-AOL, 2004), such as its signature sport publication, *Sports Illustrated*. TW-AOL's networks segment includes TNT and Turner Broadcasting System (TBS), which feature the National Basketball Association (NBA) and The National Association for

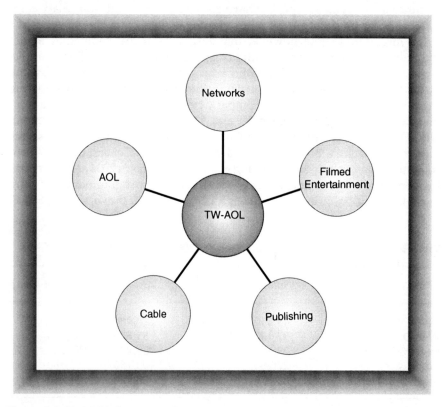

Figure 3.1 TW-AOL Corporate Segments

Stock Car Auto Racing (NASCAR) in America, as well as CNN, a global news network. Through TBS, TW-AOL also owns the Atlanta Braves, although in general TW-AOL's investment in sport media and sport broadcasting in particular is far less than the Walt Disney Company or News Corporation.

The Walt Disney Company

The Walt Disney Company (Disney) brand is synonymous with the image of Mickey Mouse, the company is famous for its theme parks in America, Europe and Asia and as Law, Harvey and Kemp (2002:285) have noted: 'Disney entertainment products are rooted in American values and tradition'. These theme parks and associated retail sales make Disney a unique media company, although like the other major players Disney also has successfully diversified its business interests.

In his letter to shareholders as part of the Disney 2005 annual report, chief executive officer Robert Iger referred to the company's establishment of three strategic priorities: creative innovation, global expansion and application of technology. These priorities are achieved through four primary business segments, represented graphically in Figure 3.2: studio entertainment; parks

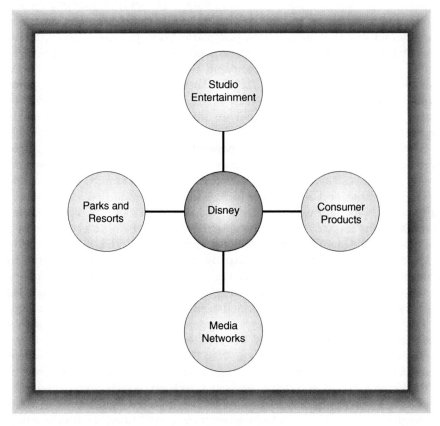

Figure 3.2 Disney Corporate Segments

and resorts; consumer products; and media networks. According to the 2005 annual report, media networks are the largest driver of the company's performance and ESPN, the company's cable sport channel, is a key element of its success. Media networks represented 41% of the company's 2005 revenue, compared with 28% and 24%, respectively, for parks and resorts and studio entertainment. Sport media content is distributed throughout the world by Disney's ESPN networks in Europe, Latin America and Asia. Sport programming through ESPN is one of the most important ways that Disney is achieving its strategic priority of global expansion. Through ESPN, Disney has purchased the rights to major American and international sport properties, including the National Football League (NFL), Major League Baseball, NASCAR and the FIFA World Cup.

News Corporation

Rupert Murdoch's chief executive officer's review in News Corporation's 2005 annual report is titled *'The Eyes of the World are On Us'*, which is a clear indication of the company's strategic direction, as well as the breadth and reach of its media products and services. According to Murdoch, News Corporation's 'diverse businesses encompass all forms of modern media: from print to broadcast to cable to satellite to film to home entertainment to the Internet' and that the company has 'learned how to integrate our content and distribution assets into a seamless whole that allows us to get the most out of each individual asset – an attribute that further distinguishes us from our peers' (News Corporation, 2005:5). These statements reflect the operations of most of the major players: media diversity; and the capacity to engage in cross promotion so that no single product is isolated from its commercial siblings.

News Corporation divides its business into eight corporate segments, illustrated in Figure 3.3: filmed entertainment; television; cable network programming; direct broadcast satellite television; magazines and inserts; newspapers; book publishing; and other. Other includes News Corporation's 50% ownership of the National Rugby League (NRL), Australia's second most popular national sport league. News Corporation's share in the NRL is a result of a merger of the Australian Rugby League and Super League, the rival rugby competition established by the company in the mid 1990s in an attempt to control the sport in Australia. The category of other also includes a subsidiary company called the Global Cricket Corporation, which holds the commercial rights to International Cricket Council events including the 2007 World Cup.

Like TW-AOL and Disney, News Corporation's filmed entertainment segment is important to its business, but it differs substantially in its significant newspaper holdings, including more than 110 newspapers in Australia where the company began. Newspapers represented 17% of consolidated revenue in 2005, behind filmed entertainment and television, which contributed 25% and 22%, respectively. News Corporation has invested significantly in sport through its FOX cable networks in America, through British Sky Broadcasting (BSkyB) in the UK, and STAR in Asia. In 2006 in America News Corporation

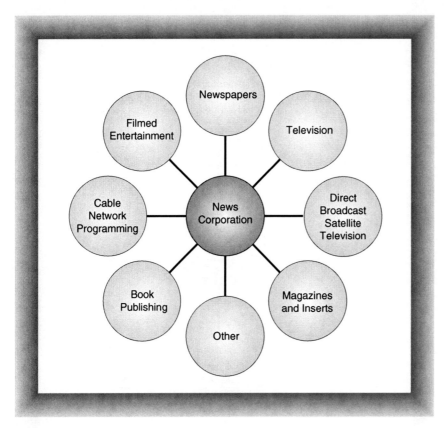

Figure 3.3 News Corporation Corporate Segments

had rights agreements with the NFL, NASCAR and Major League Baseball, while in the UK BSkyB holds the rights to the English Premier League, one of the world's premium sport properties.

Comcast

Unlike the previous three major players, Comcast's commercial operations lack diversity and are effectively limited to two segments, represented in Figure 3.4: broadband communications networks and cable television networks. In 2004 Comcast received 95% of its revenue through its broadband communications networks, which primarily provide American subscribers with access to high speed Internet and phone services (Comcast, 2004). Comcast does engage in sport programming through its cable television networks, although its investment and commitment is far less in comparison to the top three players referred to previously. Through its majority ownership of Comcast-Spectator, in America Comcast owns the Philadelphia 76ers basketball team in the NBA and the Philadelphia Flyers ice hockey team in the NHL.

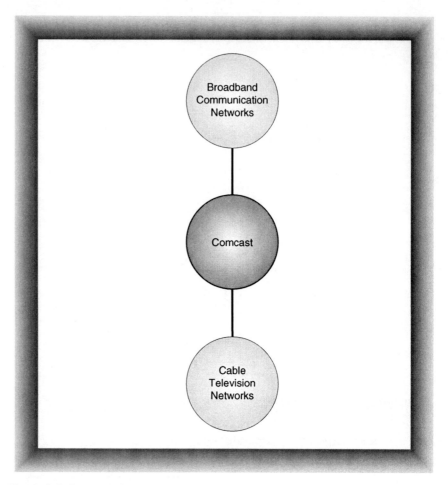

Figure 3.4 Comcast Corporate Segments

Vivendi Universal

Formed in 2000 as a result of a merger between Vivendi, The Seagram Company and Canal+, Vivendi Universal transformed itself into a media and communications company in the early years of the twenty-first century. Vivendi Universal divides its business into three core segments: media; telecommunications; and NBC Universal, although further divisions are apparent, which are represented in Figure 3.5 (Vivendi Universal, 2004). The media segment is divided into Canal+, which operates television and cable networks and Music and Games, while NBC Universal is involved in: the production of live and recorded television programmes; the production and distribution of motion pictures; the operation of television broadcasting stations; the ownership of several cable/satellite networks around the world; the operation of theme parks; and investment and programming activities in multimedia and the Internet. In 2004 the media segment contributed 42%, telecommunications 47% and NBC Universal 11%, while it resulted from the

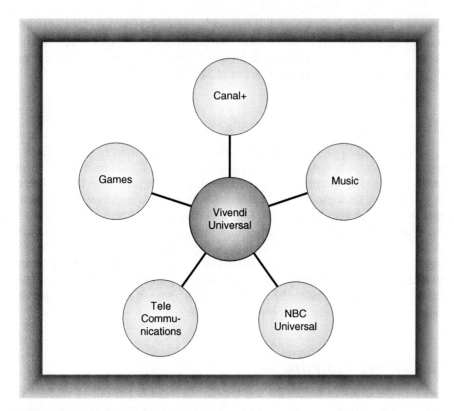

Figure 3.5 Vivendi Corporate Segments

following markets: France (56%); Rest of Europe (13%); America (17%); and Rest of the World (14%). Through Canal+, Vivendi Universal has the exclusive rights to the French national football league games and has a 98.5% share in Paris Saint-Germain, one of the league's leading teams, as well as its interests through NBC Universal previously noted.

Comparisons and connections

Filmed or studio entertainment contributed approximately 25% of revenues for the top three media players, while media networks play an important role in overall business strategy and development. Disney and News Corporation invest heavily in sport, as will be revealed in more detail in the following chapter, while sport is far less important for companies such as Comcast, in which telecommunications drive a significant proportion of overall revenue. As previously noted, Disney's parks and resorts business segment is unique, while Vivendi Universal's Music and Games are unique segments within the top five major players.

Although these major players are in direct competition in network and cable television, publishing and filmed entertainment in particular, there are commercial partnerships which make the media landscape even more complex. For example, Disney and News Corporation both own 50% of ESPN Star Sports, while News Corporation also has commercial partnerships with Vivendi and Viacom and TW-AOL has established commercial relationships with Vivendi and Bertelsmann (Law et al., 2002).

Other media players

The major media players have a significant global presence, yet there are a host of other media companies that also have a significant role in the sport media nexus. For example, Bertelsmann owns 90% of the publicly listed RTL, which in 2004 comprised 31 television and 30 radio stations in 10 countries throughout Europe. In 2004, RTL used these media outlets to broadcast the European Football Championships and the Athens Olympic Games (Bertelsmann, 2004). Mediaset in Italy, CBS in the America, ITV in the UK and PBL in Australia are all important players in their respective sport media markets. Similar sized companies exist in many other parts of the world and although they do not have the global reach of some of the big players, play an important role in covering national sports.

The media industry

Profiling the ways in which the key media players are organized and structured is useful for developing a more generalized understanding of the media, as well as identifying the points at which sport and the media intersect. Figure 3.6 graphically represents the core business dimensions of the media industry, although as the profiles of the major players illustrated, typically not all segments are fully represented in a single organization. The first dimension is providing communication services, such as telecommunications or Internet/broadband access. In the case of Internet/broadband access, the service enables consumers to access other products and services. Some of these products and services may be contained within websites owned or operated by the same media organization providing the communication service.

The second dimension is distribution, which comprises television, newspapers, radio, magazines and Internet websites. These are the means of distributing media content. Without this content, the means of distribution are simply empty vessels. For the purposes of providing clarity in relation to the sport media nexus, this content is divided into two sub-sets: sport and non-sport. Sport content is the games, matches and events that media organizations bid for the rights to broadcast on television, radio and the Internet, as well as cover in newspapers and magazines. Typically, sport content is provided by an external party. In other words, the sport organization providing the content is an independent entity. Sometimes, although not very often in the contemporary nexus, sport content is provided by an internal arm of the media organization. In this case, the sport organization is owned by the media.

Non-sport content providers can be internal or external and service the third dimension, products, as well as distribution. Products consist of film,

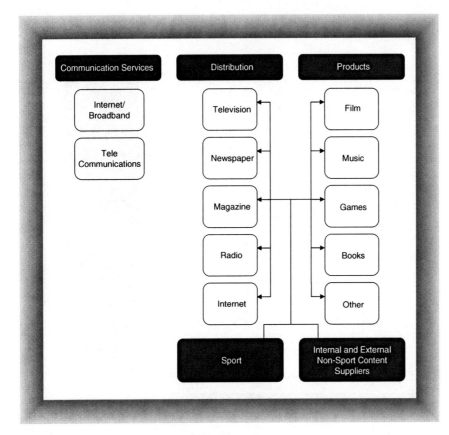

Figure 3.6 Media Industry Organization

music, games, books and other, which includes parks, resorts and associated consumer products. A media organization may produce films or studio entertainment internally for external distribution and sale, whereas it might contract external authors to provide manuscripts in order to produce books. Similarly, television drama might be produced by the media organization or be purchased from an independent production company. Sport content also services the products dimension, such as with licensed games or books, although it is a minor contributor relative to non-sport content.

Sport attracts audiences to the media's modes of distribution, but its importance is more clearly illustrated in Figure 3.7, which highlights horizontal and vertical integration as a way of producing a web of promotion. In Figure 3.7 a single media organization owns multiple distribution outlets. Sport content is able to be utilized by any distribution outlet in the web and coverage of sport in one outlet in turn creates awareness and promotes the coverage via another outlet. Sport coverage in one outlet can also be used to promote another outlet that does not cover sport, or non-sport content on the same outlet. Sometimes this occurs on the same horizontal plane (the same type of outlet, such as two television stations or programmes) or the same vertical plane (two different outlet types, such as a newspaper and a magazine).

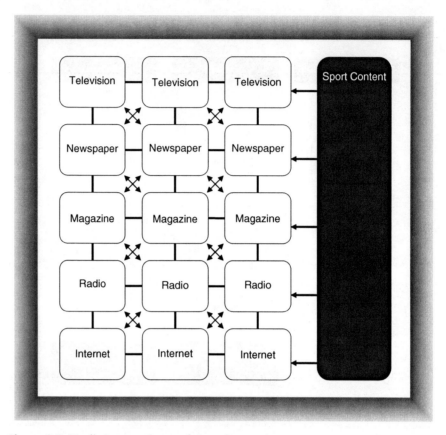

Figure 3.7 Media Integration and Cross Promotion

In some countries media ownership laws restrict the amount of vertical and horizontal integration a media organization can achieve. Both can lead to a lack of media diversity. For example, if a media organization owns all the newspapers in a single city, then it could cross promote its activities, raise prices or use its news gathering infrastructure to service all its publications. The products represented in Figure 3.6 can also be promoted through horizontal and vertical integration. For example, a film produced internally within the media organization could be promoted during sport coverage on one of its television stations, or in one of its magazines.

Key sport players

Like the media industry, there are also key players that dominate the sport industry and the sport media nexus. These sport organizations and their competitions have become valuable commercial properties, however, they are not spread evenly throughout the world and some sports have been

Table 3.2 FIFA Membership by Confederation, 1904–2005

	1904	1925	1950	1975	1990	2005
Europe	8	28	32	35	36	51
South America	0	6	9	10	10	10
North/Central America	0	3	12	22	27	35
Asia	0	1	13	33	38	46
Africa	0	1	1	35	48	53
Oceania	0	0	1	4	8	12
Total	8	39	68	139	167	207

Source: www.fifa.com

more successful at capitalizing on the media's need for content and desire to increase audiences and revenue. The following sections provide thematic discussions of the key players in the sport industry.

King football

Almost wherever it is played, football in its various forms is a leader in the sport media nexus. Globally, football is played in more than 200 countries and in many countries is the most popular spectator sport, for both live and mediated audiences. In some countries, such as America, New Zealand, Australia, South Africa, Canada and parts of the UK, an indigenous code is the dominant sport. For example, in Australia, Australian football competes with rugby league, rugby union and soccer (called football in most parts of the world). Each of these football codes has a professional league and are the top four sports in terms of their media revenue and overall popularity.

FIFA

FIFA is the world governing body for football and consists of six football confederations that span the globe: Africa; Asia; South America; North and Central America and the Caribbean; Europe; and Oceania. The history of FIFA's membership (countries), demonstrated in Table 3.2, illustrates the growth of the sport and the growing awareness of the sport outside Europe (FIFA, 2006). It is also indicative of FIFA's increasing political, economic and cultural power. FIFA is responsible for one of the two biggest sporting events in the World, the FIFA World Cup, which is staged every 4 years.

As far as its media presence is concerned, FIFA claims they 'offer broadcasting rights, as well as many unique FIFA programming opportunities. FIFA's proven sponsorship and advertising programmes across the News Media area are constantly developing. From 3G, MMS and SMS, to sponsorship of FIFAworldcup.com, the single largest sports event website of all time,

FIFA have the platforms to reach your target audience' (FIFA, 2006). In 1986 the World Cup was broadcast in 166 countries, with almost 10,000 hours of television time and a cumulative viewing audience of 13,500 million people. By 2002 these figures had increased markedly to 213 countries, in excess of 41,000 hours of television time and a cumulative viewing audience of almost 29,000 million.

UEFA

Of all FIFA's confederations, Europe is the oldest and most powerful. The Union of European Fútball Associations (UEFA) is the governing body for football in Europe. Its core mission is to promote, protect and develop European football at every level of the game. The promotion component of its mission is largely achieved through the annual UEFA Champions League and the European Championship, held every 4 years in between FIFA World Cups. These competitions are valuable media properties and UEFA derives 65% of its income from television revenue (UEFA, 2006).

European and American Football Leagues

National football leagues are among the most powerful players in the sport media nexus. They do not command global interest and awareness in the same way as major events such as the FIFA World Cup or the Olympic Games, but they do provide consistent content that commands a loyal audience. The English (Premier League), Spanish (Liga de Fútbol Professional or La Liga), Italian (Serie A) and German (Bundesliga) leagues are the most prominent, an indication of which is the worth of the competing teams illustrated in Table 3.3. Similarly, the American NFL has been a dominant player in the sport media nexus since the 1950s, which is also illustrated by the worth of the teams shown in Table 3.4. The J-League is prominent in Japan, while in South Africa and New Zealand rugby union's dominance is partly achieved through the successful Super 14 competition, which includes teams from each of the countries and Australia. The northern hemisphere also has a six nation's rugby union tournament that is popular as a live and mediated product.

Major events
Olympic Games

The Olympic Games, organized and managed by the International Olympic Committee, is one of the most recognizable global events. The American and European markets continue to be the most profitable, as will be demonstrated in the following chapter, however the Games have established a worldwide profile through the principle that all broadcasting agreements be based on free-to-air coverage. This has resulted in more than US $10,000 million in

Table 3.3 Most Valuable Football (Soccer) Teams (2006)

Team	Country	Value (US $ million)	Revenue (US $ million)
Manchester United	England	1,373	298
Real Madrid	Spain	1,012	334
AC Milan	Italy	921	283
Arsenal	England	841	207
Bayern Munich	Germany	769	229
Juventus	Italy	687	278
Chelsea	England	508	267
Internazionale Milan	Italy	504	215
Barcelona	Spain	440	252
Liverpool	England	370	219
Schalke 04	Germany	324	118
Newcastle United	England	302	156
AS Roma	Italy	263	160
Manchester City	England	222	109
Tottenham Hotspur	England	214	127
Olympique Lyonnais	France	208	112
Celtic	Scotland	196	111
Valencia	Spain	195	102
Bayer Leverkusen	Germany	189	95
Glasgow Rangers	Scotland	187	99

Source: www.forbes.com

Table 3.4 Most Valuable NFL Teams (2004)

Team	Value (US $ million)	Revenue (US $ million)
Washington Redskins	1,264	287
Dallas Cowboys	1,063	231
New England Patriots	1,040	236
Philadelphia Eagles	952	216
Houston Texans	946	215
Denver Broncos	907	202
Cleveland Browns	892	203
Caroline Panthers	878	195
Tampa Bay Buccaneers	877	195
Chicago Bears	871	193

Source: www.forbes.com

broadcast rights deals from 1984 to 2008, but has also meant that the majority of the world's population has been able to access the event freely. The inability to gain additional revenues through pay television rights deals has been offset through significant sponsorship deals with global brands such as Coca-Cola, General Electric, Johnson & Johnson, Kodak, McDonalds and Visa. These brands and products have further contributed to the Olympics' increasing global awareness.

Although not as popular or as profitable as the Olympic Games, events such as the Asian Games and the Commonwealth Games also generate significant media attention in the competing countries. Annual events such as the Tour de France are also attractive as global media events. The Tour de France has benefited in this respect from a strong European following and the success of American Lance Armstrong in particular.

Sport circuits

Although they often contain major events, sporting circuits are another segment in the collection of sport's major players. Men's and women's tennis and golf are the most prominent examples of global or regional circuits that attract significant media coverage. For example, in 2006 the Association of Tennis Professionals (ATP) Tour for men played 64 tournaments in 31 countries, while the Sony Ericsson Women's Tennis Association (WTA) Tour played 63 events in 35 countries. The WTA tour is the most prominent professional sport for women in the world and in 2006 more than 1,400 players representing 75 countries competed for in excess of US $60 million. In tennis the US Open, French Open, Australian Open and Wimbledon are the major events that capture significant media coverage.

Similarly, the men's and women's golf tours are also popular media properties. Male and female golfers compete on both the American and European tours, which have affiliated events throughout the world. For men the US Open, US PGA, US Masters and British Open are the major events that attract significant media coverage. Because of the prominence and popularity of individual golfers and tennis players, both these circuits are popular global products and feature on both free-to-air and pay television.

Motor sport

Although most of the world's major motor sports operate as sport circuits, it is worth considering them as a specific segment in order to establish their importance in the sport media nexus. Formula 1 racing is one of the most popular television sports in the world, in part because it travels to a significant number of its countries. The Formula 1 circuit includes grand prix events in Bahrain, Malaysia, Australia, San Marino, Spain, Monaco, England, Canada, America, France, Germany, Hungary, Turkey, Italy, China, Japan and Brazil. Formula 1 is broadcast in Europe on RTL, on ITV in Great Britain, SPEED Channel in America and Al-Jazeera in the Middle East.

Similarly, the second most prominent motor sport circuit, the World Rally Championship (WRC), also holds events across the globe: Monte Carlo, Sweden, Mexico, Spain, France, Argentina, Italy, Greece, Germany, Finland, Japan, Cyprus, Turkey, Australia, New Zealand and Wales. Both the WRC and Formula 1 are centred in Europe, but events are increasingly being held in growing Asian markets. Although not based on a global sporting circuit, NASCAR is second behind the NFL in television ratings in America. It manages 36 races across the country in the Nextel Cup, the premier competition. Telecast on major television networks, NASCAR claims it has a fan base of 75 million people, although its popularity is limited to North America.

The global sport media industry

Profiles of the major sport players in the sport media nexus reveal that media organizations value content that can deliver large national and global audiences. Referring back to the discussion of the three dimension of the media industry (communication services, distribution and products), sport content that is able to secure widespread distribution is valuable, but even more so is content that can be effectively utilized through vertical and horizontal integration across distribution outlets and between distribution and products. The most valuable sport content, such as the FIFA World Cup or national football leagues is able to draw audiences into a web of media consumption, rather than an isolated mediated sport experience.

Summary

This chapter has examined the sport media nexus at global and national levels by examining the special characteristics of the media and sport industries. In particular, this chapter has profiled key media and sport players, which facilitated generalizations about the way in which both industries operate. This chapter has also highlighted the dominance of particular sports and their importance to the media as content that is able to penetrate and leverage new markets around the world. Review questions and exercises are listed below to assist with confirming your knowledge of the core concepts and principles introduced in this chapter.

Review questions and exercises

1. Does the media provide entertainment, information or education in its coverage of sport?

2. Why is sport an important property for the major media organizations of the world?
3. Which organization is the most important sport media player in the world? Why?
4. What media organizations are dominant in your country of origin? Are there many or only a few major players? What is the impact of this diversity or lack thereof?
5. Which business segments are important to these organizations? How important is sport to these segments?
6. What proportion of the major television stations and newspapers in your city or nation are owned by one of the major media players profiled in this chapter?
7. What impact does the ownership referred to in the previous question have on content?
8. Do any of the media organizations in your nation have commercial interests as owners or part owners of professional sport teams? If so, what impact does this have on content?
9. What proportion of all sport broadcast rights fees in your nation are paid to football codes?
10. Were the top five rating sport broadcasts in your nation or state last year local or global? Were they based on the seasonal, circuit or event model?

Case 1 Surfing: an unusual minor player

Unlike many other sports that are able to specify a broadcast date and time and are able to play despite the conditions (such as football where the players will play in any conditions or basketball where the conditions are static and not venue specific), surfing is a sport that is heavily dependant on natural conditions. Most major competitions are scheduled over approximately 10 days, which is necessary to allow for highly variable conditions. In these competitions it is not unusual for competitors and organizers to spend a number of days waiting for the waves to reach an acceptable height to start, resume or finish the competition. This unpredictability means that a surfing competition is not an ideal product for live broadcasting.

Live television broadcasting in particular relies on predictability, as programmes need to go to air when they are scheduled and viewers expect to be entertained. A season based on weekly competition, combined with a willingness to play in tropical or artic conditions depending on the location and time of year means that football is a product that fits the predictability requirements of live television broadcasting extremely well. Surfing on the other hand is more problematic and has had to devise a broadcast strategy that suits the unpredictability and length of its competition format, as well as the commercial and cultural environment in which surfing consumers and sponsors operate.

The Association of Surfing Professionals (ASP) has been the governing body of surfing since 1976 and among its functions manages the world tours for men, women and juniors. Like tennis and golf, surfing is a global sporting circuit and the men's and women's tours visit places such as Tahiti, Japan, Brazil, Mexico, South Africa, Hawaii, Australia and France. Highlights of the competition are broadcast as highlight packages throughout the world on news and sport programmes, while highlight programmes are produced following the tournament, which are also broadcast globally on both pay and free-to-air television.

What is unusual about surfing's place in the sport media nexus is that it relies on sponsors, not media organizations to broadcast its product. All events of the men's and women's surfing world tour are available as live web casts through the websites of naming rights sponsors of each of the events. For example, the Rip Curl Pro event held annually at Bells Beach in Australia is available through the Rip Curl website. Surfing fans are able to access a live broadcast at no cost, in a similar fashion to a free-to-air television broadcast. This type of arrangement does not make surfing one of the major players in the sport media nexus, but it certainly makes them one of the more innovative.

Case 2   Mediated sport?: World Wrestling Entertainment

World Wrestling Entertainment (WWE) claims that it is an integrated media and entertainment company, a description that is very similar to media organizations such as the Walt Disney Company. WWE also claims that it is involved in the sport entertainment business, a description that might fit a number of major sport players at the start of the twenty-first century. Although WWE exhibits features of both media and sport organizations, it is neither. Its detractors argue that is fake, yet it has a massive fan base in America and is expanding into Japan and Great Britain in particular. Whether it is sport, media or entertainment, it is clear that it is very successful.

In the report to shareholders as part of the 2005 annual report, WWE founders Vincent and Linda McMahon noted that 'WWE's success emanates from our intellectual property – our Superstars – who bridge cultural, economic and social barriers around the world. Our fans around the globe understand and love our entertainment product, regardless of language and cultural differences'. This type of language and sentiment could be used to describe sport and sport stars across the globe and is an accurate representation of the way in which sport has been used to establish and develop new markets, particularly for pay television.

Listed on the New York Stock Exchange, WWE has four business segments: live and televised entertainment; consumer products; digital media; and film. WWE claims that their strategy is a simple one, which is to develop compelling storylines that involve their Superstars (of which approximately

180 are under contract), which creates television ratings, which in turn drive revenue from pay-per-view events. Once again, this formula or strategy mimics that of non-scripted sport seasons and tournaments. WWE claims that it is the largest provider of pay-per-view events in the world, with international broadcasters including SKY in the UK, Premiere in Germany, SKY Perfect TV! in Japan and Main Event in Australia. In 2005/2006, live events and television programming drove total revenues of US $400 million.

Similar to only the most sophisticated sport organizations, WWE has diversified its business operations. It produces its own home videos, magazines and music, as well as utilizes its website to promote activities and sell merchandize. According to WWE the website averages 14.5 million unique visitors worldwide per month. Finally, in 2006 WWE released its first feature film and has plans for more in the future.

Sources: http://corporate.wwe.com/; WWE 2005 Annual Report.

4

Putting up
big numbers:
broadcast rights
and revenue

Overview

This chapter examines the commercial relationship between the sport and media industries and the ways in which money drives the sport media nexus. In particular, the key features of the process of selling and purchasing the rights to broadcast sport on various media forms are examined. This chapter also investigates the ways in which sports and media organizations attempt to leverage their audiences in order to achieve greater revenues, primarily through advertising and sponsorship.

After completing this chapter the reader should be able to:

- Identify and explain the commercial relationships between sport organizations, media organizations, sponsors, advertisers and consumers in the sport media nexus.
- Describe the process by which sport and media organizations sell and purchase the rights to broadcast sport via electronic media.
- Explain the rationale behind media organizations bidding to acquire the rights for sporting events, leagues or teams.
- Explain the rationale behind segmenting rights in order to maximize revenue.

> ■ **Explain the ways in which sport and media organizations use each other to increase their revenue through advertising and sponsorship.**

Introduction

As the previous three chapters have demonstrated, the sport media nexus is robust. The evolution of the sport media nexus, its strength, and the global power and influence of both of its component industries, has largely been driven by money. The media coverage of sport has become the central means by which sport organizations obtain revenue, while sport has become one of the most valuable 'properties' for media organizations. The importance of sport is such that major national broadcasters almost always bid for the rights to high-profile sports (Hoehn & Lancefield, 2003). In fact, the rights to 'premium' sports have become such an important commercial property that not having them can adversely impact a company's financial bottom line or in extreme cases lead to the demise of media organizations. The way in which the commercial dimension of the sport media nexus operates can be divided into five interrelated components, which are represented in Figure 4.1.

First, media organizations pay for the right to broadcast a sport event, season or series of games. These broadcast rights are typically limited to free-to-air television, pay television, radio and the Internet, and of these four the two television forms are by far the biggest players. In Figure 4.1, this is demonstrated by the sport organization providing the official broadcaster with content and in return the broadcaster pays a rights fee. In contrast to most forms of electronic media, however, the print media typically reports on sport in a heavily competitive environment in a news or public interest capacity, rather than a promotional capacity via an exclusive contract or arrangement, and as such are not charged by sport organizations.

Second, media organizations that purchase the rights to broadcast a sport event, season or series of games seek to secure a return on investment. On free-to-air television this is primarily achieved through the sale of advertising space and time, which in Figure 4.1 is represented by the advertiser acquiring exposure to the consumer via the broadcaster. The number of people watching the sport is directly proportional to advertising revenue and to broadcast rights fees. On pay television a return on investment is achieved by the sale of advertising space and by attracting subscribers who, in general terms, are prepared to pay for a generic service, dedicated sport channels or pay-per-view events. In Figure 4.1, this relationship is represented by the consumer paying the broadcaster for content which has previously been purchased by the broadcaster from the sport organization. Increasingly, through developments in digital technology, television networks are also able to generate a return on investment through interactive revenue, such as gaming and gambling.

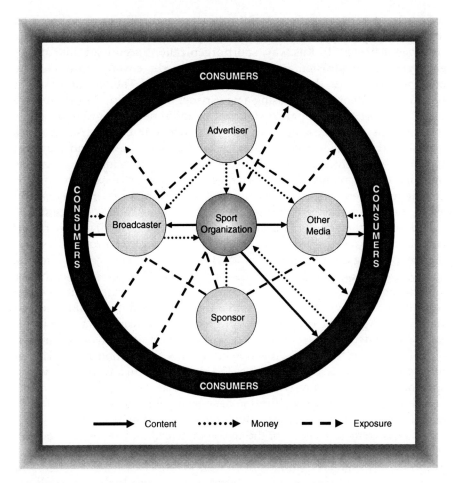

Figure 4.1 Commercial Dimensions of the Sport Media Nexus

In the case of pay television, the number of people watching sport and more specifically those who are prepared to pay is directly proportional to the broadcast rights fees. The popularity and appeal of sport also means that acquiring the rights to broadcast sport events and games can increase the broadcaster's brand awareness, which in turn might increase the demand for other non-sport related content (Hoehn & Lancefield, 2003). This phenomenon is likely to be greater if a broadcaster has held the rights for an extended period of time and consumer loyalty to both the sport and media products has been established.

Third, media organizations that do not have the exclusive broadcast rights will also seek to attract advertising revenue through coverage of sport. For example, a sport magazine or newspaper will invest in the coverage of sport in a non-exclusive and typically a non-official capacity, which will in turn attract consumers. This is represented in Figure 4.1 where consumers pay other media providers for sport related content. Based on the size and demographics of the readership, advertisers will pay the magazine or newspaper to access consumers.

Fourth, sport organizations seek to attract sponsorship revenue based on the sport's popularity, which in turn is proportional to the amount of media coverage achieved. In this way, sport organizations secure additional revenue via the broadcaster, as well as via the media coverage provided by other media outside the exclusive rights agreement. The consumer might pay for the content by purchasing a newspaper or magazine, or may receive the content for free through an Internet or radio news programme. These relationships are represented in Figure 4.1, whereby the sponsor receives exposure to consumers via the broadcaster and other media, and the sport organization receives a direct financial benefit. Thus, sport organizations must not only maximize media coverage that results from exclusive broadcast rights agreements, but must also seek to maximize general media coverage, thereby increasing exposure, awareness, interest and audience share.

Fifth and finally, sport organizations are able to provide mediated sport content directly to consumers. In Figure 4.1, this is represented by consumers paying the sport organization for the product. However, if the product is free the sport organization is able to increase their revenue through sponsorship or advertising sales. For example, a sport organization provides content on its website, through which sponsors and advertisers are able to gain access to consumers. Again, the preparedness of sponsors or advertisers to pay is primarily dependent on the size of the audience. In most situations where a sport organization is increasing its revenue in this way the relationship is with an official sponsor of the club or league. The situation of an advertiser paying a sport organization as represented in Figure 4.1 is rare. However, developments in technology and the diversification of sport organizations' media interests may increase the use and profitability of this dimension in the future.

It is clear from an analysis of the core commercial dimensions of the sport media nexus represented in Figure 4.1 that sport and media generate revenue by attracting the greatest number of viewers (as well as listeners, readers and users). The media are attracted to sport because a large number of people are interested in a variety of sport products, while sport is attracted to the media because it can generate interest and ultimately increased audiences, whether live or mediated. This connection between sport and the media is often regarded as a typical 'chicken and the egg' conundrum – it is hard to know which came first. How does a sport obtain media coverage without audience interest or awareness and how does a sport create audience interest or awareness without media coverage? For established sports that are successful media properties, however, these questions are at the periphery of their operations.

Broadcast rights

Sport and sport broadcasting rights have special features that are not exhibited by other media products, making them extremely valuable national and global commodities. Sport events and games are ephemeral products or perishable goods, which means that they endure or last for a very brief period of time (Tonazzi, 2003; Sandy, Sloane & Rosentraub, 2004). Although sport is available via delayed coverage or through highlight packages, the value of these is far less than live sport, because of the intense consumer interest in the result of the game, match or event as it is taking place. There are very few non-sport related events that are ephemeral or perishable in the same way. Occasions of state and crisis events might exhibit similar features, but they are either too infrequent or too sudden to merit legitimate comparison. Sport is also unique in that there are very few products that consumers are able to satisfactorily substitute (Tonazzi, 2003). In other words, a viewer who wants to watch televised games of a football league has little option but to consume the product offered by the broadcaster who has secured the rights. It is unlikely that the viewer will consider watching tennis or golf on another network a viable substitute. By contrast, a viewer interested in watching a criminal or legal drama is likely to be able to substitute a variety of products on a variety of networks and stations. In essence, each sport is a relatively unique product, which means that it is of more value than a product with multiple variants or imitations. Finally, unlike the multitude of news and drama that is available to television networks in particular, the amount of professional sport is finite (Tonazzi, 2003). Moreover, premium sport leagues and events are even more limited, which means that competition to acquire the rights is greater.

The limit of substitutable products and the desire of consumers to view matches or events 'as they happen' make sport a highly valued and sought after commodity for media organizations. At the 1998 annual general meeting of News Corporation, Rupert Murdoch informed shareholders that he intended to use sport as a battering ram and lead offering in all pay television operations, because sport overpowers everything else (Ferguson, 1999). The fact that sport is viewed as a key driver of direct and indirect revenues for media organizations has a significant impact on the size of broadcast rights, the competition to secure them, the ability of sport organizations to maximize their revenue through sponsorship and the service that media organizations demand from their sport partners.

Selling rights

A sport organization has a number of factors it needs to consider in negotiating a broadcast rights agreement with a media partner (Foster, Greyser & Walsh, 2006). The size of the bid is generally the most important, for if all other elements of the bid are equal then the highest will be selected. This is even more important for sport organizations in which broadcast revenues represent a majority of total revenue, in which there is increasingly a demand to continue to maintain the exponential growth experienced in the 1990s and early part of the twenty-first century. For example, in 1986 the annual rights fee for the BBC and ITV to broadcast the English Premier League was £3.1 million, whereas the 2001 deal, with BSkyB as the primary partner, was worth £550 million (Sandy et al., 2004). In Europe alone the broadcast rights fees for the FIFA World Cup and the Olympic Games increased during the 1990s by 900% and 380% respectively (Hoehn & Lancefield, 2003). For most sport organizations the size of the broadcast rights deal is the overriding factor, often to the detriment of other considerations.

The ability of the broadcaster to provide broad coverage is an important factor for most sport organizations, whether they are seeking to build their profile or further enhance the cross promotional purposes made possible by a large audience and national or global sponsors. This consideration appears to differ between sports and between countries, for some sports will opt to sign broadcast rights deals that offer no free-to-air television coverage, thereby limiting their reach to pay television subscribers only, while others will seek to capitalize on the commercial opportunities provided by increased audience awareness. Often the coverage of the sport and the amount of money available as part of a broadcast rights agreement are competing factors.

The financial solvency of potential bidders is also a consideration, for a high bid from an organization that cannot afford the price is as useful as no bid at all. This consideration is important in situations where there is a third party or broadcast rights agent involved in the process. An exemplar in this respect was FIFA's sale of the rights to the 2002 and 2006 World Cup competitions to Kirch, a German media and marketing company that negotiated rights deals with individual broadcasters (Sandy et al., 2004). In 2002 Kirch declared bankruptcy, causing FIFA and other European sport properties to re-think their broadcast rights strategies. Financial solvency is less of a concern for high-profile sport organizations that negotiate directly with large national or multi-national companies with diversified commercial interests.

Buying rights

The attractiveness of broadcast rights for a prospective buyer is dependent on the audience the broadcaster is able to capture by broadcasting the match, game or event. All things being equal, a large audience pool should equate to a willingness to pay a significant amount of money, while a small audience will generally make the acquisition of the rights package far less appealing. In a similar way that money is the overriding factor for sellers, the size of the audience is invariably the overriding factor for buyers. However, for media organizations the quality of the audience is also a major factor, and in this respect sport is also a particularly good product. Sport usually attracts male viewers aged between 16 and 35 years of age, who are both difficult to reach and typically have high disposable incomes (Hoehn & Lancefield, 2003). Some sports, such as golf, have the capacity to attract a different demographic, such as older males, who also have high disposable incomes. In other words, both the size and the quality of the audience are key variables in calculating the worth of rights to media organizations and advertisers.

Although sport and media organizations can enter into commercial relationships where the revenue is shared or the sport organization assumes the financial risk, the vast majority of sport rights sales, particularly for major sports and events, are on a fixed revenue basis. What this means in practice is that the media organization agrees to pay a fee for the duration of a contract, which might be anything from one event to ten seasons long. The media organization makes the offer based on what it predicts it can recover primarily through advertising and subscription sales. If the audience ratings for the sport product that has been purchased are less than expected, then it follows that the advertising revenue will also be less than expected, particularly if the ratings decline significantly over a 4- or 5-year period. In this situation the broadcast rights deal may result in a net loss for the broadcaster.

The value of sport rights increases in proportion to the exclusivity, scope and duration of the rights (Hoehn & Lancefield, 2003). If the rights are non-exclusive then the broadcaster must not only concern itself with maximizing its investment through advertising and subscription sales, but must also compete against rival broadcasters that are seeking to do the same. This non-exclusivity is likely to reduce advertising and subscription sales, as well as lessen the additional benefit of consumer loyalty. Non-exclusive rights are likely to increase rather than reduce churn, the process in which consumers switch from one provider to another to access preferred programmes. Similarly, it is to the broadcaster's commercial advantage to have access to the greatest number of games for the longest time. Although a long-term broadcast rights agreement shifts a significant amount of risk from the sport organization to the media organization, the trade-off is that the media organization is able to build long-term viewer loyalty.

News Corporation provides a succinct summary of the sports rights marketplace and the pros and cons of buying in:

> 'Sports programming rights contracts between the Company, on the one hand, and various professional sports leagues and teams, on the other, have varying duration and renewal terms. As these contracts expire, the Company may seek renewals on commercial terms; however, third parties may outbid the current rights holders for such rights contracts. In addition, professional sports leagues or teams may create their own networks or the renewal costs could substantially exceed the original contract cost. The loss of rights could impact the extent of the sports coverage offered by FOX and its affiliates, and the Company's regional sports networks, and could adversely affect its advertising and affiliate revenues. Conversely, if the Company is able to renew these contracts, the results could be adversely affected if escalations is sports programming rights costs are unmatched by increases in advertising rates and, in the case of cable networks, subscriber fees.' (News Corporation, 2005).

In 1998 President of NBC Sports Dick Ebersol declared in response to a new NFL broadcast deal that 'the dollar figures have reached an insane level' and 'it is a foolhardy economic venture' (Higgins, 2005). However, since then the rights for major sport properties have continued to increase and News Corporation's fear, expressed above, of the negative impacts caused by losing the rights to premium sport properties seems to be the overwhelming trend among media organizations (see Case 1).

Case 1   Fighting for the rights to Australian football

The acquisition of broadcast rights should, if a logical and unemotional cost-benefit analysis is applied, be a rational process whereby a broadcaster or cluster of broadcasters weigh up whether acquiring the rights will result in a positive or negative impact on the business. However, the broadcast rights process is often anything but rational. This was illustrated in the 2005/6 negotiations for the broadcast rights to the Australian Football League (AFL), Australia's most popular professional sport league.

In 2001, after a 43-year exclusive association with channel 7, one of Australia's three commercial free-to-air broadcasters, the AFL awarded the broadcast rights to the 2002–2006 seasons to a consortium headed by News Corporation. The consortium split the rights, valued at AUD500 million over the duration of the contract, between channels 9 and 10, channel 7's rival free-to-air broadcasters and pay television broadcaster Foxtel. In 2005 channels 7 and 10 announced that they were teaming up in an attempt to secure the next round of broadcast rights. In late 2005 channel 9, in conjunction with Foxtel and News Limited submitted a bid of AUD780 million for the rights to broadcast the 2007–2011 seasons on free-to-air and pay television. It appeared as is the significant increase in the fee would result in the channel 9 consortium winning the rights.

However, in 1997 channel 7 signed a deal with the AFL which gave them first and last rights at the negotiating table until the end of 2011, for which they paid AUD20 million. After a long and prosperous relationship between the broadcaster and the sport, this deal would have presented itself as one that delivered increased security to channel 7 and an increase in revenue for the AFL with few or no consequences. The result of the first and last rights agreement was that in early 2006 channels 7 and 10 matched the bid from the rival consortium and secured the rights.

Prior to the final offer director of corporate development at channel 7, Simon Francis, said 'we will let our heads and not our hearts make the final decision' (Barrett, 2005), but it is questionable whether the successful networks were forced into a deal that significantly overvalued the rights. James Packer, chief executive officer of channel 9's parent company PBL, said that in offering AUD780 his father Kerry Packer had 'thought about trying to put Nine and PBL into that cliche, a win-win scenario, where you pay as much as you possibly can for it, then add 15% on top of that and know that if you get it it's OK and if the other guy gets it, you know, it's going to be hopefully causing a bout of indigestion' (Ziffer, 2006). This arbitrary approach to the value of the rights and the highly competitive nature of the negotiations led some market analysts in Australia to conclude that the rights were significantly over priced and would lead to increased financial pressure on the successful networks.

Sources: Grigg (2006) and Stapleton (2005).

A competitive arena

Competition, as previously alluded to, is an important element of the broadcast rights process for both sellers and prospective buyers and has three primary dimensions. First, leagues prefer to limit internal competition between clubs by entering into joint or collective selling arrangements. The government regulation of this practice will be discussed in more detail in the following chapter, but is sufficient in this context to note that for sport organizations it is important to minimize internal competition in order to maximize external competition for the product. A broadcaster that is able to secure the rights also wants to limit internal competition within the league to maximize the benefits that flow from exclusivity. However, more internal competition between clubs within a league might benefit a range of broadcasters, particularly where high-profile football rights are concerned.

Second, in order to maximize broadcast rights fees, a league or in some cases a team must maximize the competition between prospective buyers. In other words, if there is only one legitimate buyer then it is likely that the fee will be low, whereas if there are four or five broadcasters willing to bid for the rights then the competitive process is likely to considerably raise the fees. Media organizations, however, want to create the opposite scenario, in which competition, and therefore prices are minimized. In essence, the effect of a broadcaster engaging in long-term exclusive agreements in a limited and finite market could be a reduction in competition, whereby the dominance of a single broadcaster might limit the entry of rival broadcasters or the profitability of existing operators.

Finally, sport leagues and teams are engaged in competition with competitor sports at national and international levels. Seth Blatter, president of FIFA, conceives of the final competitive dimension in the following way:

> 'The act of tendering and selling rights for mammoth sporting events boils down to a battle for the available capital. International sports federations are consequently compelled to deal in the manner of commercial corporations – in direct competition with one another – and other institutions (especially cultural ones) to procure this precious commodity' (FIFA, 2004).

The highly competitive nature of sport broadcasting invariably means that smaller sport leagues and teams attempt to make their product as attractive to broadcasters and advertisers as possible, while larger sport events, leagues and federations have the ability to demand more from broadcasters because of their superior product and audience.

Segmenting the market

Segmenting the market refers to two primary approaches by sport organizations in selling broadcast rights to sport events and games. The first approach is to offer broadcast rights to multiple providers, rather than offer all broadcast opportunities to a single media provider, which would create an exclusive relationship. In practice this means that broadcast rights might be split

63

between free-to-air television, pay television and the Internet, while maximizing exclusivity within each of the media forms. Broadcast rights might also be split on the basis of live, delayed or highlights of coverage, but the prominence of live coverage means that this segmentation has a finite ability to raise revenue. As previously noted, in segmenting the rights there is a trade off between exclusivity and competition, however, in the case of segmenting the rights based on media form, exclusivity can be maintained by offering separate broadcast packages.

The second way in which sport organizations might be considered to segment the market is where they offer the broadcast rights to multiple broadcasters across different territories or geographic areas. In a national context this might mean selling the broadcast rights to a television network that broadcasts into a state or region and at the same time selling the rights to a second or third broadcaster that operates in a different market and does not engage in direct competition. In an international context the segmenting of rights might be manifest in an organization selling to individual countries, rather than to a third party independent agent that then on-sells the rights to media organizations. For example, the 2008 UEFA European Championship broadcast rights were sold on a market by market basis, rather than selling the rights to Europe as a whole. UEFA claims that the European Championship of football is the third biggest sport property in the world, with only the Olympic Games and the FIFA World Cup as more valuable sport events, and the sale of the 2008 rights was staggered throughout 2006 across Europe. The UEFA Champions League was also sold on a country-by-country basis, resulting in the following broadcasters securing contracts for the period 2006–2009:

- United Kingdom – ITV and BSkyB
- Italy – RAI, Mediaset and Sky Italia
- Spain – Antena 3 and Canal+
- France – TF1 and Canal+
- Germany – Premiere
- The Netherlands – NOS and UPC
- Scandinavia – TV3 and Viaset
- Greece – ERT and Supersport

The value of rights

Sport broadcast rights in the top two markets, United States of America and Europe are strikingly similar. In 2002 broadcast rights for sports were approximately US $5,000 million, with football rights accounting for almost half (Hoehn & Lancefield, 2003). In America, the NFL rights were US $2,200 million in 2002, equivalent to 45%, while in Europe, rights to football (or soccer) leagues accounted for US $2,390 million, equivalent to 46%. In a smaller market such as Australia, the football codes (Australian football, rugby league, rugby union and soccer) represent more than 90% of expenditure by media organizations on sport broadcast rights. Similarly, in Spain football/soccer rights represent 72% of total broadcast rights fees (Hoehn & Lancefield, 2003). In order to gain further clarity about the extent of the rights market, it is useful to examine a range of media and sport perspectives at an organizational level.

Media perspectives

An examination of the contractual agreements and liabilities of some of the world's major media organizations reveals that a significant amount of money has been allocated to securing the broadcast rights to sport events and leagues. It also reveals the extent to which sport has become the major property for global media organizations.

For example, News Corporation's 2004–2005 annual report states that as of 30 June 2005, the company, as part of contractual agreements, was committed to US $12,273 million, including US $3,343 million in 2005–2006 and US $3,925 million in 2006–2008 for sports programming rights (News Corporation, 2005). In 2004 and 2005 television revenue contributed 24% and 22% of News Corporation's consolidated revenues respectively, while the company attributed growth in the financial year 2004–2005 to increased advertising revenues from the telecast of the Super Bowl and the Daytona 500, which were not telecast on FOX in 2004. FOX's broadcast of Super Bowl 39 was seen by 133.7 million viewers in the United States of America alone, making it the largest total audience in FOX's history and the fifth largest in American television history. The 2004 Major League Baseball (MLB) World Series averaged 25.4 million viewers across its four games, while FOX's broadcast of the 2005 Daytona 500 equalled the record for the biggest audience for a National Association for Stock Car Auto Racing (NASCAR) race on any US television network.

Similarly, Time Warner AOL's 2004 annual report states that as of 1 December 2004, the company, as part of contractual agreements, was committed to US $4,275 million, including US $1,250 million in 2005 and US $1,754 million in 2006–2007. The News Corporation and Time Warner figures are not directly comparable as Time Warner's figures include licensing arrangements with movie studios for movies on theatrical release, although the sport rights content comprises that vast majority of its contractual liabilities.

The 2004–2006 NFL rights cost the Walt Disney Company US $3,700 million, while the new agreement with the NFL for the right to broadcast Monday night football games commencing in 2006–2007 for 8 years cost US $8,870 million. In addition, the 2005 annual report notes that the Company entered into an 8-year agreement with NASCAR for ABC and ESPN to broadcast certain races and related content from 2007 onwards. The Walt Disney Company, through ESPN and ABC also acquired the rights to the men's and women's FIFA World Cups from 2006 to 2014. Through its sports networks the company also has rights agreements with The British Open, PGA Tour events, the Indianapolis 500 and the US figure skating championships. As a result of acquiring these sport properties, the Walt Disney Company claims that approximately 97 million Americans turn to ESPN media every week for their sports viewing and news. The Walt Disney Company's 2005 annual report states that as of 1 October 2005, the company, as part of contractual agreements, was committed to US $15,837 million for sports programming rights, including US $2,524 million for 2006, US $4,275 million in 2007–2008 and US $3,418 million in 2009–2010.

Finally, Vivendi Universal's 2005 annual report states that as of 31 December 2004, contractual obligations for sports rights amounted to €2,134million, comprising €531 million in 2005, €1,287 million in 2006–2007 and 316 million in 2008–2009. The 2003 and 2002 figures were €695 million and €1,065 million respectively, indicative of a fluctuating market for sports rights. Viviendi Universal's subsidiary Canal+ acquired the rights to the 2005–2008 seasons of the French National Football League for €1,800 million.

Sport perspectives

The allocation of sport rights fees, as discussed previously, is not even. Rather, the revenue that a sport organization is able to achieve through the sale of broadcast rights depends on the size and demographics of the market. An examination of a variety of broadcast rights deals reveals that rights fees are in the main proportional to the size of national and global audiences that a sport event or league is able to attract.

Globally, the Olympic Games and the FIFA World Cup are the largest sporting events in the world and capture the greatest amount of media and popular interest. The summer and winter Olympic Games each consist of approximately 2 weeks of sporting competitions held every 4 years in which all countries can compete, while the FIFA World Cup is similarly held every 4 years but consists of 4 weeks of competition for the final 32 teams that have qualified. The Olympics are an ideal case study in the growth of broadcast rights, the importance of the American and European markets to international events and the proportion of revenue that is acquired through rights agreements.

Table 4.1 illustrates the growth in broadcast rights fees paid to the International Olympic Committee by international broadcasters. The figures demonstrate the enormous growth in broadcast rights fees since approximately US $1 million was paid for the rights to broadcast the 1960 summer Olympic Games in Rome. By the 2001–2004 quadrennial period, broadcast rights accounted for approximately 52% of Olympic revenue.

Table 4.1 also shows that since the 1984 Games in Los Angeles, which marked the birth of a highly commercialized Olympics, the broadcast rights fees have increased by in excess of 500%. A more detailed examination of the figures demonstrates that a majority of broadcast rights revenue has been generated by the American market. Table 4.2 shows that although this dominance has abated somewhat and the contribution by European markets has increased, broadcast rights revenue for the Olympic Games is still dependent on Westernized countries in particular. Of the 21% represented by other in 2004 in Table 4.2, Japan accounted for 10% and Australia and Canada a further 6%, leaving 5% of broadcast revenue outside the North America, Europe, Australia and Japan.

Table 4.1 Olympic Games Broadcast Rights (in US$)

Summer Games		Winter Games	
Rome (1960)	1,178,000	Squaw Valley (1960)	50,000
Tokyo (1964)	1,578,000	Innsbruck (1964)	937,000
Mexico City (1968)	9,750,000	Grenoble (1968)	2,613,000
Munich (1972)	17,792,000	Sapporo (1972)	8,475,000
Montreal (1976)	34,862,000	Innsbruck (1976)	11,627,000
Moscow (1980)	87,984,000	Lake Placid (1980)	20,726,000
Los Angeles (1984)	286,914,000	Sarajevo (1984)	102,682,000
Seoul (1988)	402,595,000	Calgary (1988)	324,897,000
Barcelona (1992)	636,060,000	Albertville (1992)	291,928,000
Atlanta (1996)	898,267,000	Lillehammer (1994)	352,911,000
Sydney (2000)	1,331,550,000	Nagano (1998)	513,485,000
Athens (2004)	1,494,028,000	Salt Lake (2002)	736,135,000

Source: www.olympic.org

Table 4.2 Percentage Contribution of American and European Broadcast Rights Fees to the Total Broadcast Rights Fees for the Summer Olympic Games

City/Year	America (%)	Europe (%)	Other (%)
Montreal (1976)	72	19	9
Moscow (1980)	82	8	10
Los Angeles (1984)	79	8	13
Seoul (1988)	75	8	17
Barcelona (1992)	63	15	22
Atlanta (1996)	51	28	21
Sydney (2000)	53	26	21
Athens (2004)	53	26	21

Source: www.olympic.org

Table 4.3 shows a similar pattern for the broadcast rights for the winter Olympic Games, in which the dominance of the American market has been maintained, despite some fluctuations that are the result of where the event was staged (the North American percentage is higher when the Games are staged in North America). In the year with the highest figure for 'other', Albertville (1992), the broadcast rights fees paid by Japan, Canada and Australia accounted for more than half of the 18%.

Table 4.4 uses the 2006 winter Olympic Games in Torino, Italy to further demonstrate that beyond Westernized countries in which the advertising markets are strong and provide broadcasters with opportunities to maximize a return on their investment, broadcast rights fees are of a nominal value. In fact, the rights to broadcast the Olympic Games to a vast majority

Table 4.3 Percentage Contribution of American and European Broadcast Rights Fess to the Total Broadcast Rights Fees for the Winter Olympic Games

City/Year	America (%)	Europe (%)	Other (%)
Innsbruck (1976)	86	10	4
Lake Placid (1980)	75	19	6
Sarajevo (1984)	89	5	6
Calgary (1988)	95	2	3
Albertville (1992)	75	7	18
Lillehammer (1994)	84	7	9
Nagano (1998)	73	14	13
Salt Lake (2002)	74	16	10

Source: www.olympic.org

Table 4.4 Torino 2006 Olympic Games Broadcast Rights Holders

Country/Territory	Broadcaster	Rights Fee (in US$)
United States	National Broadcasting Company (NBC)	613.4 million
Canada	Canadian Broadcasting Corporation (CBC)	28.0 million
Latin America	Organizacion de la Television Iberoamericana (OTI)	1.75 million
Asia-Pacific	Asia-Pacific Broadcasting Union (ABU)	950,000
Japan	NHK + NAB	38.5 million
Korea	Korea Pool	900,000
Europe	European Broadcasting Union (EBU)	135 million
Australia	Seven Network	14 million
Africa	Supersport	600,000
Total		833 million

Source: www.olympic.org

of the world's population are only worth a few million dollars. However, the commercial growth of China and India in particular suggests that this dominance may not continue beyond the first 20 years of the twenty-first century.

As regular global events the Olympic Games and the FIFA World Cup (see Case 2) are able to acquire significant revenues through broadcast rights, however, the rights to national leagues and global circuits are at least, if not more significant.

For example, in 2005 NASCAR in America signed broadcast rights deals for the 2007–2014 seasons that were reported to be worth US $4,500 million

Case 2   FIFA's exponential growth

FIFA has experienced significant growth during its history of over 100 years. Its major event, the FIFA World Cup, has generated substantial revenue through media rights and associated sponsorship, particularly towards the end of the twentieth century and at the beginning of the twenty-first. In 1906 FIFA recorded annual revenues of approximately CHF500, which remained relatively stable for the first 20 years of its history and then increased modestly throughout the majority of the twentieth century. By 1970 annual revenue was CHF1,500,000 which subsequently increased to CHF10,000,000 by 1989 and to CHF33,000,000 by 1997. Revenue growth exploded at the end of the 1990s, as it increased to CHF389,000,000 in 1998 and to CHF963,000,000 in 2002.

The massive growth in revenue experienced by FIFA was largely due to broadcast rights generated by the World Cup. In 1930 match levies and subscriptions from its member associations accounted for 85% of its revenue, whereas by 2002 less than 1% of the organization's revenue was from the same source. The following table demonstrates that there are fluctuations in FIFA's revenue based on the scheduling of the World Cup, but the overall trend is that broadcast rights and associated marketing represent the vast majority of the organization's revenue.

FIFA Revenue 1999–2002 (CHF million – figures in brackets are percentage of total annual revenue)

Year/Income Source	1999	2000	2001	2002	1999–2002
Total	212	690	820	963	2,685
Television Rights	152 (72%)	343 (50%)	317 (39%)	813 (84%)	1,625 (61%)
Marketing	11 (5%)	304 (44%)	461 (56%)	64 (7%)	840 (31%)
Other	49 (23%)	43 (6%)	42 (5%)	86 (9%)	220 (8%)

Source: www.fifa.com

with Fox Sports, Speed Channel, TNT, ABC and ESPN (Gough, 2005; Reynolds, 2005). In deals that both segmented the rights and maintained exclusivity, Fox will broadcast the first half of the NASCAR season and the famous Daytona 500, while ESPN and ABC will broadcast the second half and the conclusion to the season. In this scenario the broadcasters are compelled to work together to ensure that the consumers, sponsors and advertisers enjoy a level of continuity that would not normally be apparent with two or more competing broadcasters.

The South African, New Zealand and Australian rugby unions (SANZAR) current broadcast deal with News Corporation and Africa's Supersport is worth US $323 million over 5 years, which includes the rights to Australia, New Zealand, Africa, the United Kingdom and Ireland (Smith, 2005). The previous deal was US $555 million over 10 years and the increase in rights fee is a result of increasing the international Super 12 competition to Super 14 in 2006, which meant an increase from 69 matches to 94 and increasing the Tri-Nations series from six to nine matches. In other words, News Corporation was prepared to pay more money for more content.

Rights agreements are not limited to both television forms, as radio and the Internet also feature in broadcast agreements between sport and media organizations. For example, in 2005 XM Satellite Radio signed a US $100 million agreement to be the exclusive satellite radio network for the National Hockey League in America over 10 years, beginning with the 2007–2008 season (Consoli, 2005). XM Satellite Radio also captured the rights to MLB in America in an 11-year deal worth US $650 million, while rival radio broadcaster Sirius Satellite Radio secured the rights to broadcast NASCAR from 2007 onwards for US $107.5 million over 5 years.

Recovering rights fees and maximizing exposure

The way in which free-to-air television recovers the money it expends on acquiring the rights to broadcast sport is primarily by selling advertising space and time. Advertisers are charged a rate based on expected ratings. These rates are calculated based on prior ratings for similar programmes, and the expected demographics of the television audience. Previous audiences that watched similar programmes can also be used in the calculation (Foster et al., 2006). Table 4.5

Table 4.5 Television Sport Audiences in 2005

Event	Audience (million)
National Football League Super Bowl	93
UEFA Champions League Final	73
Canadian Formula One Grand Prix	51
World Championships – Athletics	23
MLB World Series	22
National Basketball Association Final	20
Tour de France Final Stage	16
US masters Golf Final Day	15
Wimbledon Men's Final	12
Host City Naming for 2012 Olympics	11

Source: Goodbody, 2006.

demonstrates that television sport is a popular product with audiences, which generates high ratings and therefore, high advertising rates.

The Walt Disney Company's explanation of the connection between expenditure on rights and return on investment through advertising is succinctly expressed in the following excerpt from its 2005 annual report:

> 'The costs of these contracts [contractual commitments for the purchase of television rights for sports and other programming, including the NBA, NFL, MLB and various college football and basketball conferences and football bowl games] have increased significantly in recent years. We enter into these contractual commitments with the expectation that, over the life of the contracts, revenue from advertising during the programming and affiliate fees will exceed the costs of the programming. While contract costs may initially exceed incremental revenues and negatively impact operating income, it is our expectation that the combined value to our networks from all of these contracts will result in long-term benefits. The actual impact of these contracts on the Company's results over the term of the contracts is dependent upon a number of factors, including the strength of advertising markets, effectiveness of marketing efforts and the size of viewer audiences' (Walt Disney Company, 2005:60).

The amount that advertisers spend on sport is relative to the size of the audience, but is often also dependent on cultural context. In many cases this means that football is a dominant media product in terms of advertising revenue, however, in India approximately US $200 million per annum is spent on sport by advertisers, of which more than 90% is spent on cricket (Gupta, 2005).

In 2006 the Pittsburgh Steelers defeated the Seattle Seahawks 21-10 at Super Bowl XL, the annual championship game of America's NFL. Off the field companies competed with each other to advertise their products in the most creative and appealing ways on television network ABC. The broadcast was watched by 45.85 million homes, the second highest total in American television history, which equates to an estimated 141.4 million viewers, with an estimated average of 90.7 million viewers throughout the broadcast. Advertising rates averaged US $2.5 million for 30 seconds of time during the 2006 Super Bowl. Advertisers that paid the money, often for more than one commercial included major American products and suppliers:

- Bud Light (4)
- Budweiser (3)
- Burger King (2)
- Cadillac (2)
- Diet Pepsi (2)
- ESPN (3)
- Ford (1)
- Gillette (3)
- Honda (1)
- Hummer (1)
- Magnolia Pictures (1)
- MLB (1)

- MasterCard (1)
- Motorola (1)
- New Line Cinema (1)
- Paramount (1)
- Toyota (2)
- Walt Disney (4)
- Warner Bros (3)

Not including those commercials that promoted the NFL or network television series, companies spent approximately US $155 million during the broadcast of the Super Bowl to promote their products to an audience of 130 million people throughout the broadcast. Anheuser Busch, the company that owns Budweiser beer, spent US $20 million on eight commercials advertising beer. Notable absentees from the 2006 Super Bowl broadcast were Visa and McDonalds, companies that chose instead to advertise during the 2006 Torino Winter Olympic Games that began approximately a week after the Super Bowl. Rather than the US $2.5 million per 30-second slot being charged for the Super Bowl, rates for Olympic Games were approximately US $700,000, making them a cheaper alternative.

For pay television and associated media forms that are able to sell video or highlight packages on demand, a return on investment is achieved via direct selling to consumers. The most prevalent is the purchase of pay television, in which consumers gain access to live broadcasts. These broadcasts may be available as part of a standard package of pay television programmes, a specialized sport service or as pay-per-view events. Pay-per-view broadcasting has been dominated by boxing and to a lesser extent in America by World Wrestling Entertainment (WWE) events, although media organizations are increasingly examining and utilizing this method of revenue generation to ensure a return on expensive football rights deals around the world.

Sport sponsorship and media

As illustrated in Figure 4.1, sport organizations derive revenue from sponsors based on the exposure to consumers through exclusive (official) and non-exclusive (unofficial) media coverage. Like the relationship between advertisers and media, sponsors are prepared to pay sport organizations to promote their products and services depending on the number of consumers they will be able to access.

For example, the extent of NASCAR broadcast rights deals referred to previously are reflected in the level of the organization's sponsorship revenue. In this respect both broadcast rights and additional sponsorship revenue are proportional to the same variable, the number of spectators and fans of the sport. In 2003 NASCAR signed a US $700 million agreement over 10 years with Nextel Communications, a company seeking access to NASCAR's estimated fan base of 75 million Americans and 5 million Canadians (Hunter, 2005). Primary sponsorships for NASCAR cars are valued at between 10 and 20 million dollars depending on the success of the team and driver. By contrast, in the early 1960s, sponsorship of a car for the entire season was approximately 6,000 dollars (Hoye, Smith, Westerbeek, Stewart & Nicholson, 2006). The massive increase in NASCAR sponsorship is due to companies gaining increased access to consumers through media organizations, as well as the loyalty of fans. A *Sports Illustrated* poll found that more than 80% of NASCAR fans make an effort to purchase the products of their favourite team's sponsors and after Coca-Cola began sponsoring NASCAR, market research indicated that the company sold an additional 55 million bottles of soft drink per month (Hunter, 2005).

An extension of sponsorship arrangements is the ownership of teams, although this is a relatively limited phenomenon. The United States Major League Soccer (MLS) has been a professional football league since its inception in 1994, and the New York/New Jersey MetroStars were one of the league's original teams. In 2006, however, the team was purchased by Red Bull Energy Drink, renamed Red Bull New York and the uniform was changed to reflect the team's new ownership. Red Bull also owns other sporting properties, including Red Bull Salzburg, a team in the Austrian Bundesliga and a team on the formula one racing circuit. The purchase of these teams is predicated on the ability of the purchaser to gain a return on investment through increased exposure and product sales.

Because of the constant exposure during games, uniform sponsorship is a particularly significant method of capitalizing on media coverage. The shirt sponsor of Italian football club Juventus is energy company Tamoil, which pays £15 million per season, while Spanish club Real Madrid is paid £14 million per season by BenQ for shirt sponsorship. In Germany Bayern Munich's shirt sponsorship from T-Mobile is worth £11.4 million per season and in the English Premier League Manchester United signed a deal in 2006 with insurer AIG for £14 million per season after previous long associations with Vodafone and Sharp.

In 2003–2004 Cricket Australia, the national governing body for the sport, generated AUD82.5 million, of which 64% resulted from the sale of media rights and a further 22% from sponsorship. By contrast, gate takings accounted for only 4% of annual revenue. Hutchinson 3G is the major sponsor of Australian cricket, with the home Test series branded as the '3 Test Series'. In addition, Hutchinson has exclusive rights to mobile wireless communication and subscribers to Hutchinson's 3G network are able to access live cricket on their mobile phones. '3' is Hutchinson's premier brand and Australia's first third generation mobile telecommunications service, which has the capacity for face-to-face video calling and mobile Internet at broadband speed. As a result of 3's sponsorship of the Australian cricket team and its home test series, 3 mobile customers are able, for the cost of AUD8 per month, to obtain unlimited access to the television broadcast of the cricket via their mobile phones. In this case, the sponsor is paying for exposure as well as paying for content as a broadcaster. Further advances in mobile communication technologies are likely to exacerbate this trend in the future.

As illustrated in Figure 4.1, sport organizations also provide content direct to consumers. Fans of MLB in the America are able to access radio broadcasts and archives of the 2,400 games played each season through the league's website. Similarly, the World Rally Championship (WRC) offers a premium content service called WRC+ through its website. For £40 per year WRC fans can get access to live rally action, highlights, interviews and insider information and specials. The ability of sport organizations to capitalize on selling content and meaningfully segmenting the market beyond free-to-air and pay television is largely dependent on the availability and take-up of new high-end broadband speeds. In this respect developments in technology are likely to be an important aspect of the broadcast rights market of the future.

Summary

This chapter examined the commercial relationship between sport and media organizations. In particular, the process by which sport broadcast rights are bought and sold was discussed and the amount of money expended on broadcast rights was examined from both media and sport perspectives. It was clear from an analysis of the world's major professional sport organizations that broadcast rights are now a significant component of overall revenue and in many cases represent a majority of income. Importantly, it is also clear from this chapter that money is the most important driver of the sport media nexus. Review questions and exercises are listed below to assist with confirming your knowledge of the core concepts and principles introduced in this chapter.

Review questions and exercises

1. What is the role of a sport organization in the commercial dimension of the sport media nexus? Do they access consumers directly, or via media organizations?
2. What is the role of an exclusive broadcaster in the sport media nexus? How do they ensure a return on investment?
3. What is the role of non-exclusive media such as magazines and newspapers in the sport media nexus?
4. How do sponsors access consumers within the sport media nexus?
5. How do advertisers access consumers within the sport media nexus?
6. What factors do sellers consider in the broadcast rights process?
7. What makes a broadcast right deal more valuable for a prospective purchaser?

8. Choose a sport organization not referred to in this chapter and find out the amount paid for the rights to broadcast the sport. Is it an exclusive agreement? Is it split between free-to-air and pay television and is there provision for radio and Internet rights? Have the fees to obtain the rights increased or decreased over the past 5–10 years?

9. Choose a sport organization not referred to in this chapter and find out the amount paid to sponsor the organization. Is the sponsor visible or mentioned frequently in media coverage of the league or team?

10. Access a major sport organization's website. Are sponsors or advertisers featured on the site? Is this an effective way to access sport consumers?

5 Balancing the scales: sport media regulation

Overview

This chapter examines the regulation of the sport media nexus and in particular the broadcasting of sport on both free-to-air and pay television. The chapter explores the rationale for government involvement in the regulation of sport broadcasting, government objectives and the regulatory mechanisms applied to govern sport broadcasting in different national contexts. This chapter also examines the impact of sport broadcasting regulations on the sport and media industries and their respective operations.

After completing this chapter the reader should be able to:

- Understand why governments seek to regulate sport broadcasting.
- Describe the ways in which governments regulate sport broadcasting.
- Evaluate the impact of sport broadcasting regulation.
- Contextualize the rationale of governments to regulate sport broadcasting in terms of a desire to protect the interests of consumers and prevent anti-competitive behaviour.
- Contextualize sport broadcasting regulations within geographical, cultural and national perspectives.

> ■ Speculate on the impact of changing sport broadcasting regulations in terms of the interests of consumers, the profitability of sport organizations, the place of sport in society and the competition between and within media organizations.

Introduction

The sport media landscape, outlined in the first four chapters, is both complex and dynamic. It has also altered dramatically, marked by the advent of television, the hyper commercialization of sport since the 1970s and the introduction of pay television and the Internet in the last two decades of the twentieth century. The increasingly commercial nature of the sport media nexus and the relationship between sport and television in particular has presented a series of challenges for governments all over the world. These challenges have included ensuring that its citizens have reasonable access to sport broadcasting on television and that media and sport organizations do not engage in practices or behaviour that is anti-competitive. Governments have responded to these challenges by regulating sport broadcasting, albeit in different ways depending on cultural, national and geographical contexts. The regulatory mechanisms and their impact are indicative of both the special social significance of sport and the commercial power of the media.

The regulation of sport broadcasting attempts to ameliorate the problems that result from often divergent interests of audiences, broadcasters, sport organizations and governing bodies. Hoehn and Lancefield (2003:566) note that the 'pre-eminent position of sports programming in a channel's offering and as a key driver of a TV delivery/distribution platform has forced governments to intervene in media merger proposals, sports-rights contract negotiations, and disputes among TV distribution systems over access to content'. This government intervention has had a significant impact on the way in which sport is broadcast, the amount of sport that audiences have access to via free-to-air television, the ways in which sport organizations are able to sell broadcast rights and in some celebrated cases the ownership of sport teams. Like the sport media industry generally, the regulation of sport broadcasting is not static, but rather has been evolving dynamically since the introduction of pay television in particular. This process has been exacerbated by a shift from a industry paradigm in which content, such as sport, was competing for broadcast time on media outlets that were scarce to one in which a multitude of outlets and forms are competing for scarce content (Cowie & Williams, 1997). This shift is graphically represented in Figure 5.1.

BISHOP BURTON COLLEGE

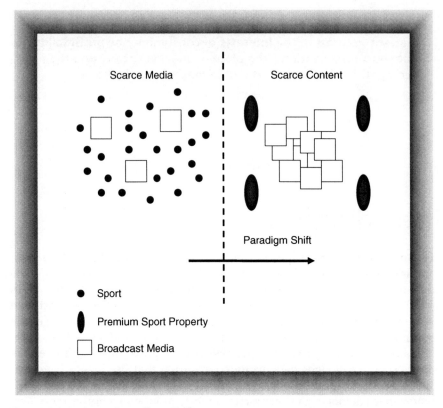

Figure 5.1 Industry Paradigm Shift

Government intervention

In market driven economies, resources are allocated through the interaction of demand, supply and prices. There are occasions where the full benefit of the market is not realized because of an under supply of socially desirable products or an oversupply of less desirable products (Cooke, 1994). This situation is known as market failure, in which the market does not deliver the best outcome possible and where the allocation of resources is distorted (Michael, 2006). In this instance the market does not operate in the best interests of the community or nation, and a government may intervene if it believes that it can engineer a better outcome. This intervention can take the form of market participation, market regulation, financial intervention or economic intervention (Michael, 2006).

In market participation governments provide goods or services in competition with private providers, which often serves to keep prices low. Market regulation typically refers to enacting legislation in order to dictate the way in which an industry operates and in particular the way in which specific companies are able to do business. Financial intervention is where a government allocates financial resources to specific industries. This might occur through investment in infrastructure or awarding grants. Finally, economic intervention is where governments implement tariffs and subsidies to stimulate production, protect markets or alter the costs of a product or service.

Sport broadcasting on free-to-air television, as demonstrated in the previous chapter, is subsidized by advertising revenue. Aside from the cost of a television set and an antenna to receive a broadcast signal, sport broadcasts are available at no cost to the consumer. In this case the consumption of the product by one consumer does not adversely impact the consumption of other consumers and the service or product has a non-excludable feature. The number of consumers simply raises or lowers the revenue that is able to be generated either from the sale of advertising time or the sale of additional goods and services being advertised. In the case of free-to-air broadcasting of sport, the benefits of watching sport, which is often of considerable social and cultural significance, are able to be enjoyed by a substantial majority of the population.

In contrast, sport broadcasting on pay television is predicated on the notion that consumers will pay to consume the product. In this case the migration of sport matches and events from free-to-air television to pay television transforms sport from an essentially free consumer product subsidized by advertisers to one that requires payment. This migration and transformation in the product will cause market failure, for the cost imposed on a product that was previously delivered at no cost is likely to result in significantly less people having access to the product. The same is likely to occur if a single broadcaster is able to secure sufficient sport rights to reduce competition in the market place and subsequently increase costs above market value. Many governments regard sport events of national and international significance to be merit goods, where community demand for the product is high because of social benefits, 'but the normal market cost would be intolerable for an individual consumer' (Michael, 2006:63). Governments intervene where merit goods are concerned to ensure that a wide public distribution of the product is achieved, in order to maximize the number of people able to receive a social benefit from the product or activity.

Of the four intervention strategies referred to previously, market regulation is preferred by governments seeking to avoid or limit the extent of market failure in sport broadcasting. For example, many governments around the world have regulated the migration of sport matches and events to pay television by legislating that events of national and international significance are broadcast on or offered first to free-to-air television. This is referred to variously as anti-siphoning legislation or the listing of sport events.

Broadcasting regulation generally and sport broadcasting regulation more specifically is an attempt to balance social, cultural and economic objectives (Productivity Commission, 2000). All three objectives can be achieved, but it is rare that a government does not make compromises to ensure that one objective does not dominate or overwhelm the others. In the case of sport broadcasting, government, sport and media organizations often disagree on the balance between the three. Not surprisingly, sport and media organizations often argue that broadcasting regulation is skewed in favour of social and cultural objectives and does not allow them to maximize economic returns available through the transaction of sport products, such as the sale of broadcast rights or the purchase of access to pay per view events.

The regulation of sport broadcasting is dependent on commercial, cultural and geographic contexts. In other words, governments apply a different set of regulations depending on the country, the importance of sport, the historical relationship between free-to-air and pay television, the access of consumers to pay television and the proximity of different national and regional markets. Sport broadcasting regulation may be divided into three distinct components. First, government regulation attempts to prevent sport events migrating exclusively from free-to-air television to pay television. Second, government regulation attempts to ensure that sport and media organizations to do not engage in anti-competitive behaviour in the buying and selling of broadcast rights. In particular, monopolies created through the sale of broadcast rights are to be avoided, as they will necessarily restrict supply, which in turn will raises price to a level that will exploit consumers (New & Le Grand, 1999). Third and finally, government regulation attempts to limit or prevent any negative consequences of the vertical integration of the sport and media industries, such as the purchase of a sport team or league by a media organization (see Case 1). The following sections outline sport broadcasting regulation in various regions and nations in order to contextualize its impacts on the sport and media industries.

Case 1 Manchester United and BSkyB

On October 29, 1998 the British Secretary of State referred the proposed acquisition of football club Manchester United by British Sky Broadcasting (BSkyB, a News Corporation subsidiary) to the UK Competition Commission (formerly the Monopolies and Mergers Commission). In its final report the Commission noted that BSkyB was 'a vertically integrated broadcaster which buys TV rights, including those for sporting events, makes some of its own programmes, packages programmes from a range of sources into various channels and distributes and retails these channels to its subscribers using its direct-to-home satellite platform as well as selling them wholesale to other retailers using different distribution platforms'. It also noted that Manchester United by any measure was the strongest club in the English Premier League.

In considering the competitive effects of the proposed take-over bid, the Commission discovered that BSkyB was essentially the only provider of premium sports channels on pay television and that entry into the premium sports channel market was dependent on the ability of the broadcaster to acquire the rights to live sport events. Furthermore, it noted that there were insufficient rights to sustain a significant number of channels and BSkyB's high market share meant that it had market power. Given this market power was essentially a monopoly, the acquisition of Manchester United was likely to contribute to the broadcaster's ability to raise prices above competitive levels with impunity.

The Commission noted that 'because of its financial strength, the size of its supporter base and recent sporting success, Manchester United has greater influence within the Premier League than any other club and that, in the event of the merger, it would use this influence to persuade other members of the Premier League to support the sale of rights to BSkyB. Many parties felt that it would be objectionable if BSkyB, or indeed any other broadcaster, bought any Premier League club, because it would give it a seat on both sides of the table when rights sales were being negotiated. For BSkyB, the incumbent broadcaster of Premier League football, to acquire the most influential club was widely seen as particularly detrimental'. The notion that BSkyB could be both a club owner and a bidder for the broadcast rights was just one of the anti-competitive impacts of the proposed merger that led the Commission to conclude that it should be prohibited.

The Commission concluded that the proposed take-over of Manchester United by the United Kingdom's primary pay television sports channel provider would result in BSkyB acquiring a significant advantage in the marketplace at the expense of its competitors. In particular, BSkyB would have an advantage in gaining the rights to broadcast the English Premier League and other broadcasters would be at a competitive disadvantage in establishing sports channels on pay television. The Commission noted in their final report that their public interest conclusions were based mainly on the effects of the merger on competition between BSkyB and other broadcasters. However, they also noted that they believed the merger would also adversely affect football by reinforcing 'the existing trend towards greater inequality of wealth between clubs, thus weakening the smaller ones' and would also give BSkyB 'additional influence over Premier League decisions relating to the organization of football, leading to some decisions which did not reflect the long-term interests of football'. In both instances the Commission believed this would damage the quality of British football.

The Commission argued that it was unable to identify any public interest benefits from the proposed merger and was therefore likely to act against the public interest. As a result, the Commission recommended that the acquisition of Manchester United by BSkyB be prohibited, which it duly was. By contrast, the 2005 acquisition of Manchester United by Tampa Bay Buccaneers (National Football League (NFL)) owner Malcolm Glazer in a £790 million take-over was not referred to the Competition by the British Office of Fair Trading as it was not considered to have any adverse impact on competition.

Source: Competition Commission (1999); http://europa.eu

Europe

The European Commission seeks to ensure that sport leagues, clubs and broadcasters do not engage in anti-competitive behaviour. In particular, the Commission regulates the practice of joint selling, which the Commission describes as a 'situation where sports clubs assign their media rights to their association, which sell the rights on behalf of the clubs' (Toft, 2003). The Commission notes that as a result of joint selling leagues and associations have traditionally packaged all media rights and sold them to a single broadcaster in each territory. This practice enables the league or association to control the sale of the broadcast rights and maximize the exclusivity of the contract, however, the European Commission believes that joint selling is a horizontal restriction of competition, whereby clubs are unable to compete for broadcast rights fees on an individual basis (see Case 2). This lack of

---

Case 2   Joint selling

In order to regulate what it views as anti-competitive behaviour, the European Commission has focused its attention on the joint selling of rights by and within European football competitions. In particular, the way broadcast rights were sold by Union of European Football Association (UEFA), the English Premier League and the German Bundesliga were subject to investigation by the Commission.

In 1999 the European Commission objected to the fact that UEFA sold the rights to all Champions League games in an exclusive contract to a single broadcaster for up to 4 years at a time. As a result of these arrangements not all games were seen live on television, while Internet and telephone operators were denied access to the rights. In the opinion of the Commission this situation restricted competition between broadcasters, as well as hindered the development of new technology, which was regarded as a disadvantage to broadcasters, individual clubs and spectators.

UEFA's amended joint selling arrangement, which was approved by the Commission in 2003, consists of UEFA centrally selling the rights to live television transmission of midweek night matches in two separate packages. These packages give the broadcaster the right to select the best of the available matches, while UEFA has the exclusive right to sell the remaining matches. If it does not manage to do this then individual clubs are given the opportunity to sell the rights to matches themselves. In response to the Commission's additional concerns, the amended rights arrangement also enabled Internet and phone operators to purchase Champions League content. Finally, as way of counteracting the potentially negative effects of long-term broadcast rights agreements, UEFA agreed to limit contracts to a period not longer than 3 years.

The European Commission also investigated the joint selling of broadcast rights by the English Premier League and found that individual clubs were prevented from selling rights, even to matches that were not included in the collective package. The result of this situation was that approximately 25% of matches were broadcast live and that these matches were limited to a single broadcaster. As a result of discussions between the Commission and English Premier League, the League agreed to an amended arrangement for the selling of rights for the

2007–2009 seasons. Essentially, the League agreed to offer six balanced packages of rights, with the additional clause that a single bidder not be allowed to buy all six. This arrangement would ensure that at least two broadcasters would televise Premier League matches, ensuring greater competition and consumer access.

Finally, the German Bundesliga also agreed to an amended arrangement to sell the rights to its matches after the European Commission determined that arrangements prior to 2003 restricted competition and exacerbated trends in media concentration. The amended Bundesliga rights process included the sale of discrete packages to matches in the first and second division that were able to be purchased by free-to-air and pay television, as well as packages for free-to-air broadcasters exclusively. The rights arrangements also included provisions for the sale of live rights and high-light packages to Internet and mobile phone providers, as well as the ability for individual clubs to sell the rights to its home games. The amended process by which the Bundesliga sells broadcast rights, like the UEFA and English Premier League arrangements, ensures that multiple broadcasters will have access to valuable sport content.

Sources: Toft (2003).

---

competition creates an additional lack of horizontal competition between broadcasters, which in turn limits public access. The process and implications of joint selling are graphically represented in Figure 5.2.

The Commission acknowledges that the joint selling of sport broadcasting rights is accepted practice and in many instances facilitates exclusivity, which in turn maximizes the return that sport leagues and clubs can achieve. However, joint selling also facilitates long-term contracts and if the broadcaster is dominant in the marketplace, this can lead to market foreclosure. The practice of joint selling long-term exclusive rights packages results in a minority of media organizations being able to afford the rights. In other words, the act of selling the rights can be anti-competitive, while long-term exclusive contracts can result in a lack of competition between broadcasters, which in turn might result in an increase in prices and a further reduction in competition between broadcasters.

Individual European governments have responded differently to the challenge of regulating the practice of joint or collective selling of rights by football leagues. In France the national football federation was granted legislative protection as the sole authority responsible for the sale of broadcast rights (Cave & Crandall, 2001; Rumphorst, 2001). By contrast, the Netherlands competition authority prohibited the joint selling of rights to the Dutch Football Association. Similarly, in 1999 the Italian competition authority prohibited the collective selling of live rights by the national football federation (Tonazzi, 2003). However, the collective sale of highlight packages was allowed due to the logistical difficulties in selling these rights on an individual basis (Rumphorst, 2001). Case 2 of this chapter examines the regulation of joint selling in selected European leagues and associations by the European Commission.

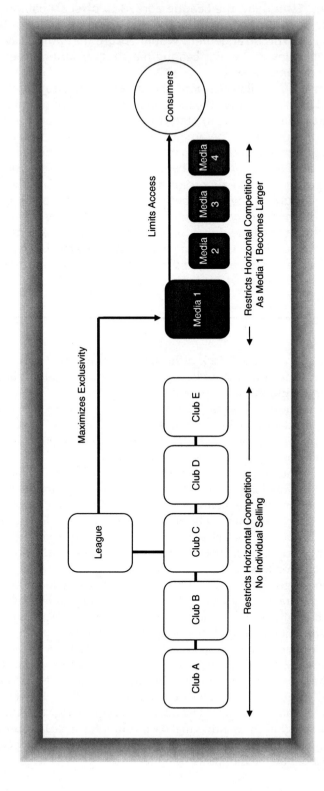

Figure 5.2 Joint Selling

The European Commission has adopted legal measures to ensure that events of major importance are available on free-to-air television and that major sport events do not migrate exclusively to pay television, thereby maximizing public access and attempting to avoid market failure. In Member States of the European Union these legal measures are enshrined in the Television Without Frontiers Directive (henceforth referred to as 'the Directive'). The Directive was established in 1989 and then amended in 1997. Article 3a of the 1997 version of the Directive states:

> Each Member State may take measures in accordance with Community law to ensure that broadcasters under its jurisdiction do not broadcast on an exclusive basis events which are regarded by that Member State as being of major importance for society in such a way as to deprive a substantial proportion of the public in that Member State of the possibility of following such events via live coverage or deferred coverage on free television. If it does so, the Member State concerned shall draw up a list of designated events, national or non-national, which it considers to be of major importance for society. It shall do so in a clear and transparent manner in due and effective time. In so doing the Member State concerned shall also determine whether these events should be available via whole or partial live coverage, or where necessary or appropriate for objective reasons in the public interest, whole or partial deferred coverage.

The European Commission notes that events such as the FIFA World Cup, the European Football Championship and the Olympic Games are of major importance to society, and article 3a of the Directive is designed to prevent instances such as the final of the FIFA World Cup being broadcast exclusively on pay television.

As a result of article 3a, individual Member States are able to construct a list of events that should be available on free-to-air television. These lists are constructed using different criteria and also reflect different national sporting and cultural preferences. For example, the Austrian listed events are dominated by the Olympic Games, football and skiing, although the latter is not a feature of any other European list. In Austria the following events are listed:

- The Summer or Winter Olympic Games.
- FIFA World Cup football Matches (for men) if the Austrian national team is involved, as well as the opening match, the semi-finals and the final of the football World Cup (for men).
- European Championship football Matches (for men) if the Austrian national team is involved, as well as the opening match, the semi-finals and the final of the football European Championship (for men).
- The final of the Austrian Football Cup.
- FIS World Alpine skiing Championships.
- World Nordic skiing Championships.

By contrast, in Belgium 20 sporting events are listed as being either popular, culturally or nationally significant or have traditionally been broadcast on free-to-air television. Of these 20 events, 6 are related to the broadcast of football at national or international level and 8 are cycling events. This preference for cycling events is not reflected in any of the other European lists. The German list, like many of the European lists, is dominated by football:

- The Summer and Winter Olympic Games.
- All European Championship and World Cup Matches involving the German national football team, as well as the opening match, the semi-finals and finals, irrespective of whether the German team is involved.
- The semi-finals and final of the German FA Cup.
- The German national football team's home and away matches.
- The final of any European football club competition (Champions League, UEFA Cup) involving a German Club.

The notion that the listing of events is dependent on the national importance and heritage of particular sports and events is confirmed by Ireland's list, where unlike central European countries the Winter Olympics has been excluded and Hurling and horse events have been added. The Irish list is as follows:

- The Summer Olympics.
- The All-Ireland Senior Inter-County Football and Hurling Finals.
- Ireland's home and away qualifying games in the European Football Championship and the FIFA World Cup tournaments.
- Ireland's games in the European Football Championship Finals tournament and the FIFA World Cup Finals tournament.
- The opening games, the semi-finals and final of the European Football Championship Finals and the FIFA World Cup Finals tournament.
- Ireland's games in the Rugby World Cup Finals tournament.
- The Irish Grand National and the Irish Derby.
- The Nations Cup at the Dublin Horse Show.

Like the German list, the Italian list is relatively short and is dominated by football, but also includes two events of national importance, the Tour of Italy (Giro d'Italia) cycling competition and the Italian Formula One Grand Prix. The most complex regulation in Europe is in the United Kingdom, where the list is divided into Group A and Group B events. The UK Television Broadcasting Regulations of 2000 state that Group A events must be made available for acquisition by a free-to-air broadcaster and that the channel or broadcaster must have a minimum 95% penetration. By contrast, Group B events are those that may not be broadcast live on an exclusive basis unless an adequate provision has been made for secondary coverage. The minimum acceptable service in this respect is edited highlights or delayed coverage of the event of at least 10% of the event or 30 minutes of coverage for an event of 1 hour or more in duration, whichever is greater. The UK Group A listed events are as follows:

- Olympic Games
- FIFA World Cup Finals tournament
- FA Cup Final
- Scottish FA Cup Final (in Scotland)

- Grand National
- The Derby
- Wimbledon Tennis Finals
- European Football Championship Finals tournament
- Rugby League Challenge Cup Final
- Rugby World Cup Final.

Australia

The Australian Broadcasting Services Act 1992 and its amendments are the primary mechanisms by which the Australian federal government has regulated Australian broadcasting generally and sport broadcasting more specifically. The Act included the following aims: to promote the availability to audiences throughout Australia of a diverse range of radio and television services offering entertainment, education and information; to provide a regulatory environment that will facilitate the development of a broadcasting industry in Australia that is efficient, competitive and responsive to audience needs; to promote the role of broadcasting services in developing and reflecting a sense of Australian identity, character and cultural diversity and to encourage providers of commercial and community broadcasting services to be responsive to the need for a fair and accurate coverage of matters of public interest and for an appropriate coverage of matters of local significance.

Part 7 of the Act describes how the responsible government Minister may protect the free availability of certain types of programmes. In practice, these programmes are sporting events which are considered to be nationally significant and in 1994 the Minister for Communications, Information Technology and the Arts was given the power to list in a formal notice, known as the anti-siphoning list, which sporting events are to be available on free-to-air television. This list gives free-to-air broadcasters the first option to purchase the rights to these events and sports, but does not compel them to do so and in the event that no free-to-air broadcaster wishes to purchase the rights then they are offered to pay television. The anti-siphoning law is designed to prevent pay television operators from acquiring the rights to sporting events of national significance and to prevent the migration of these sports to pay television (Stewart et al., 2004). In short, the anti-siphoning law protects the interests of commercial free-to-air broadcasters to ensure that sport is available to the Australian population at little or no cost. In doing this, the Australian government has placed pay television operators at a commercial disadvantage. Pay television was introduced to Australia in 1995 and free-to-air television networks expressed concerns that pay television would capture the rights to sport and free-to-air television would lose advertising revenue. In 2002 pay television advertising revenue was less than AUD100 million, while free-to-air advertising exceeded AUD2,000 million.

An investigation into Australia's sport broadcasting regulation by the Australian Broadcasting Authority (2001) concluded that 'Australia's anti-siphoning scheme and its list of events are both more extensive and restrictive than those in operation overseas'. The Australian 2006–2010 anti-siphoning list includes the following sports and events:

- Each event held as part of the Olympic Games.
- Each event held as part of the Commonwealth Games.
- Each running of the Melbourne Cup (Horse Racing).
- Each match in the Australian Football League.
- Each match in the National Rugby League, State of Origin Series and International Test Matches.
- Each International Rugby Union Test Match and each match of the Rugby Union World Cup.
- Each International Test and One Day Cricket Match played in Australia or the United Kingdom and each match of the One Day World Cup.
- The English Football Association Cup final.
- Each match in the FIFA World Cup.
- Each match in the Australian Open tennis tournament.
- Each match in the Wimbledon (the Lawn Tennis Championships) tournament.
- Each match in the men's and women's singles quarter-finals, semi-finals and finals of the French Open tennis tournament.
- Each match in the men's and women's singles quarter-finals, semi-finals and finals of the US Open tennis tournament.
- Each match in each tie in the Davis Cup tennis tournament when an Australian representative team is involved.
- Each International Netball match involving the Australian team.
- Each round of the Australian Masters golf tournament.
- Each round of the Australian Open golf tournament.
- Each round of the US Masters golf tournament.
- Each round of the British Open golf tournament.
- Each race in the Fédération Internationale de l'Automobile Formula 1 World Championship (Grand Prix) held in Australia.
- Each race in the Moto GP held in Australia.
- Each race in the V8 Supercar Championship Series.
- Each race in the Champ Car World Series (IndyCar) held in Australia.

It is clear from the above list that there are some inconsistencies, particularly if the strict criterion of national importance is applied. For instance, the final of a football competition held in the United Kingdom is considered to be of national significance to Australians, while the US Masters and British Open golf tournaments are on the list but the United States Professional Golf Association (USPGA) Championship and US Open are not, despite recognition that they comprise golf's four 'majors'. Furthermore, the final three rounds of the French and US Open tennis tournaments are listed, but in each case would only be of interest if an Australian was successful in the early stages of the tournament. Australia's anti-siphoning laws are an example, by international standards, of extreme government regulation in the area of sport broadcasting. While it is true that the Australian government has prevented market failure, it has also provided sustained assistance to one set of commercial providers in preference to another for more than a decade.

United States of America

Cave and Crandall (2001:F13) have noted that 'throughout the modern history of sports broadcasting in the United States of America there has always been controversy over the ability of leagues or sports associations to limit individual members' rights to broadcast their games'. In particular, court rulings in 1953 and 1960 determined that league wide television contracts that benefited the collective at the expense of the rights of individual teams were a violation of the Sherman Act. In response, the government enacted the Sports Broadcasting Act in 1961, which gave sport leagues the ability to offer rights as a package to a national network on the grounds that it was in the interest of spectators and the leagues' health and competitive balance (Cave & Crandall, 2001; Sandy et al., 2004). As a result, the NFL signed its first national television contract in 1962, which was worth US $4.7 million annually.

The Sports Broadcasting Act has allowed the NFL to offer collective rights to national networks since 1962. Cave and Crandall (2001) have demonstrated that no other professional sport in America relies solely on national rights and that the NFL has the highest proportion of total revenue derived from broadcast rights. Although the Sports Broadcasting Act legalized collective selling, it did not legalize other forms of restrictive practices by sport leagues and associations in the sale of broadcast rights. Cave and Crandall (2001) referred in particular to the Supreme Court's ruling that the National Collegiate Athletics Association's (NCAA) plan to control the broadcast rights to all college football games was unlawful. As a result, colleges were able to break from national broadcast rights contracts and sign their own rights agreements.

A league or association's capacity to limit or prevent the individual sale of rights by teams to local and regional broadcasters is related to the league or association's ability to make the argument that it is necessary to maintain competition within the league. In reality, this is a difficult argument to sustain and almost all basketball, baseball and hockey teams in the United States of America sell broadcast rights in this way. The concerns that surround joint selling in Europe are also partly ameliorated in the United States of America by the segmentation of rights deals in order to maximize revenue, which in turn increases competition, as well as consumer choice and access. For example, the NFL's rights for the 2006–2012 seasons are shared by ESPN, NBC, CBS, Fox and DirecTV.

China

Until the beginning of the 1980s, there was little competition in European broadcasting, as it was generally dominated by state-funded monopoly broadcasters (Tonazzi, 2003). The impact of the entry of commercial broadcasters into the marketplace was increased competition, as well as the increased importance of sport properties. Unlike most of Europe and the United States of America, China is yet to experience the impact of commercial broadcasting, as it is almost exclusively controlled by the central government, however, sport is an important feature of national and state broadcasting. China Central Television (CCTV), which began in 1958, is effectively a government department that broadcasts on both free-to-air and pay television. CCTV has satellite television stations that are available to all Chinese people who own a television, while it also provides a range of other specialist stations that are available at a cost. Although there is a financial return to the government, the key tenets underpinning broadcasting are public and political benefits. In other words, broadcasting in China is not a commercial enterprise in the same way as it is in Westernized countries, despite the fact that advertising revenue is significant.

The Chinese broadcasting system is further complicated by the fact that there are a multitude of Chinese states, which also provide public broadcasting in the form of free-to-air and pay television stations for the citizens of that state. In both the case of CCTV and state run television networks, sport is available on both forms, depending on the sport and its importance. The majority of major international events such as the Olympic Games or the FIFA World Cup are broadcast on one of CCTV's satellite stations, in order to provide public access. In this way CCTV regulates the broadcast of events of global or national significance, in much the same way as the listing of events does so in other countries. CCTV-5, China's sport channel established in 1995, broadcasts sport 24 hours per day, 7 days per week to 700 million people, while CCTV also controls external access to Chinese sporting events. Finally, the purchase of sport events by state run networks is ad hoc, where different states purchase rights based on particular interests or historical anomalies. For example, one state run cable station may elect to purchase the rights to the English Premier League, while another in a different part of the country might purchase the rights to the Serie A in Italy, while CCTV might purchase the rights to the Bundesliga. The regulation of these broadcasts is inconsistent, however, as citizens of one state can often receive sport broadcasts from stations in other states.

Summary

This chapter has examined the regulation of sport broadcasting. In particular, it has examined the ways in which governments regulate the broadcasting of sport on free-to-air and pay television, the vertical integration of sport and media organizations and the practice of anti-competitive behaviour by sport and media organizations in the sale and purchase of broadcast rights. This chapter has demonstrated that governments, sport organizations and media organizations are engaged in a complex activity, where often it is difficult to achieve a balance between social, cultural and economic objectives.

Governments throughout the world are attempting to achieve parity between the public interests of its citizens and the commercial interests of sport and media organizations at a time when broadcast rights represent an increasing proportion of overall revenue for sport teams and leagues. It is unlikely that these competing forces will abate, as live sport is a highly sought after product by broadcasters and consumers alike. As pay and digital television providers achieve greater market penetration it remains to be seen whether the concept of national significance will be able to sustain the practice of listing events in an increasingly globalized sport market. Finally, it is also likely that cases of vertical integration will confront governments more often in the future as the convergence of the sport and media industries continues. Review questions and exercises are listed below to assist with confirming your knowledge of the core concepts and principles introduced in this chapter.

Review questions and exercises

1. Why do governments regulate sport broadcasting?
2. What is market failure and how does it relate to sport broadcasting in particular?
3. What are the ways in which government can intervene and what is the preferred method of intervention where sport broadcasting is concerned?
4. What are the three main areas in which government seeks to regulate the practice of sport broadcasting?
5. What are anti-siphoning laws and listed events designed to avoid and what are they designed to achieve?
6. What is joint selling?
7. How does joint selling restrict horizontal competition in sport and media?
8. What is a potential impact of the vertical integration of sport broadcasters and sport teams? Is it sufficient to legislate against?
9. Are any sport teams in your region, city or nation owned by media organizations? If so, does the media or sport organization have any advantages as a result?
10. Identify if your country of origin has any legislation that enables the listing of events of national significance. If so, what are the events and why have they been chosen? If not, what is the proportion of major sport events on pay television?

6  Content is king: sport media texts

Overview

This chapter examines the content of sport media, the sport text. In particular, this chapter explores the ways in which the media uses frames, narratives, modes of writing, personification and photographs to make sport texts meaningful and entertaining. This chapter also examines the representation of gender, race and nationalism as examples of the way in which sport texts can construct personal and collective identities and influence the ways in which people view the world around them. This analysis is undertaken in order that sport managers are able to decode and deconstruct the representation of sport in the media.

After completing this chapter the reader should be able to:

- Generalize about the importance of decoding sport media in order to understand broader social themes.
- Explain what a text is.
- Identify the ways in which sport texts are constructed to make them meaningful and entertaining.
- Generalize about the way in which sport is represented in the media, with specific reference to various social themes such as gender, race and nationalism.

Introduction

At the end of the twentieth century Real (1998:15) noted that ignoring sport media in contemporary society 'would be like ignoring the role of the church in the Middle Ages or ignoring the role of Art in the Renaissance'. In other words, sport media is an omnipresent feature of contemporary societies and without the ability to analyse sport media we cannot hope to understand the societies in which we live. Real also argued that the saturation of media sport makes it difficult to analyse. Thus, the paradox is that understanding sport media is crucial to an understanding of broader society, but its place in society makes it almost impossible to do so. Because we are bombarded with images and sounds from sporting events and contests of the past, present and future, we are in a difficult, if not impossible place from which to establish a reference point. Often, and this is particularly true for people engaged in the study of sport or who are employed within the sport industry, people grow up immersed in sport and have been inculcated into sport's particular and peculiar rituals and routines from an early age, by family, friends and peers. For many, sport and sport media have become important vehicles for creating and understanding a series of individual and collective identities. These identities make it difficult to analyse sport media, but all the more important to develop the skills to understand sport media texts.

What is a text?

A sport media text is not just the written or printed word, although a text can be a book, such as the one you are currently reading. Rather, a text is anything in audio or visual form that presents or represents sport to an audience. Thus, a sport media text could be a billboard on a freeway advertising a particular brand of deodorant used by a well known athlete, a live radio broadcast of a rugby union game or a pop song performed by the wife of a footballer. In each of these examples the audio or visual text can be understood differently by different people. The interpretive possibilities of sporting texts are infinite because they refer to a wide variety of people and events, were constructed by journalists, editors, producers, commentators and photographers with particular personal and professional agendas, and are able to be examined in a variety of contexts by readers, viewers, listeners and users who have unique ways of reading the text.

As a result of these different contexts in which sport media texts are created and experienced, the way in which sport texts are understood can vary markedly. For example, one person driving their car past the advertising billboard may subconsciously believe their performance in a social basketball game later that evening will be improved because their choice of deodorant is that of the well known athlete, while another may experience self loathing because they discover they use the same brand as an athlete from a team they hate.

In developing an understanding of the ways in which the media represent sport, it is important to note that texts 'foster specific ways of seeing the world, hinder other ways, and even structure ways of relating to the text itself' (Dahlgren, 1992:13). In other words sport media texts can influence the way in which people understand the world around them. For example, an emphasis on male sport within media coverage may encourage young men and women to see the world as a place where men are rewarded for being active and women are passive. Sport media texts might also prevent people from interpreting or understanding the world in particular ways. For example, an emphasis on nationalism and patriotism may encourage division and combativeness, which prevents or limits a view of the world as one without borders. Finally, the ways in which a text is constructed may influence the way it is interpreted. For example, a newspaper article might consist of a story, a headline, a photograph and a caption. The boldness of the headline and the angle of the photograph might arouse anxiety in the reader, which will affect any reading of the story.

In daily life we use sport media texts to make sense of sport, the world and our place in it. These texts are not neutral and objective. Rather, they are infused with political, cultural, commercial and social ideologies. These ideologies influence our readings of the texts consciously and subconsciously. In order to understand how we make sense of sport, the world and our place in it, an analysis of these ideologies and how they are deployed is essential. This requires the ability to decode or deconstruct sport media texts, to discover the codes and structures that are both hidden and obvious.

Decoding media

Hartley (1982:81) suggested that events need to be assigned a 'proper' place in the order of things and that the media do this by using 'cultural maps of the social world'. Maps prevent the world from being seen as a jumble of random and chaotic events by assigning them a social context, relating them to other known events and placing them with a frame of meanings that are familiar to the audience (Hall, Critcher, Jefferson, Clarke and Roberts, 1978). These maps have also been referred to as codes, which according to Hall (1973) are configurations of meaning that enable a sign or text to signify additional implied meanings, and formats, which are the devices journalists use to 'categorize, choose, organize and represent knowledge as news' (Ericson, Baranek & Chan, 1991:149). Finally, Gitlin (1980:6) referred to 'frames', the 'principles of selection, emphasis and presentation composed of little tacit theories about what exists, what happens and what matters'. He argued that these frames, like 'maps of meaning', organize the world for the media and their audiences. Gitlin suggested that recognizing the existence of frames prompts several questions, including what is the frame being used, why this frame and not another and how are different frames used by different media at different moments?

In order to answer these questions it is important to have an understanding of some of the devices used by the media to construct sport texts and make them meaningful or entertaining. The following sections examine some of the devices which are particularly relevant to sport media.

Narratives

Manoff (1986) suggested that in reading the news, readers are being told a tale, while Bell (1991:147) argued that 'journalists are the professional story-tellers of our age'. An important feature of these stories or tales is that there are a limited number of basic patterns and variations, or narratives, to which they conform (Dahlgren, 1992). Newspapers make use of familiar narrative codes to present different content and contexts in similar terms, in order that they are able to be easily understood by the audience (Bignell, 1997).

Narratives have ingredients that 'culturally competent audiences' can recognize, noted Dahlgren (1992), as well as a relatively finite range of possible meanings. Similarly, Manoff (1986) suggested that narratives are organizations of experience, and that the sense of the world that they make is invariably conventional. Decoding the way in which newspapers create familiarity, routine and convention through the use of narrative is, however, a complex task (Ericson et al., 1991). Often a single news item is no more than a segment of a narrative that is sustained by 'wrapping', a process in which a news item is placed and juxtaposed with other items.

Like other media narratives, those deployed within sport media have a relatively finite range of possible meanings. In many cases the narratives are used often and well known to audiences. For example, rivalry is a key narrative that is a regular feature of the sport media. The rivalry can be local, national or global, between individuals, teams or countries and can used to construct a story or a series of stories of the course of a week, months or years. Rivalries such as those between boxers Muhammad Ali and Joe Frazier, or tennis players John McEnroe and Jimmy Connors or athletes Steve Ovett and Sebastian Coe provided the media with a frame to contextualize sporting events that took place over many years. Each new event only made sense because the narrative placed it in a meaningful context. As will be illustrated later in this chapter, often events outside sport such as political conflicts and wars can be used to develop narratives that frame national rivalries and provide them with heightened meaning.

Personification

The process of framing news and constructing media narratives typically involves an emphasis on people, rather than institutions. Although the content of routine news may contain information about or reference to institutions, it is invariably made meaningful by the action or inaction of people. Stories that interest readers, viewers and listeners are inevitably personal and the human-interest story has been a perennial feature of the media (Hughes,

1981). The good human-interest stories, Hughes argued, begin in situations that are familiar to the reader's own experience as a human being and might, for example, revolve around family, marriage, death or coincidence. The extreme case is tabloid journalism, in which events and issues are personalized to such an extent that it makes every news story a human-interest story (Knight, 1989).

In the mass media, organizations, bureaucracies, movements and other large or enduring social formations are reduced to personifications (Gitlin, 1980). Galtung and Ruge (1988) argued that personification is a result of the need for identification and that people can serve more easily as objects of positive and negative identification, while people and not 'structures' act within a time-span that fits the frequency of the media. In other words, it far easier to ascribe attributes to the actions of people than in it is for institutions and structures.

Sport is an unusual case because leagues and clubs, which are institutions, are often the subjects of media coverage as a result of their history and tradition. Clubs like Manchester United in the English Premier League or Real Madrid in La Liga are iconic brands, however, their media coverage invariably revolves around the actions of players, managers and administrators. Like the film and music industries, sport is an ideal vehicle for personification because the athletes and players are generally well known to the audience. The ways in which sport professionals act as objects of positive and negative identification is exaggerated by the fact that fans and spectators invest sport in the their personal identities. The implications of this are discussed in greater detail in later chapters that examine crisis and star management within the sport media nexus.

Modes of sport writing

Sport reporting has distinct features that contribute to the ways in which the sport text is constructed, which can be understood through Rowe's (1992) comprehensive theoretical examination of newspaper sports reporting. In order to better understand the diversity of styles, formats, modes of address and writer/reader positions that exist within the discipline of sports journalism, Rowe argued that there are four different modes of sports writing – hard news, soft news, orthodox rhetoric and reflexive analysis.

Hard news usually appears on the back page of newspapers, accompanied by banner headlines and striking photographs. In approach it mirrors the news that appears on the front page and adheres to the principles of neutrality, balance and accuracy. The standard technique of documenting who, what, when, where and why of a particular story is emphasized, while editorial comment is subordinated. This style of reporting, suggested Rowe, lends itself to a third person narrative, an objective record of events that invokes a tone of authority, as well as a depersonalization and naturalization of the stories. Results, match statistics, individual performances and an overall evaluation of the game are typical formats, but as Rowe noted, the 'transfers of players, injuries, changes to rules and, increasingly, announcements of sponsorships and contracts for television' also feature (100).

Soft news, by contrast, is more entertainment orientated than hard news. It is highly selective, sometimes referred to as 'infotainment' and emphasizes celebrity. In doing so, it typically focuses on biographical information and the recounted experiences, tastes and opinions of sporting stars.

Orthodox rhetoric, the third mode of sports writing, adopts the advocacy of editorial journalism. In an attempt to generate and promote controversy or conflict and benefit from the consequent increased circulation, the function of the sports journalist in this mode is not to record newsworthy sports information, but to 'consciously and actively intervene in the sports discourse' (104). Unlike either hard or soft news, orthodox rhetorical writing seeks to assert the subjectivity of the writer, in a process that is part persuasion and part antagonism.

The final mode, reflexive analysis, is characterized by a shared experience between the reader and writer. It seeks to understand or deconstruct the social influences on the way sport is 'seen', as well as the ways in which sport is socially constructed. Furthermore, in this mode, sport's inherent contradiction as a unifying discourse that transcends the struggles of everyday life on the one hand and as a basis for the reproduction of social hierarchies on the other, referred to by Rowe as the split discourse of sport, is not only recognized by the writer, but attempts are made to heal the split.

Of the four modes, hard and soft news are the most prevalent, with hard news representing vital on-field information in the main and soft news comprised of off-field feature stories and profiles. The amount of soft news has increased as the profile of professional athletes has risen, yet the irony is that the increase in the amount of soft news has been a significant contributing factor in constructing and embellishing these profiles. The incidence of orthodox rhetoric is also increasing, as the sport media nexus becomes more competitive and sport media commentators and reporters become celebrities themselves. By contrast, reflexive analysis is the rarest of the modes and does not appear to be increasing.

Photographs

Photographs are an essential part of the process by which newspapers make news salient by personifying events, because people are essentially interesting and can be vividly and concretely depicted in images (Hall, 1973). The use of a photograph to elaborate a story is a complex process, however, for as Barthes (1977:19) noted, by the time the press photograph is published, it has been 'worked on, chosen, composed, constructed, and treated according to professional, aesthetic or ideological norms'. News photographs, argued Hall (1973:241), operate under a hidden sign marked 'this really happened, see for yourself' and can guarantee and underwrite the perceived objectivity of the newspaper despite the fact that the selection of a particular photograph is a highly ideological procedure. The news photograph is not the representation of an objective truth, but rather a single moment that has been selected to represent a complex chain of events (Hall, 1973). This is further complicated by the acknowledgement that the photograph represents an event or person and the choice a particular angle, pose and selection of objects, where any number of other combinations could have been chosen.

The majority of photographs in the tabloid press are very plain (Becker, 1992). Typically, they present people who are quite ordinary, in their everyday surroundings and serve to make the people in them accessible to the viewer. Although Becker argued that the plain photograph is most common, she acknowledged that photographs are sometimes published from the time the event was taking place. Candid photographs are structured 'to reveal how people react when the comfortable façade of daily life is torn away' (Becker, 1992:143). These photographs are thought to reveal the truths of human nature, suggested Becker, as people expose themselves in the wake of great joy or tragic loss. Gripsrud (1992) noted that that media utilizes a standard-ized representation of emotions in order to convey a message to its readers. For example, certain poses, such as the bowed head that stands for 'grief' or 'sorrow' or particular poses and angles, such as the extreme close-up that stands for 'intensity' are well-established signs.

Rowe (1999) suggested that an analysis of sports photography is an inte-gral part of deconstructing the sports text. In addition, the sports photo-graph is usually accompanied by headlines and captions that help to 'anchor and relay' the photographic message. Hence, the photographic text must also be examined as the sum of a number of interrelated parts. The meaning of the photograph is dependent on 'the caption, headline, the positioning of the item in relation to other items, the reputation of the publication and, importantly, [the way in which readers] respond to the subjects with which they deal according to [their] own "reading positions" as male or female, black or white, young or old, working class or bourgeois, and so on' (122). Rowe argued, therefore, that 'reading' the photographic text is a complex process in which one social construction, the 'reader', is 'taking in' another, the photograph.

Themes in sport media texts

Kinkema and Harris (1998) found that a number of salient themes have been dominant in the analysis of sport media texts. First, global, national and local relations; second, race relations; third, gender relations; fourth, com-mercialization; fifth, winning; sixth, drugs; and seventh, violence. An earlier identification of the major tenets in sport media analysis by Jhally (1989) pro-duced similar results: militarism and nationalism; competition and the rules of the game; labour; the team and authority; gender; race and sports culture; and the culture of consumption were guiding the majority of work in the field. Similarly, in an assessment of the main ideological effects of the media, McKay and Rowe (1987) noted that the media legitimates masculine hegem-ony, capitalist rationality, consensus and militaristic nationalism and that it acts to marginalize, trivialize and fragment alternative ideologies of sport.

Gender

The representation of gender within and by the sport media has been a topic of intense academic scrutiny. In particular, researchers have examined the amount of media coverage received by women's sport and representations of masculinity and femininity.

A notable example of the research that examines the amount and content of media coverage of women's sport is Duncan and Messner's (2005) study of gender in televised sport. Their 15-year longitudinal study (1989–2004) revealed that the coverage of women's sport on television news and highlight programmes was exceptionally low and had not improved greatly from 1989 to 2004. Table 6.1 illustrates that despite some minor fluctuations, the distribution of sport news by sex on three network affiliate stations in a major American city has remained stable across the 15 years. The trend across media forms is confirmed through Bishop's (2003) examination of American magazine *Sports Illustrated*, in which the percentage of articles about women, which was typically about 5% of total sport coverage, dropped between 1980 and 1996.

The results of American national and regional highlight programmes such as ESPN's *SportsCenter* or FOX's *Southern California Sports Report* show an even greater disparity in the coverage of men's and women's sport. The proportion of men's sport in 2004 was 97% and 96.3% on the ESPN and FOX programmes, respectively. Duncan and Messner's (2005) study also examined the way in which women's sport was reported. They noted that the quality of reporting had improved in the 2004 sample, but that themes of sexualization and humour that had characterized previous studies were still prevalent (Messner, Duncan & Cooky, 2003). In particular, Anna Kournikova (1999) and Maria Sharapova (2004) were athletes who were overtly sexualized by the media coverage, a feature that was exacerbated by the fact that tennis accounted for approximately half of all televised media coverage within the sample.

The amount of coverage and the ways in which female athletes are sexualized through the media coverage of sport are both important as we attempt to decode sport media texts. However, they are only pieces of a broader puzzle. In order to deconstruct these texts in terms of their impact on audiences it is necessary to dig deeper. Duncan and Messner (1998) have explored three key themes that they argued have been central to media descriptions of sport.

Table 6.1 Television Sport News by Sex, 1989–2004

Sex/Year	1989	1993	1999	2004
Men (%)	92	93.8	88.2	91.4
Women (%)	5	5.1	8.7	6.3
Neutral/Both (%)	3	1.1	3.1	2.4

Source: Duncan and Messner (2005).

First, male athletes are often represented as larger than life. The descriptors 'big', 'large', and 'huge' are often used to describe male athletes and male sport, which may contribute to the ways in which masculine identities are constructed. Second, attributes that connote strength such as 'powerful', 'confident', 'gutsy' and 'dominant' are used far more frequently in male sport than attributes that suggest weakness, such as 'weary', 'frustrated', 'panicked' or 'dejected'. By contrast, in female sport the weakness descriptors are used far more frequently. Third and finally, explanations for success and failure tend to be different in men's and women's sport. For example, a male victory might be attributed to the player's competence (talent, power, size, speed, ability to read the play, etc.), whereas a female victory is more likely to be explained by reference to emotions, luck, togetherness and family.

The themes referred to above are not prevalent in every sport text and they might not be evident by examining one or two pages of the newspaper sport section. In fact, the use of language may have become so natural that the ways in which it might influence individual and collective identities, or the way we view the world around us might not be readily apparent. It may take a detailed examination of a variety of sources over an extended period of time to discover the ways in which 'appropriate' masculine and feminine qualities are being constructed by the sport media. This is what makes decoding sport media difficult, but also both necessary and rewarding.

Race

Like gender, the media representation of race is often difficult to decode. Whannel (2000) has identified two major themes in the area: first, whether the media provides stereotypical images of black athletes; and second, whether positive images reinforce stereotypes of athleticism at the expense of other human qualities and attributes. Davis and Harris (1998:157) have argued that a stereotype 'is a generalization about a category of people that is negative and/or misleading'. In the case of Americans from African descent, they suggested that stereotypes such as ignorant, lazy, happy-go-lucky, savage and animal-like have been prevalent in American society, although where they were once publicly articulated, they are now far more subtle and elusive. The sport media is one place where these subtle stereotypes might be constructed and communicated. For example, in a range of different sporting contests and contexts, black and indigenous athletes are often referred to as being more naturally gifted. White athletes might be described by commentators as 'workmanlike' or 'hard working', while the feats of black and indigenous athletes might be described as 'magical', 'mercurial' or 'instinctive'. In each individual instance it might be unclear whether it is an overt form of racism, a naturalization of language or a perpetuation of stereotypes. But, what we do know is that through the media, various frames or cultural maps are competing. Sport media management has an important role to play in ensuring that generalizations that are negative or misleading are not perpetuated and that our social reality is more accurate and equitable.

Nationalism

Sport media is also an important part of constructing national identities, particularly with the global importance and influence of events such as the Olympic Games and the FIFA World Cup. Sporting events are by their nature combative and territorial and often the media coverage serves to reinforce particular ideologies and stereotypes. Sometimes the broad theme of the media coverage is as simple as 'us against them', but the way in which messages are conveyed are often more complex. For example, Blain, Boyle and O'Donnell (1993) have argued that throughout European journalism on the World Cup, football has been interpreted as a substitute war. However, the military metaphor is applied to the German team more than any other. Its type of football is described as powerful and ruthless and opponents are killed off. Maguire, Poulton and Possamai's (1999) study of the media coverage of the semifinal between Germany and England in the 1996 European Football Championships revealed that the English media often referred to the Second World War, while the German media were more likely to refer to contemporary politics to assert their superiority. They concluded that the media coverage of global sport was being used to reassert national identities at the expense of European integration.

Summary

This chapter has examined the sport text and the devices used by the media to make sport media meaningful and entertaining. This chapter also explored the key themes of gender, race and nationalism in order to explain the ways in which the sport media influences the construction of the social world in which we live. Importantly, being able to decode and deconstruct sport texts places those involved in the management of sport media in a more powerful position. The deconstruction of sport texts enables a more complex understanding of the role of the sport media nexus in broader society and potentially avoids being bombarded with images and texts that naturalize stereotypes or particular ways of seeing the world. This knowledge might assist in engaging in more effective sport media management, but might also be used in changing the sport media nexus to ensure it is more equitable and less stereotypical. Review questions and exercises are listed below to assist with confirming your knowledge of the core concepts and principles introduced in this chapter.

Review questions and exercises

1. What is a sport text?
2. What are the key devices used by the media to construct meaning and entertainment?

3. Locate a contemporary sport photograph in which the subject is active. Decode the photograph from the perspectives of the reader of the text, the subject(s) and the photographer. Are they different? Why?

4. Using the same photograph, decode it from the position of a different gender, race, ethnicity or nationality than your own? Would it be interpreted in different ways? Why?

5. Locate a contemporary sport photograph in which the subject is passive. Are there more or less possible meanings than the photograph in which the subject was active? Why?

6. Locate a black and white sport photograph in an old newspaper. What are the differences between the old and contemporary sport photographs that might create a different reading of the text for an audience?

7. Choose a sport section from a major daily newspaper or a sport news programme on television. What themes were most prominent throughout the section or broadcast?

8. Did you detect any gender, race or national stereotyping in the section or broadcast? If so, describe it.

9. How were women and female athletes represented in the section or broadcast? Was there a disparity between the amount of male and female sport covered?

10. Overall, what was the message about the purpose of sport from the section or broadcast?

Case 1   Super Bowl men and women

In 1975 the following was observed about the Super Bowl, the championship game of America's National Football League (NFL):

> The structural values of the Super Bowl can be summarized succinctly: North American professional football is an aggressive, strictly regulated team game fought between males who use both violence and technology to gain control of property for the economic gain of individuals within a nationalistic entertainment context. The Super Bowl propagates these values by elevating one game to the level of a spectacle of American ideology collectively celebrated. Rather than mere diversionary entertainment, it can be seen to function as a 'propaganda' vehicle strengthening and developing the larger social structure (Real, 1975:42).

Wenner (1998) noted that Real's observations were just as relevant at the end of the twentieth century. More than 30 years after and well into the twenty-first century, the comments are still an accurate reflection of the power and influence of a single mega sport media event. Several other analyses of the Super Bowl have been conducted since, which provide further insights into the ways in which the media coverage of American Football's Championship game might influence the ways audiences think about themselves and their place in the world.

Through an examination of advertisements aired during 2002 and 2003 Super Bowls (and *Sports Illustrated* swimsuit issues in the same years), Messner and Montez de Oca (2005) have suggested that male consumers are encouraged to see beer and liquor products as essential to creating stylish and desirable lifestyles. Furthermore, they argued that four dominant gender themes are evident in the advertisements. First, men are presented as losers, in which they are 'always on the cusp of being publicly humiliated'. Second, male friendships and their emotional stability is a core feature of many advertisements. Third, women appear as 'highly sexualized fantasy objects', who according to Messner and de Oca, 'serve as potential prizes for men's victories and consumption choices'. Fourth and finally, women whom men are emotionally committed to are absent from the advertisements or threaten men's freedom to enjoy the pleasures of the male group. Importantly, Messner and Montez de Oca have argued that these themes are part of process of constructing versions of men and women (and their relationships) that encourage men to 'remain more open to the marketing strategies of the industry'.

In his analysis of the media and public reaction to the uncovering of singer Janet Jackson's breast during the coverage of the 2004 Super Bowl's half-time show, Wenner (2004) has argued that in hiring MTV to produce the half-time show, CBS (broadcaster) and the NFL were treading a fine line in attempting to attract young male viewers and provide appropriate family entertainment. Wenner noted that the other acts that appeared with Jackson in 2004 provided an 'edginess' that CBS and the NFL were looking for with sexually explicit lyrics, crotch grabbing and sexually suggestive dance routines. However, the incident with Jackson and Justin Timberlake resulted in public consternation, over 500,000 complaints to the federal regulatory body and a federal investigation on indecency. In many respects the juxtaposition of the acceptability of highly sexualized women in advertisements throughout the Super Bowl and the unacceptability of a semi-naked breast of a celebrity illustrates an unresolved tension in the sport media nexus.

Sources: Real (1975); Wenner (1998); Messner and Montez de Oca (2005); and Wenner (2004).

Case 2 The Olympic ideal

The Olympic Games are one of the largest sporting events in the world. They are also one of the largest media events in the world and like many mega media events, their construction reveals much about the ways in which the media frames the world in which we live. As Billings and Eastman (2003:574) noted in their study of the media coverage of the 2002 Salt Lake City Winter Olympic Games, 'what television audiences see is not an Olympics itself, but an event that has been framed by producing organizations that cultivates societal values as a part of prolonged media exposure'.

In order to examine the gender, ethnic and national parity of network television commentary in the United States of America, Billings and Eastman formulated six hypotheses, listed below, which they tested by examining 52 hours of prime-time broadcast, which represented 100% of NBC's coverage over 17 evenings. The results are in parentheses:

1. Comments by NBC commentators regarding the gender of the athletes will tend to magnify men's effort and diminish women's effort (women athletes were more likely to be viewed as succeeding because of athletic skill, but were also more likely to have failure attributed to a lack of experience).
2. Comments by NBC commentators regarding the nationality of the athletes will flatter American athletes but diminish the achievement of athletes from other nations (American athletes were depicted as succeeding because they kept their composure and had superior courage, while non-American success was attributed to experience).
3. Men and women will receive the same amount of clock time within NBC's prime-time Olympic coverage (male athletes received twice as much time as female athletes, the largest gap of the previous five Olympics).
4. The majority of the top 20 most mentioned athletes will be males, Whites and Americans (70% of the top 20 and top 10 most mentioned athletes were male, with majorities of white and American athletes in the top 20).
5. The majority of host and reporter or announcer name mentions of athletes will be of males, Whites and Americans (the hypothesis was true for males and Whites, but not for Americans, as non-Americans were mentioned more often).
6. Host commentators will be significantly more successful than on-site reporters in achieving gender and ethnic balance in mentions of athletes by name (male reporters were more likely to mention male athletes, female reporters were more likely to mention women, while host commentators were found to disproportionately favour American athletes).

Billings and Eastman suggested the discrepancy in clock time between men and women was a major finding, because this is the 'ultimate framing function of the Olympic telecast' (583), which was supported by the dominance of men in the most mentioned athletes. The dominance of white athletes at the Olympic Games and the attribution of superior courage to particular nationalities are not surprising, but the important question, for sport managers more than most, is what are the consequences of this type of framing? For African America children? For recent migrants? For female athletes? For prospective sport participants?
Source: Billings and Eastman (2003).

7 Working the beat: sport media production

Overview

This chapter examines sport media production and in particular the institutionalized routines and work practices of sport media professionals. This chapter explores a number of themes, including the profession of sport journalism, the concept of newsworthiness and the beat model of sport reporting. The information within this chapter is contextualized by an analysis of the way in which the institutionalized work practices and routines of sport journalists, editors, reporters and commentators impact the media coverage available to different types of sport organizations and the strategies required to achieve media coverage in this environment.

After completing this chapter the reader should be able to:

- Describe the special features of sport journalism and the work of sport media professionals.
- Relate the theoretical concept of newsworthiness to practical sport media management practices.
- Understand the beat model of sport reporting and the ways in which sport media professionals have institutionalized their work practices to manage available time and resources.

> - Utilize knowledge of the work practices and routines of sport media producers in order to inform sport media management strategies and planning.

Introduction

The previous four chapters in this part have examined sport media industries and practices, such as the sale of broadcast rights and sport broadcasting regulation, which impact the nexus at the macrolevel. By contrast, the previous chapter examined sport media texts, the content that consumers interact with on a daily basis at a microlevel, while this chapter is an analysis of the way in which sport media is produced.

This analysis of sport media production necessarily involves an investigation of the work practices and routines of sport media professionals, the people who produce the texts. An understanding of these practices and routines is important, for it informs and shapes effective sport media management at an instrumental level. The way in which sport media texts are produced and selected influences the amount of media coverage that different types of people and organizations receive. For example, the previous chapter noted that sport media texts often privilege the position of hyper-masculine sports, while at the same time tending to marginalize female athletes and sports. A sophisticated understanding of these trends and themes must include an analysis of texts, but also of the way in which they are produced.

In order to operate effectively within the sport media nexus, it is essential for a sport media manager to have an understanding and knowledge of who produces sport media, how they choose what is newsworthy and what is not, as well as how they organize their professional lives in order to make their jobs easier, provide them with increased status and credibility or conform to accepted routines and practices. An analysis of the work routines and practices of sport media producers enables sport organizations to tailor their media management strategies and target appropriate media outlets. For example, the two cases in this chapter demonstrate how two organizations have put in place media management (a facility and media protocol) that makes the media's job easier, which in turn results in more and better media coverage. An analysis of newsworthiness informs the practice of sport media management that will be dealt with the detail in the following chapters.

Sport media producers

According to Herbert (2000), newsrooms consist basically of editors and reporters. In a newsroom, journalists collect, report, edit and distribute a special category of information called news (Newhagen & Levy, 1998). The definition of a journalist traditionally included all full-time reporters, writers, correspondents, columnists, newsmen (and women) and editors, although technological changes in the twentieth century have meant that it also includes radio and television editorial personnel in news and public affairs programming (Weaver & Wilhoit, 1986). In other words, the term journalist has come to signify a range of occupations associated with the production of news within a wide variety of media outlets. It is clear, however, that the term is increasingly losing its currency, and with advances in communication technologies in particular, the notion of a sport media producer is more relevant at the start of the twenty-first century.

The sport media nexus is a significant field of employment, within both sport and media organizations. In many countries sport is the largest journalism speciality, yet the phrase 'toy department' has often been used to describe and denigrate the field of sports journalism (Garrison & Salwen, 1989; Rowe, 1992). Various explanations have been proposed for this lack of occupational credibility, including the lower class of origin of sport journalists, the lack of educational qualifications relative to other specializations and sport's non- or anti-intellectual ethos (Rowe, 1992). During the latter half of the twentieth century both print and broadcast sport journalism were transformed from mostly fun and games to serious journalism. However, inherent contradictions still exist, such as the popularity of sport journalism versus credibility within the broader profession and the seriousness of work versus the fun of sport. Perhaps the most significant barrier to professional credibility is the notion that sport media producers are more likely to promote sport through their coverage, rather than report objectively. This criticism could be levelled at most media professionals, who often have vested interests or explicit ideologies that inform their work, yet it seems to be sharper when directed at sport media producers.

A recent study of the attitudes of sports editors at daily newspapers in the United States of America has demonstrated practices that would be questionable outside the sport section (Hardin, 2005). In particular, the study highlighted the occurrence of 'boosterism', which describes bias in the coverage of home teams. A significant 39% of the editors surveyed believed that sport journalists should cheer homes teams and 43% believed that accepting 'freebies' from sport teams such as free tickets and travel would not compromise a reporter's objectivity. It is clear from this study and research on the beat model of sport reporting, which will be discussed later in this chapter, that the commercial interdependence of the sport and media industries has created some unique professional practices.

Further evidence of this special relationship is evident in the 2005 national study of the American Project for Excellence in Journalism (APEJ, 2006), which revealed the content and practices of sport journalists were in marked contrast to their non-sport colleagues. The study of the content of the front pages of newspaper sport sections found that planned events dominated newspaper coverage of sport, with reporting on games contributing 70% of the total and media conferences and releases contributing a further 18%. Furthermore, the study found that newsroom initiated stories, whereby a journalist conceived of and then investigated a topic made up only 10% of the total, which was half the amount in other comparable sections of the newspaper, while unplanned events accounted for the final 2%. Moreover, the study revealed that relative to other sections of the newspaper, these figures did not change greatly depending on the size of the newspaper and its circulation. In other words, those newspapers with greater resources and more staff were engaged in the same practices as sport media producers at smaller organizations.

The study referred to above also reported findings related to the content of articles. In particular, results demonstrated that 88% of articles contained only one viewpoint, while this figure was an average of approximately 50% for other comparable sections of the newspaper. The amount of opinion and speculation, as opposed to hard facts, was also much higher in sport section articles. Furthermore, football, baseball and basketball dominated coverage, with two out of every three front-page stories related to these sports. By contrast, articles that focused on more controversial sport issues, such as drugs and crime, represented only 3% of the total. The findings also showed that there was a significant disparity between men's and women's sports, with 5% of articles reporting on female athletes and 3% of female teams, which confirms the results of research referred to in the previous chapter.

In a national survey conducted in the early 1990s, Henningham (1995) found that Australian sports journalists were:

> Overwhelmingly male and Caucasian, slightly less well educated than other journalists, more conservative in their political values, less professional, but less inclined to support ethical breaches. They [were] happier in their work, less stressed, more supportive of traditional 'objective' models of journalism and less supportive of investigative roles for the media.

Similarly, Garrison and Salwen (1989; Salwen & Garrison, 1998) found that sports section managers in America were typically young, white and male. A clear profile of sports journalists emerged from these surveys, but it is less clear what role they perform, or what role they should perform. Koppett (1981) argued that the reporter's job is to gather news and deliver some fraction of that news to the public as quickly as possible. They should not be advocates, he suggested, because this compromises the function of delivering information. Rather, they are more accurately and usefully viewed as conduits between the source and the reader. His views are in contrast to those of Rowe and Stevenson (1995), who suggested that in producing the sports text, a journalist necessarily involves her or himself in a series of complex negotiations, with media management, other journalists (inside and outside the discipline), editors, sports organizations (from coaches through to media managers), athletes and finally, their readers. This notion of a sport media producer's complex negotiations is an ideal way to explore their work practices and routines and the ways in which news is selected and rejected.

Newsworthiness

The sport media environment is highly competitive, with enough print and broadcast space for only a small percentage of events and happenings. Media producers rely on mechanisms, both conscious and subconscious to determine what is newsworthy and what is not. Galtung and Ruge (1988) suggested that twelve factors impact upon the structure and selection of news, eight of which are culturally indistinct and four that are culturally specific or culture-bound. The following is a list of those factors that are not dependent on a cultural context, which means that it is reasonable that news organizations anywhere around the world, will respond in a similar fashion based on these factors:

- The more similar the *frequency* of the event to that of the news medium, the more likely it is that is will be recorded as news.
- The louder the noise, or *amplitude*, the more chance that an event will be recorded as news.
- An event with a clear interpretation, that is *clear and unambiguous*, is preferred by the news media to one that has a possible multitude of meanings.
- If an event is able to be interpreted within a clearly defined cultural framework, it is *meaningful* and is likely to receive more attention than an event that is culturally distant and is therefore not as relevant.
- News must be *consonant*, in that the expectation of the event should meet with the reality. An event that is too far removed from what is predicted or wanted may not be covered, or may be distorted to fit to expectations.
- The more *unexpected* an event is, within the confines of being meaningful and consonant, the greater the chance of being considered newsworthy. The corollary of the sixth factor is that events that are regular, institutionalized, continuing and repetitive will not generally attract attention.
- Unless the amplitude of an event is reduced drastically, once an event is defined as news it establishes *continuity* and will remain as news.
- The *composition* of news determines its selection. If a large number of similar items have been reported on, a report of similar nature will be unlikely to be regarded as news, whereas an event of a different nature will.

The following is a list of four factors that are culturally specific:

- The more an event contains *elite nations*, the more likely it is to be recorded as news. The perception of an elite nation will differ markedly within regions.
- The more an event contains *elite people*, the more an event is likely to attract attention.
- The more the event is able to undergo *personification*, whereby it is able to be viewed in personal terms, or due to the actions of specific people, the more likely it will be recorded as news.
- The more *negative* an event or its consequences are, the more likely it is to be perceived as newsworthy. Negative news by its very nature is more unexpected than positive news, is less predictable, is often sudden and immediate, has a range of possible consequences and undermines the potentially positive meta-narrative.

Furthermore, Galtung and Ruge (1988) suggested that the more an event satisfies the twelve criteria listed above, the more likely that the event would be selected and registered as news. Once a news item is selected, what makes it newsworthy according to the twelve factors will be accentuated. Similarly, Hall, Critcher, Jefferson, Clarke and Roberts (1978) suggested that events that score high on a number of news values will have greater news potential and that journalists will play up the extraordinary, dramatic or tragic elements of a story to enhance its newsworthiness.

The newsworthiness criteria explain in part why sport is a significant and regular feature of media news. It also highlights the ways in which sport organizations can maximize their media coverage. For example, continuity and composition are both important for sport organizations. However, the application of the criteria is likely to be markedly different depending on the size of the organization. Small sport organizations or athletes that come to prominence sporadically or unexpectedly often have peaks of media coverage, followed by long troughs. What these organizations and athletes often fail to realize is that the strategies to maintain the continuity are as important, if not more so than achieving the initial coverage. Gains achieved by a team, league or sport through increased participation or commercial interest can quickly dissipate when the media coverage falls away. Similarly, small sport organizations that attempt to compete with larger sport organizations in the same media market often disregard the composition of news. These organizations pitch or present the media with stories and news ideas that are effectively the same as those organizations with greater amplitude. A better strategy might be to adopt a targeted approach, where less but more unusual stories are pitched or presented.

Deviance

Shoemaker, Danielian and Brendlinger (1991) have argued that newsworthiness indicators can be broken down into three general theoretical dimensions. First, the deviance dimension, which refers to whether an event is novel, odd or unusual, whether the event is prominent, whether it has a sensational feature and whether the event exhibits conflict or controversy. Second, the social significance dimension, which refers to whether the event is important, has a high or low impact or consequence and is of public interest. The third and final dimension consists of the contingent conditions of timeliness and proximity. If an event is highly deviant, and has a social significance, the event will receive a high level of media coverage. On the other hand, if an event has a low deviant level, and is of low social significance, it is likely to receive little or no coverage. Shoemaker, Danielian and Brendlinger suggested that deviance is the essential criteria for newsworthiness because deviant people and deviant events receive a lot of attention. Furthermore, they suggested that human beings have an innate interest in deviance and that attention to media content is at its highest when the content deviates from an individual's existing schemata. Similarly, Schudson (1995) referred to three news zones, that included legitimate controversy, deviance and shared values, while Hall, Critcher, Jefferson, Clarke and Roberts (1978) noted that the construction of a topic in terms of a debate in which there are oppositions and conflicts is one way of dramatizing an event in order to enhance its newsworthiness. This notion of deviance, controversy and conflict is important when sport organizations have to deal with issues of crisis or scandal, which will be discussed in further detail in Chapter 12.

Celebrity

In his study of the American media, Gans (1980) suggested that there are two types of people who appear in the news: the 'knowns' and the 'unknowns'. The 'knowns' are familiar names among the audience, or those who have appeared frequently in the media. An examination of any media form, from tabloid newspapers to gossip magazines to investigative political television programmes reveals that a significant proportion of print and broadcast news is occupied by the 'knowns'. It is clear that authoritative sources make the news and that the better the source is, the better the news is perceived to be (Sigal, 1986). By contrast, the 'unknowns' constitute a minority of newsmakers and are typically engaged in unusual or controversial activity, or have been victims of crime or disaster. In contemporary society, both the celebrity and the victim have enormous cultural currency, illustrated by the trend of the contestants of reality television programmes becoming famous for simply being famous, while the suffering of people as a result of hurricanes and tsunamis is magnified by blanket media coverage. The theme of celebrity and stardom will be discussed in greater detail in Chapter 11.

The beat system

One of the criticisms of sport journalism and a reason for low credibility that has resulted in the tag 'toy department' is that the frame that is often utilized by sport media producers is an uncritical and promotional discourse. In other words, unlike other more serious aspects of the media that engage in objective investigative journalism, sport media producers have often been accused of adopting work practices and routines that institutionalize the promotion of sport and its related activities. The intimate connection between sport and the media and their reliance on each other for commercial success has resulted in the development of particular professional codes and work practices.

The 'beat' is a particular way that media organizations prioritize their time, resources, personnel and money, as well as the way in which they ensure that there is enough news to publish or broadcast. In essence, a media organization creates a beat by assigning a reporter or reporters to cover an institution or area of human endeavour full-time. The beat reporter's job is to provide news about the people, businesses, issues, events and controversies on the beat, in order that the media outlet can establish a regular feature or section in the area. The beat is essential to the manufacture of news and is not limited to sport news production. For example, the winner of the Pulitzer Prize for beat reporting in 2003 was Diana Sugg of the *Baltimore Sun*, who is a health reporter, while in 2002 Gretchen Morgenson of the *New York Times* won for her regular coverage of Wall Street. Beat reporters can cover crime, politics, sport, religion, science issues, weather, foreign affairs, or a whole range of other topics, depending on the interests of the audience, or the specific nature of the region, city, state or country.

Unlike other beats, however, the sport beat has particular and peculiar implications for the management of sport. Whereas politicians might vary what they say or do because of the media coverage, they rarely have to consider the impact of the way in which news is manufactured. For sport organizations the reality is very different. The routines and ideologies that underpin the beat reporting model mean that some sports get covered while others do not. The beat model of sports reporting also has specific implications for sport reporters and editors, as it relies on the reporter or journalist maintaining very close relationships with people at the heart of their beat.

The beat model of sport reporting places media professionals in a precarious position, and although this is true of all beat reporters, it is particularly true in sport because of the inextricable commercial link between sport and the media. On the one hand they need to satisfy their audiences, who demand interesting and at times provocative/controversial stories. On the other hand they need to keep their sources (their beat) onside. Without the audience they have no job and without the sources they have no job. In other words, it is sometimes difficult to determine the more powerful master.

Similar to other news departments, the sports newswork environment, suggested by Lowes (1997, 1999), is one in which there are daily pressures to produce a sufficient amount of quality copy and constraints within which the sport journalists must operate, such as time, money and resources. In response to these conditions and to cope with the demands placed on them, sports journalists have institutionalized their work routines. The major component of this institutionalization is the beat system, whereby a reporter is assigned to cover one or more sports on a full-time basis. The large commercial spectator sports could have several journalists working their beat, depending on the size of the sport, the media outlet and the market. As Theberge and Cronk (1986) noted, journalists must have ready and frequent access to reliable news sources in order to do their work. The beat is a way of both formally and informally organizing a journalist's access to information, in order that the information is regular, newsworthy and is attributable to credible news sources.

Lowes (1999) explained that the beat system is a huge investment of the financial and human resources of a media organization. As such, beat reporters must produce, whether the story is newsworthy and whether the quality of the writing is good or not. The result is that only the major commercial spectator sports are assigned beats, because they are seen to attract the greatest audience share. These sports have the resources to act as a constant source of information for journalists, through the employment of media, communication and marketing managers, as well as finances to support facilities that make the sports journalists' job easier, such as media facilities with telephones, data points or wireless Internet access. Commercial spectator sports are also able to make their athletes, coaches and administrators available to the media more often than amateur or semi-professional sports. As a consequence, minority and women's sports are often neglected or ignored, because they are not supported by, and do not support, the routinization of sports news gathering.

Lowes identified two primary categories of sources for the sports reporter – major commercial sport organizations and their clubs and personal contacts on the beat. These routine sources could be athletes, coaches, administrators or managers, player agents, team doctors, trainers, equipment managers, administrative staff, or in some circumstances, other sports reporters. Lowes noted that over a period of time a reporter would more than likely develop affection for the players or for the team as a whole. These sentiments he argued, are precisely what sport organizations seek to exploit. However, the intimacy of this relationship means that sports journalists must be careful not to offend their routine sources, thereby cutting them off from a reliable and constant source of information. Lowes suggested that in the most extreme cases sports reporters can be subjected to physical intimidation and violence as a result of a negative story, however, the more likely consequence of overt criticism is that the reporter will be cut-off or ostracized. It is important to note that Lowes conducted his research in North America, where typically cities have only one professional team in any one sport. In other contexts where teams are not so geographically disparate, a beat might refer to a league or teams from a league based in the same city. It is possible that this might change the nature of the beat reporting relationships, because a reporter will necessarily have more sources and contacts at their disposal, yet the need to establish strong and intimate links with the respective teams is unlikely to be obviated.

Lowes argued that sports news is a discourse that serves the promotional interests of the primary stakeholders in the commercial sports industry. Furthermore, he suggested that there is limited space for news that does not promote the industry, because it is very difficult to create a culture of consumption, both of sports and the media, if the news questions the functioning or existence of the sports industry. Likewise, Klatell and Marcus (1988: 210) argued in their analysis of television sport journalism that no one likes to hear bad news, such as the tragic drug induced death of a basketball star, corruption scandals at Universities and colleges or athletes with drug, alcohol and financial problems from high school through to professional sports. They noted that 'athletes and sport executives often react worst when the news is broken by a seemingly friendly source, a sports reporter. There is often a very real sense of betrayal, accompanied by a feeling that one's privacy has been violated by the very people who should have been guarding the secrets most assiduously'. Their analysis of audience is complemented by Henningham's (1995) assessment that sports journalists have a 'neutral', rather than a 'participant' concept of journalism and that they prefer not to engage in investigative journalism or to stir up trouble. It is reasonable to conclude that in general sports journalists avoid making explicit or critical value statements and that socially critical commentary is not usually a feature of their stories (Trujillo & Ekdom, 1985).

The concept of a promotional discourse and set of work routines and practices that suppress negative or controversial stories is contrary to components of the newsworthiness criteria presented earlier. This disparity is indicative of the institutionalization of the sport beat and the commercial interdependence of the sport and media industries. The strength of this interdependence is not sufficient to ensure all sport news is positive, for negative news is reported. Rather, the relationship between the two industries ensures that reporting is generally positive and readers, viewers and listeners continue to consume. If the media continually reports negative news about politicians, consumers are likely to vote them out of office, rather than stop accessing the media. By contrast, continually negative news about players, coaches and managers might cause people to cease their media consumption of sport. The end result would be a downturn in profits, which the media will do almost anything to avoid.

Implications for sport media management

Lowes (1999) used Tuchman's (1978) apt analogy of the fishing net to explain the process by which media organizations structure their news gathering and selection practices. News gathering is like casting a fishing net, where the size of holes in the net will determine the size of the fish that are caught. Most news gathering nets are made to catch only the biggest fish only, as there is limited media space and they have limited resources with which to gather the news. The sport media environment is no different and in general the net that is cast invariably lets the small fish through the large holes in the net. In order to catch more and smaller fish, the media organization would need to make the holes smaller, which essential means employing more journalists. The reality is that most media organizations are content to invest as much as it takes to catch the big sport fish.

This model of sport news gathering and selection has significant implications for the practice of sport media management within large and small sport organizations. First, large sport organizations in major professional leagues have a distinct advantage within the beat model of sport reporting because they invariably have both the time and money to devote to supplying the media with information and resources required to undertake their work in a timely and professional manner. In other words, large organizations are simply able to service the media more easily and effectively (Case 1 is a good example of a large organization constructing a purpose built facility to make the job of the media easier, which in turn will result in more extensive coverage). Second, small sport organizations must ensure that they are mindful of the realities of the beat reporting system in developing and enacting sport media management strategies. Importantly, small media organizations must make it as easy as possible for the media to report on their events and achievements. Case 2 is an example of a strategy employed by a women's sport organization in order to encourage better sport media relations and in the process improve the amount and quality of coverage. Third and finally, the promotional nature of the sport media relationship must be dealt with honestly and ethically. The relationship is predicated on mutual commercial benefit, and although the organization can make it as easy and comfortable for the journalist to do their job, at the end of the day, bad news will be interesting to the general public because of its deviant quality.

Major professional sport leagues and events have a distinct advantage in the media marketplace because they are inherently newsworthy. The regularity and consistency of sport allows media organizations to plan effectively, while its ephemerality provides a continuous flow of unexpected results. Furthermore, because of their exposure, athletes are invariably considered celebrities by the media and the public, whether or not they want to be. This enables the sport media to create and report moments of heroism, but conversely means that moments of deviance can quickly turn the hero into the villain. These themes will be dealt with in more detail in Chapters 11 and 12.

Case 1 NatWest Media Centre at Lord's Cricket Ground

Lord's Cricket Ground in England is considered by many to be the home of cricket, with a long and proud history. Like any sporting arena with a long history, however, the facilities at various times have been unsatisfactory and in need of repair or replacement. By the end of the twentieth century this was particularly true of the media facilities at Lord's. Brian Thornton, Marylebone Cricket Club (MCC) committee member and chairman of the Lord's estates sub-committee, which had responsibility for developing the ground and managing any building projects, noted that by the mid-1990s 'facilities for the media were pretty rudimentary. There was room for about 90 journalists, and the commentators were in little wooden shacks dotted around the ground' (Future Systems, 2001). With the 1999 Cricket World Cup approaching, the MCC decided that a new facility would be designed and constructed, giving the media the most up-to-date facilities that the club could afford.

Commissioned by the MCC in 1994 and designed by architectural company Future Systems, the NatWest Media Centre at Lord's Cricket Ground in England was opened in time for the 1999 Cricket World Cup. Built in a boatyard, the media centre is the world's first all aluminium semi-monocoque building, made from 26 three-metre aluminium sections that provide both structural integrity and protection from the elements in one design.

Importantly, the media centre has been designed so that cricket journalists, reporters and commentators have an unparalleled view of any game at Lord's. The interior of the centre is free of columns, and the front of the building is entirely made of glass, which provides an unobstructed view of the field from any position within the centre. The glass is inclined at 25 degrees to ensure no sunlight is reflected into the eyes of the players.

On the lower floor of the centre there are 118 seats for the print media, with a hospitality box for 18 people on either side. The top floor consists of two in vision TV studios, two large TV commentary boxes, two large radio boxes (each accommodating around 6 personnel) and 6 two-person radio boxes. The back of the building is used on match days for media catering and a bar area, with an additional room set aside for use by photographers for filing their images and storing equipment. The building also has a communications room with facilities such as a photocopier and fax. Lockers are provided at the back of the print media area and in the photographers' room. The photographers' room is equipped with chairs and bench tables around the walls, with power and phone sockets available, although most photographers use wi-fi or mobile cards to send their images back to their agencies via their own laptops.

The 118 workstations in the print media area each have two phone sockets, one for PC and one for telephone. It is the responsibility of the media organization to have a line installed at their allocated workstation, although the ability exists to connect them into the MCC phone and PC network should technical problems arise. The building has floor panels throughout, which give access under the floor to the ducts for the TV and radio broadcaster to lay cables. There are two large plasma screens at each end of the print media area, as well as television monitors along the front of the print media area, in the bar, in each of the television and radio boxes and the photographers' room. Finally, ambient sound is played within the media centre so that crowd noise and the general atmosphere outside can be felt within the building.

The NatWest Media Centre at Lord's is a clear example of a sport organization allocating significant resources to provide the media with state of the art facilities and an enviable physical space to conduct their work. Not all organizations have the financial wherewithal to undertake or complete a building of this type, yet the principles are the same, for the MCC and Lord's as much as for smaller organizations that have no professional staff or players – make the media's job easy and enjoyable.

Source: Future Systems (2001).

Case 2   WTA All-Access Hour

The Women's Tennis Association (WTA) Tour is one of the largest and most successful professional sport circuits in the world. In 2006, the Sony Ericsson WTA Tour played 63 events in 32 countries, including 26 tournaments in Europe, 15 in North/Central America and 14 in Asia, with total prize money of approximately US $60 million. The Tour features internationally recognized athletes such as Serena and Venus Williams (USA), Maria Sharapova (Russia) and Amelie Mauresmo (France). Over the past 10 years the tour has increased its popularity and global profile, in part through athletes such as Steffi Graf, Martina Hingis, Jennifer Capriati and Anna Kournikova. In 2005, the WTA signed Sony Ericsson to a US $88 million sponsorship agreement over 6 years, the largest ever in women's professional sport and the largest ever in tennis.

The WTA recognizes that its media profile is one of its greatest assets. Athletes such as the Williams sisters are not just sporting celebrities, but have been 'mainstreamed'. In other words, Serena and Venus Williams are famous outside of the world of tennis and outside the world of sport. They are famous as global celebrities and just happen to play professional tennis. As WTA chief executive officer Larry Scott has noted, 'one of the greatest assets [the WTA has] is our players who have an appeal beyond sport'. Rather than be concerned about the players having other interests, such as modelling or acting, Scott believes that these activities are a marketing asset for the WTA. As a result, female tennis players not only appear on the cover of magazines such as *Sports Illustrated*, but also generic women's and news magazines that have broader appeal and reach. This mainstreaming of female tennis stars has occurred because of a series of marketable and visible stars, as well as increasing media coverage. Sony Ericsson's sponsorship of the tour is a tangible measure of its success in a global sport market.

In 2003, under the leadership of recently appointed Chief executive officer Larry Scott, the WTA put in place an All-Access Hour, designed to improve media coverage and communication between athletes and the media in particular. The all-access hour consists of the top seeds at a tournament being involved in media roundtable interviews for 1 hour on the first day of tier 1 and 2 WTA events and prior to the main draw of grand slam events. The number of seeds made available by the tournament depends on the number of players in the draw and the level of the event. Players are seated at individual tables around a media centre at the same time. Television and print media are able to interview players for 1 hour, as well as conduct one-on-one interviews and take photographs of the players.

According to Scott, the 'WTA Tour features many of the most extraordinary and exciting women athletes in the world, and making them accessible to the media will help bring [the] biggest stars even closer to … fans worldwide' and that the all-access hour concept 'creates an efficient and high-impact interview process for … players, tournaments and the media'. The WTA All-Access Hour is an example of a professional sport organization putting in place strategies to provide the media with greater access to players, which is needed to produce media content. The way in which this access is structured makes it easier for sport media producers to do their jobs, which eventually results in increased coverage.

Source: www.wta.com

Summary

This chapter has examined the way in which the sport media produces content that is printed or broadcast as sport news and entertainment. In particular, the chapter has examined who produces sport media, the criteria that are used to select and reject news, as well as the institutionalized work practices routines that sport media professionals use to acquire and select news and content. These production features and practices have been explored in order to contextualize the sport media management practices examined in the following chapters. Review questions and exercises are listed below to assist with confirming your knowledge of the core concepts and principles presented in this chapter.

Review questions and exercises

1. What are the reasons that sport journalists might be considered less credible or professional than their non-sport colleagues?
2. Is it reasonable for sport journalists to accept freebies or to present a biased coverage of the home team? Why?
3. In your experience as a media consumer, is sport media generally more positive or negative? Is the deviance model of newsworthiness relevant to the production of sport media?
4. Are deviant events and happenings more or less prominent in sport news relative to political or financial and business news? Why?
5. Which of Galtung and Ruge's newsworthiness criteria are more prominent in sport media? Why is this so?
6. Choose a series of sport-related articles from the newspaper and identify which newsworthiness criterion is strongest. Is there a pattern or trend you can identify and if so, what is the explanation?
7. Choose a series of sport-related articles from the newspaper and identify the source of the article. Is there more than one source and does the article contain more opinion or fact?
8. What is a beat?
9. Why might a sport journalist be reluctant to report negative aspects about people on their beat?
10. Examine the articles in a sport section of a major daily newspaper. How many of the articles have more than one source? How many or more opinion than fact? How many are about a sport celebrity? How many are about a planned event? How many refer to a controversial issue?

PART THREE

Sport Media Strategies

8 Sport media planning and promotion: the foundations of coverage

Overview

This chapter examines the importance of media planning and the specific tools and strategies that a sport media manager can use to ensure effective and consistent media coverage for a sport organization or individual athlete over the course of a year or season. In particular, this chapter will discuss media lists, media plans and tools to plan and evaluate media coverage, such as the media grid. This chapter also provides practical information related to promotional strategies and campaigns, including the necessity to create a visual hook to obtain media coverage in a highly competitive market.

After completing this chapter the reader should be able to:

- Devise media planning goals for a sport organization event or season.
- Generalize about the differences between advertising and publicity.
- Use media planning tools and strategies to ensure that a sport media organization or individual athlete is well positioned to acquire media coverage.

■ **Evaluate the success of media planning and promotion strategies in order to implement improved practices and systems.**
■ **Structure an event or media opportunity to maximize the potential for media coverage.**

Introduction

It is often said that those who fail to plan, plan to fail. When this saying is applied to the sport media nexus, it simply means that those who fail to plan get no media coverage. As previous chapters have illustrated, the sport media nexus is highly competitive. Sport organizations compete to acquire mass audiences, increased revenue and media coverage, while media organizations compete to acquire premium sport content and access to its consumers. In this context failure to plan will have three important implications. First, the sport organization that fails to plan will surrender any promotional advantages to its competitors. Second, a failure to plan will result in an organizational mind-set in which the essential sport media relationship will be subsumed by other management functions that are perceived to be more important and pressing. Third and finally, these organizations will be reactive, rather than proactive, and therefore at the mercy of the media with respect to the amount and quality of the media coverage they receive. Media planning and strategy are essential for sport organizations, whether small or large, that want to operate effectively and competently within the sport media nexus.

Advertising and publicity

In sport media and the media generally there is a distinction between advertising and publicity. In general, advertising is media coverage that an organization pays for, either in cash or kind. Advertising is necessarily defined by the commercial relationship between the media outlet and the organization or individual purchasing space (in the case of print media and the Internet) or time (in the case of broadcast media). By contrast, publicity is free. In essence, publicity is the coverage that media outlets devote to an organization or individual in the form of news, whether positive or negative. The distinction between advertising and news-based publicity often appears superficially simple, but can be far more complex. In a newspaper or television broadcast, advertisements are generally very clearly delineated from news. On television, advertisements are generally grouped together or occur in single units during breaks in a sport broadcast, while in a newspaper the distinction between advertisement and news type is usually obvious. The confusion arises when media news is infused with advertising content, either consciously or unconsciously. For example, prominent radio broadcasters in Australia have been paid by commercial organizations to talk positively about products under the guise of news. In these cases the media consumer has no way of distinguishing between advertising and news-based publicity as the distinction between the two is unclear.

Publicity has the advantage that it is considered a credible source by consumers. In other words, consumers might ignore advertising because it has a blatantly commercial dimension, but be attracted to, or at very least influenced by publicity because it is typically viewed as news. The distinction between advertising and publicity means that competition for publicity is fierce, because of the cost benefit and because of the status and credibility conferred by the coverage. Sport is atypical in this respect, because professional high-profile sports in particular already have interest value as news. This high interest value means that sport organizations are readily able to generate regular free publicity through television broadcasts or newspaper reports on forthcoming events or past games. This publicity might in turn lead to an increase in the number of fans at the game and subsequent gate revenue, or an increase in interest from sponsors wishing to purchase naming rights, thereby increasing total revenue. A telecommunications company, by contrast, might be able to generate free publicity sporadically, from the launch of a new product for example, but the media are unlikely to report on the daily or weekly business of the company. Thus, the telecommunications company is more likely to advertise through the media and use sport as a vehicle for promotion because of the publicity it receives (Case 1).

Case 1   Tennis and Golf at Dubai's Burj Al Arab Hotel

The exclusive sail shaped Burj Al Arab hotel has become one of Dubai's most recognizable symbols, as well one of its most expensive, with guests paying from US $1,000 to US $15,000 per night. The hotel, which has been built on a man made island off the coast of the United Arab Emirates, has become prominent because of its distinctive look, as well as the creative and effective staging of two publicity stunts involving three of the highest-profile athletes in world sport. The hotel, which is in excess of 300 metres tall, includes a helicopter landing pad at the front of the hotel, 200 metres from the ground. In two separate publicity stunts, the pad has been used as a sport facility.

In March 2004, in a promotional event for the hotel and the Dubai Desert Classic golf tournament, Tiger Woods drove golf balls from a tee on the helipad into the Persian Gulf. Jumeirah International, the luxury hospital group that owns the Burj Al Arab hotel was highly commended for the publicity stunt in the public relations category of the 2005 Gulf Marketing Effectiveness Awards. The selection panel recognized the hotel group for the stunt that had created global media attention. Chief sales and marketing officer Bill Walshe noted that 'the event, staged in association with the Dubai Desert Classic, brought together two great icons, Tiger Woods and Burj Al Arab, creating an image that continues to be reproduced around the world'.

As a result of the success of the Tiger Woods publicity stunt, the Burj Al Arab became the site for a second and more adventurous event. In conjunction with Dubai Duty Free and the Association of Tennis Professionals (ATP), Jumeirah International organized in February 2005 for Andre Agassi and Roger Federer to play an exhibition match of tennis on a temporary grass court laid on the helipad. According to Jumeirah International both players were in Dubai to compete in the Dubai Duty Free Men's Open tennis tournament and 'couldn't resist the temptation to have a friendly knock about on the world's highest tennis court, the helipad of Burj Al Arab, the world's most luxurious hotel'.

The match was filmed by Sportsbrand, the TV production company responsible for the filming of the Dubai Duty Free Men's Open and tournament photographer Jorge Ferrari took still photographs. The 4 hour photo shoot resulted in still and moving images being broadcast globally. A photograph of the match was published on the front cover of newspaper *USA Today* in America, while in the United Kingdom eight national daily newspapers published photographs of the event. The response was similar throughout most European newspapers, while it proved to be an equally good television story. It was broadcast by CNN, ESPN, BBC World, CNN Asia and CCTV among others. The depth and breadth of media attention achieved by this publicity stunt makes it hard to assess its financial worth, but it is clear that for the hotel and the events it associated with, the benefits far outweighed the cost.

Sources: http://www.ameinfo.com; http://www.burj-al-arab.com; www.7days.ae; http://www.jumeirah.com/press_centre; www.sportsillustrated.cnn.com.

The value of publicity as a generator and barometer of wealth and public perception means that it is highly sought after. High-profile professional sport organizations might engage in advertising to increase public awareness, ticket sales and merchandise sales, but in the main sport organizations are desperate to acquire publicity. In even the smallest markets this is difficult because there is simply not enough media space and time to report on every event, match or achievement. As discussed in the previous chapter, the media are constantly required to make decisions about what is news. The reality is that only a minority of sport organizations and athletes achieve media coverage and in doing so they compete with a wide variety of organizations and individuals from sport and non-sport fields such as politics, the financial markets and the arts. Organizations that engage in media planning and promotion have a better chance of acquiring media publicity. Furthermore, the publicity they acquire is usually better quality and better positioned and they are able to evaluate the success of the media activities more effectively.

Setting media goals

Prior to beginning an examination of the specifics of the media planning required to achieve consistent media coverage for a sport organization, it is important to understand the distinction between strategy and planning. Strategy can be defined 'as the process of determining the direction and scope of activities of a sport organization in light of its capabilities and the environment in which it operates' (Hoye, Smith, Westerbeek, Stewart & Nicholson, 2006:70). In this context the amount and quality of media coverage is dependent on factors such as the level of the sport organization (national, state, regional or local), the team or individual's performance, as well as its location. In other words, the strategic direction of the Beijing Dolphins under 14 girls softball team to gain international media coverage for its championship season in B division is unrealistic, but regular coverage in the local newspaper, with the specific goals of one article published per month and a feature article on the best player, is achievable. By contrast, planning is the process by which the organization makes the strategy or direction happen, by documenting what has to be done, by whom, with what resources, within a specific timeframe.

Prior to media planning, a sport organization must set goals for the organization or athlete. These goals will be most useful and relevant when they are tied directly to the sport team or league's strategic plan. In other words, an organization's media goals do not exist in isolation. Rather, the media performance of the organization should be intimately connected to its overall vision and objectives. The entire media strategy a planning process is graphically represented in Figure 8.1.

The overall role of Cricket Australia's public affairs department is 'to win the support of cricket's stakeholders via planning and implementation of the organization's strategic communications programmes' (Cricket Australia,

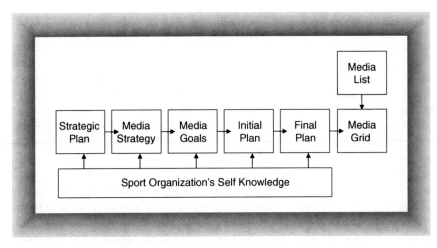

Figure 8.1 Media Planning and Strategy Flow Chart

2005), which is directly related to the overall goals of the organization. The media are one of the Cricket Australia's key stakeholders and importantly, are able to influence other stakeholders through their coverage of the game. Prior to 2000 the media relations department of the National Basketball Association (NBA) in the United States of America had two overall objectives, which were to 'make the NBA the easiest sport in the world to cover', and to 'help grow the sport of NBA basketball' (Fortunato, 2000). Each of the objectives provided direction for all the department's actions. The first objective related directly to the way in which the organization dealt with the media, while the second related to the media's influence in reaching new audiences and markets.

Media strategy and specific goals or targets for a season or event will differ from organization to organization, but whatever the size and type of sport organization, it is essential that the goals are as realistic and specific as possible. A goal for a large sport organization might be to increase the number of major daily newspaper articles published about the team by 10%. On the other hand a small sport organization might set a goal of six local newspaper articles throughout the course of the season. In both cases the goal will determine the media planning and in particular the types of media opportunities the organization attempts to create. The larger sport organization might set the goal of increasing the number of spectators through media coverage, which might mean that a major focus of media planning is to create regular media opportunities prior to games or matches. By contrast, the smaller sport organization might seek to attract participants to the organization, which means that the media planning focuses on creating stories that illustrate how much fun the sport is to play, as well as its social benefits.

Getting to know the media

One essential planning and promotion tool is getting to know the media on a personal level. Getting to know sport media producers by name and treating them as individuals rather than cogs in the media machine are ways of establishing a sound professional relationship. This relationship will strengthen the already essential connection between media and sport personnel referred to in the discussion of the beat model in the previous chapter. A strong personal connection may minimize harsh criticism at a time of crisis, or may simply enable the sport organization to have their perspective of an issue more easily heard.

The first chapter in this book highlighted that the term media can be used to describe institutions, people and the texts we interact with on a daily basis. For the purposes of media planning, it is essential to dig deeper and discover that the media is a multi-layered set of institutions and outlets (Johnston, 2004). Media planning and promotion relies on being able to target ideas, stories and events so that specific media respond by providing positive media coverage. Planning will be hindered, however, if the media is viewed as a homogenous entity, where each institution or outlet will respond in the same way. This thinking will result in wasted opportunities, time, resources and money. Rather, it is important to view local, regional and national television networks as having different needs. Similarly, television will have distinctly different needs to the Internet, radio or a magazine. For example, a television news bulletin may require a 30-second story that is highly visual, whereas a radio station may require an athlete, coach or manager to participate in a 15-minute interview.

The formal component of the process of 'getting to know the media' is the formulation of a media list (Helitzer, 1999). A media list, as the term suggests, is a list of all media organizations and contacts that are likely to cover the activities of the sport organization throughout the course of an event or season. For large events, a media accreditation process is the major mechanism by which a sport organization develops a working media list, as well as determines who is authorized to cover the event. Events such as the Olympic or Commonwealth Games have online accreditation systems, whereby journalists, editors, camera people, commentators and photographers are able to register. Once accepted, the media employee will have access to specific media facilities and resources. At the 2006 FIFA World Cup an entourage of more than 1,000 media personnel followed the Brazilian football team (see Case 2), while the summer Olympic Games accredits more than 20,000 media personnel in total. As a result of the accreditation process, a sport organization will have a comprehensive list which can be used to disseminate information.

Case 2   2006 FIFA World Cup

The 2006 FIFA World Cup was arguably the biggest sporting event ever held in the world. Staged through Germany in June and July, the FIFA World Cup created enormous media and public interest. Even a large event, such the World Cup, requires media planning and a series of events to stimulate public interest and awareness. Throughout the lead-up and during the event, media opportunities and publicity stunts were conducted. The following are some examples:

1. Giant football boot shaped dodgem (bumper) cars driven by footballers and celebrities.
2. A global tour of the World Cup trophy. The World Cup trophy tour, organized by FIFA and Coca-Cola, started on January 5 in Accra, the capital of Ghana. The tour lasted 3 months and visited 32 cities in 30 different countries before arriving in Germany. According to FIFA, the tour was viewed live by 200,000 people, but perhaps more importantly generated in excess of 1,000 newspaper articles and was featured in 45 specially broadcast television programmes.
3. Mandatory public training sessions for each of the 32 teams in their German home base city. In the case of Brazil, some training sessions prior to their first game attracted approximately 40,000 spectators and the trainings were broadcast live on Brazilian television. The

German team's public training session in Duesseldorf attracted a crowd in excess of 42,000 people.

4. Hot air balloon flights in the colours of the 32 national teams competing at the World Cup.
5. Unveiling the new Adidas ball to be used during the 2006 World Cup, named the + Teamgeist.
6. Draw of the teams in Leipzig in December, which FIFA estimates was watched by 350 million people and at which at least 2,000 journalists were present.

Similarly, large sport organizations that participate in major leagues, such as the NFL in America, the Premier League in England or the Australian Football League (AFL), also have accreditation processes to determine the eligibility of media personnel and provide access to media events, games and special media facilities. In a relatively small country like Australia, the AFL accredits in excess of 1,000 media personnel for a single season. As with a large event, the accreditation process enables the AFL to determine whether an individual is employed by a media organization in an official capacity, or whether they are attempting to gain access to the league, teams or players by deception. At the conclusion of the accreditation process, which occurs prior to the start of the season, the league has acquired a comprehensive list of media personnel, which may then be used throughout the season. This process is not limited to the major football codes, as many sport organizations provide media access to events and athlete information through their websites. For example, the World Rally Championship website has a section reserved for the media. To gain access, media personnel must register through the website and provide details of their organizational affiliation. Once again, the end product of the process is the sport organization has vetted the media and developed a useful resource for future use.

For smaller sport organizations that do not have the resources to implement an accreditation process or design and service a website that requires media registration, a media list must be developed manually. Essentially, a media list must include all media personnel and organizations that the club or league is likely to have contact with during an event or season. In practice, when the media manager wants to send out a media release about the captain of the team breaking the league's goal or point scoring record, they are able to send it to all the media on the list. Without the list, the process of communicating with the media would be slower, which would result in wasted time and resources, as well as less media coverage.

For a media list to be an effective tool for a sport organization it must exhibit two key features. First, it must be updated constantly. The media is a fluid industry, in which media personnel switch employers, so it is essential that sport organizations, through their media manager, keep track of the location of key journalists, producers, editors and commentators. New media outlets will also need to be added to the list as they are developed, launched or released. In this respect some media forms are more easily monitored than others. Major television networks and daily newspapers remain relatively stable, yet at the other end of the spectrum new Internet sites are launched on a daily basis, making it difficult to keep the list current.

Second, the media list must be segmented. In other words, a media list must be divided into the various media types, such as television, newspapers, magazines, radio and Internet, and sizes, such as local, regional, national and international. This segmentation is essential to ensure that news items or story ideas are pitched at the appropriate media. If the media list is not segmented, then news items and story ideas will go to all media outlets, regardless of whether the item or idea will be considered newsworthy. Sport organizations need to be more selective in their media communications and the media list is an important way of organizing and prioritizing information.

Constructing a media list is achieved primarily by examining the media outlets and identifying the journalists that cover a sport on a regular basis (Helitzer, 1999). For major sport organizations, this will include beat reporters and general sport reporters. For minor sport organizations, which may not have beat reporters assigned to the league or team, this will be general sport reporters only. Other personnel such as newspaper editors and sub-editors, magazine editors, television producers, radio producers and Internet site editors should also be included. Broadening the media list beyond major media organizations requires a considerable amount of research, in order to locate appropriate outlets, their employees and their contact details. Fortunately, in most major media markets, media guides and directories have been developed for commercial purposes. These guides and directories contain lists of media organizations and personnel, usually segmented by media type, size and topic (sport, business, finance, travel, politics, etc.). From these guides and directories, a sport organization should be able to construct a working media list, however, it is advisable that small sport organizations do not make their media list too large. The size of the media list should be proportional to the size of the organization and its audience. Table 8.1 is a mock media list, which illustrates how one might be formatted.

Media coverage opportunities

Once the organization's media goals have been set and a media list developed, the organization must decide which of its activities it wants the media to cover. Importantly, for most sport organizations the media will not be able to cover everything and activities must be prioritized. Helitzer (1999) suggested that the most effective way to do this is for the organization to construct an initial and final plan prior to the season or event. The initial plan is essentially a list of ideal media opportunities in an ideal world. The final plan is arrived at by sifting through the ideas contained in the initial plan and prioritizing them based on the media strategy, the size of the events required to attract media coverage, the organization's budget, availability of

Table 8.1 Mock Media List

Newspaper		
Fred Reports	Email	f.reports@mchronicle.com.ru
Journalist	Mobile	555 6666 777
Moscow Chronicle	Landline	334 556 667
	Fax	334 556 668
	Address	6 Main Street, Moscow
Television		
Julie Anchor	Email	j.anchor@S2S.com.ca
Producer	Mobile	0770 663 425
S2S Broadcasting	Landline	61 944 45676
	Fax	61 944 45678
	Address	345 Puck Drive, Calgary
Magazine		
Chuck Stevens	Email	chuck@bigwave.com
Editor	Mobile	932 008 7650
Big Wave Monthly	Landline	4378 996 553
	Fax	4378 996 550
	Address	6/88 Coral Reef Road, Hawaii

the players or athletes, likelihood of attracting media coverage, health and safety considerations and competition from other teams, leagues and sports.

For example, the initial plan might include the team conducting its annual pre-season training camp at a military base, where the players will skydive from an aeroplane and do some white water rafting. This event will probably attract significant media coverage because it contains visual elements necessary for television, newspapers and magazines. However, not all sport organizations will have the resources to fund such an activity and the safety risks might outweigh the benefits. In this case, the organization might exclude this idea from the final plan, but retain the idea of securing media coverage of pre-season training by staging a weightlifting competition that a selection of fans can participate in by entering a competition on a radio station. This event will be extremely low cost, but will still provide good media opportunities. Similarly, the initial plan might contain a family day with players dressed as clowns interacting with circus animals. Again, the media are likely to cover the event, but the cost might be exorbitant and the chance of an elephant trampling a fan too great. Thus, in the final plan the family day might be excluded but the clown theme retained in a visit to a local children's hospital by some of the players.

The final plan is not an end point. Rather, it requires execution. In evaluating the constitution of the final plan and constructing smaller action plans for each of the items on the final plan, it is advisable to consider the following:

■ Are the media opportunities well spaced throughout the course of the season or event?

- Is there a mix of stories prior to, during and after the event or season?
- If the final plan is for a season, are there regular media opportunities in the lead up to games or matches?
- Are there any competing demands at that stage of the season or event that would reduce the coverage or impact of the story?
- How will information be communicated to the media for each of the story ideas (media release, media conference, media event, etc.)?
- How much will each media opportunity cost (keeping in mind that ideas that were over budget were excluded from the final plan)?
- Which players or athletes will be required?
- What logistical planning is required for each media opportunity (location, time, props, staff, resources, etc.)?
- Are there enough human-interest stories?
- How can the visual element of the story be enhanced to generate greater television and print media coverage?

Media grids and charts

Media grids, or flow charts as they are sometimes referred to, are a media planning and evaluation tool. Helitzer (1999:234) refers to the media grid as a 'visible and ever-changing document' that allows large organizations to check their daily media progress and small organizations to check their progress throughout weeks, months or an entire season. At its core, the media grid is a way of organizing and allocating news items and story ideas to specific media outlets. Table 8.2 is an example of what a media grid might look like at the end of an event, using examples from Case 2 in this chapter. Media organizations or individuals are listed across the top and news items and story ideas are listed down the side (from the final plan). The news items or story ideas are listed as published/broadcast or rejected, but during the season or event, other terms might be included such as discussed or reworking, in order to indicate that the story is still a possibility of being published or broadcast.

The media grid can be used as a planning tool which matches stories with organizations, a cue for action or an evaluation tool. At the end of a month, event or a season, a sport organization can examine the grid to discover which types of stories where successful or unsuccessful, which media outlets published or broadcast many stories and which published or broadcast none, and which stories were suited to particular media types and sizes. For example, the grid might reveal that throughout the course of the season the organization achieved significant media coverage in newspapers and on radio, but none on television. This might indicate that the stories or events did not have a strong visual element. The grid might also reveal that one media outlet published almost all the organization's news items or stories, but another media organization of the same type and size (such as two newspapers) published very little. This might indicate that personal and institutional relationships

Table 8.2 Mock Media Grid

Story Ideal / Media Outlet	USA Today	BSkyB	Sports Illustrated	STAR	CNN
Dodgem (Bumper) Cars	Rejected	Broadcast	Rejected	Broadcast	Broadcast
Launch of Trophy Tour	Rejected	Rejected	Rejected	Broadcast	Rejected
Hot Air Balloons in Team Colours	Rejected	Broadcast	Published	Broadcast	Rejected
First Brazilian Training in Germany	Published	Broadcast	Published	Broadcast	Broadcast

need to be fostered and improved prior to the next season. Finally, a sophisticated grid might reveal that media releases were a successful communication tool for some media outlets, with others responded to more personal communication.

Knowing yourself

To undertake successful media planning and promotion a sport organization must have a well-developed knowledge of the media industry, media outlets and individual media personnel. Equally so, the organization must have an excellent knowledge of itself. On the surface this seems to be self-evident, for an organization should know itself better than anyone. However, in terms of media planning, promotion, communication and interaction, this means having detailed information about the league or the team and its players. This detailed information enables any organization to respond quickly and effectively to media questions. Many small to medium sport organizations have been caught out when one of their athletes or teams breaks a record or wins a tournament unexpectedly. A lack of detailed information can result in the organization being viewed as unprofessional, losing potential media coverage, or not capitalizing fully on the benefits of a good news story. In order to assist the media planning and communication processes, sport organizations should have:

- An up-to-date detailed history of the sport organization or event, including key milestones and achievements, such as season by season champions and major award winners.
- Current profiles of athletes, including their history and significant achievements, as well as interesting facts that could be used in a feature story.
- Current still and action photographs of athletes that can be provided to media organizations as part of a news item or story idea.

This information will be used in responding to the media, or included in media communications such as fact sheets and media releases, which will be examined in greater detail in the following chapter.

Strategies specific to small- to medium-sized sport organizations

Professional sport organizations that operate at the elite level typically have sophisticated media planning and promotion departments and strategies. The vast majority of sport organizations, however, have limited budgets, a small staff and are constantly searching for ways to increase their media management capacity. Small state or national sport organizations might only have one to three staff employed, with each staff member allocated a wide range of tasks and responsibilities across the organization, while a local or regional sport organization will likely be managed exclusively by volunteers. In these sport organizations media planning and promotion are often critical, particularly for smaller state and national sport organizations seeking greater profile and resources. Strategies must be simple, targeted and time compressed in order to be effective. If there are complex and lack strategic focus then they will be abandoned in favour of other business activities such as financial management or athlete development.

The following are a range of strategies that can be applied in small to medium sport organizations to achieve increased media management capacity (adapted from Phillips, 1996):

- Identify a hook that might create media interest in your sport, event or players. This will require the organization establishing a greater knowledge of the personalities within the sport in particular, as a human interest story is often most appealing for the media.
- Develop a one-page profile of each member on the national, state or representative team. Use these profiles at championships or events, when records are achieved or when the media enquires about an athlete.
- Make the media employee's job as easy as possible by providing timely results and information in electronic format.
- Divide your media communication into three phases (pre-event, event and post-event) and focus on one story from each that the media might be interested in.
- Select a media officer from among the best volunteers within your organization and make them responsible for communicating with the media and generating publicity. If possible, allocate funding for this person to receive basic training in media skills and management.
- Utilize students studying University level sport management, media or marketing courses in the role of media officers or as part of short-term

projects, such as events or championships. These students will be learning on the job, so there may be mistakes, but the long-term investment will be worth it.

Summary

This chapter has examined specific strategies and tools that sport organizations can use to plan for media coverage. In particular, the chapter discussed setting goals, differentiating media types and outlets, developing media lists, creating media coverage opportunities and using evaluation tools. The chapter also examined the ways in which sport organizations can promote themselves by adopting creative visual and event based strategies to attract media attention. Review questions and exercises are listed below to assist with confirming your knowledge of the core concepts and principles introduced in this chapter.

Review questions and exercises

1. What is the difference between advertising and publicity?
2. Do large sport organizations need to plan more or less than small organizations for media coverage? Why?
3. Choose a small sport organization in your local area. Identify five key media coverage goals.
4. Choose a large sport organization in your region, state or nation. Identify five key media coverage goals.
5. How do the goals of the small and large sport organization developed in the previous two exercises differ in terms of quantity, type of media and audience awareness? Do you need to alter the goals as a result of considering these factors?
6. Choose a small sport organization and develop a media list. Organize the list by media type (television, radio, newspaper or Internet) and size (local, regional, state, national).
7. Based on the five key media coverage goals, create a list of 20 media coverage opportunities throughout the course of the season that would be included in an initial plan.
8. Using the 20 items from the initial plan, choose five that would form the final plan and expand each of the ideas to make them functional.
9. Use the five media coverage opportunities identified in the previous exercise and 10 journalists or organizations from your media list to create a media grid.
10. Explain how the media grid can be used to evaluate media coverage acquired by a sport organization.

134

9

Feeding the media: communications

Overview

This chapter is the first of two chapters that examine the specific tools used by professionals who manage the media, public relations or promotional activities of a sport organization. Each of the chapters focus on sport organizations or individual athletes receiving as much media coverage as possible, with strategies and approaches tailored to their particular level and context (elite or community and profit or non-profit are two major distinctions that impact the type of media coverage being sought in a particular context). This chapter provides practical information related to media releases, fact sheets, media advisories and media guides.

After completing this chapter the reader should be able to:

■ Use a set of guidelines or rules to write a media release.
■ Use a set of guidelines or rules to write a fact sheet.
■ Use a set of guidelines or rules to write a media advisory.
■ Use a set of guidelines or rules to develop a media guide.
■ Evaluate the quality of media communications using a range of criteria, in order to improve the quality and impact of media communications.

Media communications

There are a variety of ways that sport organizations can manage their media communications. The last chapter demonstrated that an organization's media planning will determine when and how the organization communicates or interacts with the media. However simple or complex the plan, it is likely that a sport organization will need to use media releases, fact sheets, media advisories and media guides as the basis of all its communications. A large professional sport organization will use these communication strategies repeatedly throughout the course of a season or circuit, particularly media releases and fact sheets. By contrast, a small sport organization may only use these communications infrequently and might never compile a media guide. However, it should be noted that while a small sport organization may not use media guides because they are perceived to consume vital resources that could be used in the operational side of an event or competition, a media release and two or three fact sheets might form the basis of an embryonic media guide. It might be useful to release this information in a package, even to local media in a small town. It is important to be aware that these forms of communication can be hard copy or electronic. In other words, a media guide can be provided to media organizations as a printed document, or a version of the document can be sent via email or uploaded to a website in HyperText Markup Language (HTML) or portable document format (PDF). In each instance, hard copy or electronic, the same principles of communication apply, even if the end product or format differs. Furthermore, improvements in technology (from desktop publishing software to the storage capacity of hardware) have meant that the difference between hard copy and electronic versions is increasingly limited.

Releases

Media releases (sometimes referred to as news or press releases) are a direct and effective way for a sport organization to communicate with the media. They are often considered as a way of disseminating information to the media in ready-to-publish form (Wilcox, Ault, Agee & Cameron, 2000), central to media communications to the point that Bivins (1995:43) refers to them as the 'workhorse of public relations'. By following set formats and guidelines, they can be written with relative ease after some practice. Because of this ease and apparent simplicity, organizations often assume that bombarding the media with releases is a sure fire way to get media coverage and thus valuable publicity for their organization. These organizations are working on the principle that if they fire off enough shots, at least one will hit the target. Unfortunately, in hitting the target once, the organization will not only have wasted valuable time and energy, but in all likelihood will have damaged its credibility in the eyes of the media. Like the boy who cried wolf, these organizations are constantly crying 'news', when the reality is that very few people outside the organization would be interested in the story they are pitching. When they finally have a story that the public would find interesting and newsworthy, the media aren't interested because they have spent too much time wading through releases filled with tedium. A better approach is to focus on quality rather than quantity and continually ask whether the issue will interest people outside the organization and whether you would read the release if you were not employed within the organization (Denton, 2000). Although sport organizations, because of an overwhelming interest among the general public, have an advantage over generic business organizations, applying a stringent newsworthiness criteria to media communications is likely to result in better long-term coverage quality and better media relations (Case 1).

Case 1   WRC previews and reviews

The World Rally Championship (WRC) releases previews and reviews of each of its rallies through its website. These previews and reviews are in the form of media releases and in 2005 contained a range of information for use by media organizations. The rally previews featured a full listing of the driver and manufacturer championship standings, as well as a theme. For the rally of Japan, the theme was that Citroen star Christian Loeb had back-to-back world titles in sight, while for the rally of France the theme was that Citroen and Peugeot were set to 'battle for supremacy on home turf'.

The previews provided a succinct description of the location of the rally, which would be useful in print and broadcast media reports: 'The Japanese round of the WRC takes place on Hokkaido, Japan's northernmost island and is based in the relatively new city of Obihiro on the outskirts of the forested hills that host the rally's gravel stages'; and 'The Tour de Corse (Rallye de France) is considered one of the most technically challenging events in the WRC with constantly changing weather conditions and varying grades of asphalt playing havoc with tyre choices'.

The reviews provided descriptions of the event, with information on almost all the competing drivers, to suit a variety of international audiences, such as 'Marcus Gronholm drove his way to a surprise victory on Rally Japan as Subaru's Petter Solberg, who led for almost the whole rally, damaged his suspension on the penultimate stage of the event, and handed Peugeot's Finnish two-time World Champion a win'. Importantly, the reviews also contained quotes from the top three placegetters, such as the following from Loeb after his victory in France: 'I really wanted to win here, not only because this is my home rally but also because I love the Corsican stages. What makes me even happier is having been able to share my joy with that of the Citroen team during this extraordinary season'.

Source: www.wrc.com.

A media release should follow a series of rules or guidelines, in order that it conforms to media expectations and so that media releases from a single organization are consistent over time:

▓ The **headline** of the media release should summarize the most important information in the release. A good headline is often plain, precise and informative. A common mistake that media release writers make is to imagine that they are a sub-editor and provide a headline that will appear in a newspaper. The reality is that this is unlikely to happen and people involved in sport media communications should not waste their time creating catchy headlines. Sub-editors create newspaper headlines, not journalists, so if the media release is transformed into an article it will appear without a headline in the first instance (Tymson & Lazar, 2002). It is true that the headline should attempt to capture the attention of the journalist, but the journalist is likely to be struck by the newsworthiness, rather than a clever headline. Furthermore, clever headlines that appear in newspapers often obscure the content of the story that follows and the meaning of the headline only becomes apparent if the reader reads on. The media release writer cannot take the chance that the media might not read on.

- A media release must have a **date**. If the media release is clearly dated then journalists and editors know when it was sent and are able to assess its worth accordingly. Without a date a journalist or editor has no way of knowing when it was written, when the release was received by the media organization or whether another media organization might have covered the story in the intervening period. The currency of the release and its information is extremely important to the media.

- The media release must contain a summary of the most important information in the **lead** paragraph. If this information is 'buried' in the body of the media release and is not readily apparent to the reader, then the media are unlikely to search for it, particularly with tight deadlines and an abundance of competitor releases. The lead paragraph must contain who, what, when, where and why of the release and must be confirmed prior to writing the release. The following is an example of the details that should be included for the fictitious signing of Former San Francisco 49ers star quarterback Joe Montana to the Berlin Thunder, a team in the National Football League's (NFL) European league:

Who: NFL Europe
What: Ex-NFL Quarterback Joe Montana signs on as coach of Thunder
When: 3-year deal beginning next season
Where: Berlin Thunder, World Bowl Champion 2001, 2002, 2004
Why: To consolidate the Thunder's performance and increase the League's profile in Germany

- An effective media release invariably includes a high level of **statistical and factual information**. This information has the twofold benefit of improving the credibility of the release and increasing the chances of it resulting in media coverage. In the case of the above signing of Montana to the Berlin Thunder, it would be useful to include some details in the body of the release related to Montana's career in the NFL and the history and record of the Thunder. The release might be complemented by a fact sheet on each (Montana and Thunder), but the release will still need to exist as a stand-alone document.

- A media release, wherever possible, should be no more than one page in **length**. The essence of most stories should be able to be conveyed in one page. Follow up contact from either the sport or media organization should result in further information being distributed, or an interview or series of interviews being arranged. If the complexity of the story is such that it demands more than one page, the pages prior to the final page should clearly say 'continued' on the bottom of the page. The final page of the media release (whether this is the first or the third) should include the word 'END' at the bottom to denote that there is no more information to follow.

- The release should form what is known as an **inverted pyramid**, where the bulk of the information is found in the base or the foundations of the pyramid. In this way, the information in the lead is the foundation of the release. The least important information is at the point of the pyramid. If the release is structured like an inverted pyramid the media can assess the newsworthiness by looking by scanning the foundations and should they want to investigate further they can delve deeper towards the point. A good way of reviewing a media release and checking that it has the shape of an 'inverted pyramid' is to omit the last two or three paragraphs, then re-read the release. If it still has all the important details and could be sent without those paragraphs, then the chances are that your release is well structured. If, on the other hand, you discover essential information in the deleted paragraphs, then you should edit your release so that any essential information is included in the lead paragraphs, not buried in the body of the release or at the end. Another method of ensuring the release is well structured is to assume the media will not read beyond the first two or three paragraphs. This should provide a necessary focus.

- A media release should contain **quotes**, particularly if the release features the achievements, exploits or activities of an individual. An example might be 'Berlin is a city of wonderful history, architecture and culture. I look forward to living here and making the Thunder the best franchise in Europe', said Joe Montana, member of the NFL's Hall of Fame. The media will usually contact an organization for further information and in particular for quotes that can be used in a published article. For broadcast media (radio and television) the quotes will serve as a guide for an interview that will result from the release.

- It is imperative that a media release contains a complete list of **contacts**, so that the media are able to contact the sport organization for further information. Releases without current contact details are useless and a waste of the journalist's time. In fact, a release without the necessary information will lower your credibility with the journalists, thus making it harder when you next send out a release or pitch a story idea. The names of at least two people should be included with their landline phone number, mobile phone number and email address. If the media release is being distributed by a large sport organization then it is likely that there are enough people in the media, communications or marketing department to include at least two contacts on the release. For smaller organizations, who have limited paid staff or might be run entirely by volunteers, the name of the person who wrote the release should be the first contact, while the second contact can either be the most senior person in the organization, such as the president, the person most intimately connected with the issue addressed by the release or the person within the organization most comfortable being interviewed by the media.

▪ A media release should conform to a range of **formatting** conventions. The release should be printed on A4 paper with substantial margins for the media to make notes in. It should also be double spaced and the media should be able to quickly and easily distinguish between sentences and paragraphs. In this respect each sentence might equate to a paragraph, the beginning of each paragraph might be indented or a line break might be included after each paragraph. It is not necessary to be overly prescriptive here, but it is important to recognize that the approach needs to be consistent.

▪ Media releases vary in the type and quality of **header**. Some organizations prefer to use a complex header, which is similar to an organizational letterhead. The use of an organizational logo or letterhead can convey credibility and status, but the header shouldn't overwhelm the release. In this respect, organizations that include logos of major (and sometimes minor) sponsors on the release can often produce media releases that are cluttered to the point that the text and the message it is attempting to convey are lost. An organizational logo or a letterhead that incorporates the logo is sufficient. This is particularly important if the release is being distributed electronically, as too many logos or photographs embedded in the file may result in it being too large to be of practical use.

▪ **Embargos** are to be used only when they cannot be avoided. An embargo is a way of a sport organization stipulating a date and time that the media are able to use the information contained in the release. Because the media is a highly competitive industry, embargos may not be adhered to, or the media might legitimately make a mistake and use the information prior to its release date. In general, it is better if the majority of media releases are marked 'for immediate release', which is a clear and unambiguous sign that the information can be disseminated from the time the release is received. If this is not the case, then a phrase such as 'for release March 25, 10:00 a.m.' should be included.

Improving the media release

A media release should not be distributed to media personnel and outlets until it has been critically reviewed, either by the writer or a third party within the organization. The following checklist is a useful starting point for conducting the review (adapted from Tymson & Lazar, 2002):

▪ Are you certain that all of the information contained in the release is correct (in the cases where a public relations or communications firm have been subcontracted to produce media releases and other communications it is wise that the release is checked internally prior to distribution)?

▪ Is it newsworthy (try to be as objective and critical as possible)?

▪ Is it truthful (if it isn't then it shouldn't be distributed, not only because it is unethical, but it will damage the organization's credibility)?

- Do you have enough factual information to interest the media (is there enough detail to write a newspaper article)?
- What is the hook and is it strong enough to sustain media and audience interest?
- Does the first paragraph contain who, what, where, when, why and how (if it doesn't re-write the release and start the checklist again)?
- Has the release been spell checked and proofread (not just by the writer, but by a fresh set of eyes)?
- Is the media release objective or subjective in tone (keep in mind that the media will not be able to write a subjective article)?
- Can you make the language stronger, more precise or more colourful?
- Can you shorten any sentences in order to make the writing tighter?
- Can you shorten the media release (if it is more than one page and the story is relatively simple then you must shorten it)?
- Does the media release need to be checked by the legal department (this might be necessary in crisis situations, when the organization is involved in a legal dispute or might be, or when an employee is being discharged)?
- Does it contain unnecessary jargon (this is unlikely to be a positive unless the media release is pitched at a detailed trade journal, such as the description of stadium design features or amenities)?

Why didn't the release make the cut?

There are likely to be a variety of reasons why a media release was not used by the media and why no coverage in either the print or broadcast media was secured. The above checklist is a good starting point for working out where a media release might have been structurally deficient. On the other hand, the following reasons are more contextual and should be considered as part of both the planning and evaluation processes.

First, the media release was competing against other media releases for media attention. More to the point, the organization was competing against other sport organizations for media coverage. On the particular day or week when the media release was distributed, a major announcement might have been made by another club within the league, or by another league or sport within the city or nation. Or, the media release was distributed on a sport rich media day rather than a sport poor media day. Put simply, the media release might have been distributed on a Friday afternoon when journalists were busy putting the finishing touches on their previews for the weekend's games, instead of a Tuesday or Wednesday morning, when the opportunities for coverage are greater, particularly for smaller sports. In other words, the story might have been newsworthy, but was swamped by other stories that were more newsworthy. In this respect, the media manager within the organization needs to be aware not only of his or her own club, league or association, but must also be aware of other clubs, leagues and associations. For example, it makes no sense to distribute a media release on a topic that has marginal newsworthiness value the week prior to the start of the season of a major league sport. This can be moderated by good planning, but the media manager must still have a good awareness of the local sport landscape in order to pitch media releases at the right time.

Second, the media release might have been newsworthy, but didn't have a strong enough hook. The media release might not have had enough human interest or might not have had a strong visual element that would have been required to convert the story that had marginal newsworthiness into a viable media story. Although in part these are structural issues referred to in the checklist, the broader issue of newsworthiness relates to planning. In this respect, rather than pitching a story about increases in seat size and leg room at the club's renovated stadium as one of advances in plastics technology, it might have been better to illustrate how long-time supporter 'BIG Max' can now be accommodated in comfort, rather than being restricted to the 'standing room only' section at the back of the grandstand. The human-interest story, visual element and newsworthy development can be incorporated to secure valuable media coverage. The story that emphasizes technological development could probably be pitched (via a release) very quickly by the media manager, while the story that incorporates a strong human-interest angle or a visual hook will invariably require more development and more time.

Third, the media release might have been pitched at the wrong level of media. In their examination of newsworthiness, Galtung and Ruge (1988) propose that an item must be 'meaningful' in order to be newsworthy, which relates to its cultural and geographic proximity. In other words, the story must be meaningful to the audience, otherwise it is not newsworthy and the media will not be interested. At a practical level this means that the recruitment of a new player to the local handball team will be meaningful to those living in the local area and surrounding districts. Therefore, it is likely to be considered newsworthy by local print and perhaps local broadcast media. The same story is not meaningful for a regional, city, state or national audience. For these audiences the story is not newsworthy and the media release, no matter how well written, will not result in media coverage. On the other hand, a story about a junior basketball player making the national training squad might be meaningful for national audiences, or even local audiences from the area in which she grew up, but has little or no meaning outside these contexts. The challenge is for local sport organizations to pitch their media releases and stories at the appropriate media level and for large national or international sport organizations to localize their media releases and content.

Fourth, the sport organization needs to make an assessment of whether the media release is to undergo macrodistribution or microdistribution (Wilcox et al., 2000). In macrodistribution the media release is distributed as broadly as possible, to as many media outlets and sources that resources and time will allow. In microdistribution the media release is distributed to targeted media organizations. Both these methods have potential negatives and positives. In terms of assessing why a media release did not make the cut, the type of distribution might provide some answers, which in turn will improve efficiency and use of limited resources. It is likely that only the most significant stories within large organizations will require macrodistribution. In the majority of sport organization media communications, microdistribution should be the typical approach, which relies on an awareness of which media outlets are appropriate for specific issues and within particular contexts. The extreme of microdistribution is to provide a single journalist or media organization with an exclusive media release. This has the potential benefit of gaining coverage because the media organization might be attracted to the notion of gaining a competitive advantage. However, the exclusive might also create resentment among the media organizations that did not receive the exclusive, which might in turn mean that future media releases are ignored.

Fact sheets

Fact sheets are another effective, yet simple way of communicating information to the media. In general, they are used to present some of the information contained within a media release in a different format and are typically suited to sport events, rather than issues. Where a media release might announce that Coca-Cola have been signed as the naming rights sponsor for the world darts championships from 2010 to 2015 and might include some information about the event to give context to the story, the fact sheet would focus on the darts world championship and would mention that Coca-Cola is the major sponsor, but only as one of a range of facts provided.

Similar to the lead paragraph of a media release, a fact sheet should include items that address the questions of what, who, where and how. It is not necessary to answer the question why. There are no hard and fast rules that determine the content of a fact sheet, but the following headings are a useful starting point for an event, which could be a single game in a season, a single race in a sporting circuit or a major event such as world championships:

- **Event overview:** This section might include information about when the event is being held, the history of the event, previous winners and its place in the international profile of the sport.
- **Event location:** This section might include information about where the tournament is being played and how media and spectators can access the facility (such as public transport, distance from the closest airport, etc.), special features of the location and how it is being for used for any complementary activities (cultural activities or landmarks to be used for photographic opportunities with star players), as well as any specific media facilities that can be accessed.
- **Event athletes:** This section might include information on the players or teams who will be competing, such as the key players or teams and their international ranking or special characteristics. Players or teams to have won the event previously might be included, as might the star players who could attract media interest.

- **Event statistics:** This section might include a range of event and game statistics that the media might be able to use in an article or broadcast such as the number of spectators that attended last year's event, the record number of spectators at the event, the longest and shortest games played at the event, or the biggest winning margin by an individual or team.
- **Event partners:** This section might include information on major sponsors and media partners. Key details about the naming rights sponsor could be included, as might information about the broadcast partner and the way in which spectators can access a mediated version of the event.

The event's context, as well as the level of media for which the fact sheet is being written, will determine the type of information that is included in each of the sections. For example, a fact sheet released by an international sport federation hosting a world championship might highlight that the event is being broadcast in 130 countries and identify specific broadcasters in some of the key markets, whereas one distributed by a minor sport league promoting its championship game might highlight some local businesses that have donated products to be auctioned at the game as part of fundraising activities.

Like the media release, a fact sheet can be presented in hard copy or electronic form. The Melbourne 2006 Commonwealth Games provided media releases and fact sheets online (www.melbourne2006.com.au), one of which was titled '20 things about the Melbourne 2006 Commonwealth Games'. The fact sheet was presented as a series of numbered bullet points and included information such as number 6, 'Athletics, Boxing and Swimming are the only sports to have been on the program at every Games – they will continue their unbroken participation in Melbourne', or number 18, 'The Queen's Baton Relay carries the Queen's message to the athletes competing in the Games which is traditionally read at the Opening Ceremony. The Queen's Baton will travel 16,936 kilometres from Buckingham Palace through the Commonwealth, before travelling around Australia on its journey to the MCG'.

Whatever the format, the fact sheet should be presented clearly and simply. Bolded headings are an effective way to organize a fact sheet, as well as present the information. Furthermore, the nature of the information lends itself to bullet point presentation, rather than paragraph structure, which is typical of media releases, although the information need not be presented in this way. A fact sheet should not exceed two pages in length, while many of the formatting rules that apply to a media release also apply to a fact sheet. The fact sheet should include an organizational logo and contact details if it is presented in hard copy form or is designed to be printed, however, it need not be dated as the information is likely to be far less timely than that contained within a media release.

Media advisories

A media advisory is a way of alerting the media to a potential media opportunity. Like a fact sheet it outlines some basic facts, but unlike a fact sheet is not intended as a stand-alone document that is able to provide the media with sufficient background information about an event or individual. Rather, a media advisory, also called a media alert, outlines interview prospects, as well as opportunities for photographic and video coverage (Wilcox et al., 2000). Media advisories are usually much shorter than media releases and fact sheets, and are essentially a way of making contact with the media in order to make them aware of a forthcoming event, media conference or when particular athletes, coaches or administrators will be available for interviews. The what, when, where, who and why elements, which also form the basis of media releases and fact sheets, may also be included in media advisories. Furthermore, these categories can be used to provide a critical review of the media advisory prior to distribution. In other words, assess the advisory to ensure, for example, that the time of the media conference or the names of the athletes scheduled to provide interviews are not missing.

The information below was included in a media advisory sent to media organizations and personnel for the 2006 Rip Curl Pro Surf and Music Festival Media Launch, held at the Melbourne Aquarium prior to the famous Bells Beach tournament in Australia. Importantly, after a brief introduction, information in the advisory focused on four key areas: attendees, schedule, location and contacts. Email addresses and mobile telephone numbers were included for Rip Curl's media manager, team manager and public relations officer. The sections on attendees and schedule illustrate that brief information is sufficient to attract media attention. The shark dive by Fanning and Munro provided a good photo opportunity, as indicated in the advisory, which resulted in significant media coverage of the event.

The attendees

Kelly Slater – 2005 world #1, seven time world champion, 2006 Gold Coast WCT champion, 1994 Rip Curl Pro champion
Andy Irons – 2005 world #2, three time world champion, 2002 & 2003 Rip Curl Pro champion
Mick Fanning – 2005 world #3, 2001 Rip Curl Pro champion
Trent Munro – 2005 world #6, defending Rip Curl Pro champion
Nathan Hedge – 2005 world #8

The schedule

10.00 a.m. – Mick Fanning, Trent Munro and Nathan Hedge to meet with Rip Curl staff at Melbourne Aquarium
10.20 a.m. – Mick Fanning and Trent Munro to do a 20 min shark dive with the famous Rip Curl Pro Bell trophy. *GREAT PHOTO/FILM OPPORTUNITY
10.40 a.m. – Kelly Slater, Andy Irons, James Tomkins, Jimeoin and Nick Barker to meet with Rip Curl staff at Melbourne Aquarium
11.00 a.m. – Official Group Media Conference, hosted by Rip Curl Pro commentator Neil Ridgway (Rip Curl Marketing Manager) *GREAT PHOTO/FILM OPPORTUNITY

11.30 a.m. – End of Group Media Conference. Media has 30 min opportunity for 1-on-1 interview requests. *GREAT PHOTO/FILM OPPORTUNITY

Media guides

Media guides, sometimes referred to as press kits, are an ideal way to provide the media with information they need to produce content, particularly for large sport organizations. Rather than have each individual reporter or editor approach staff for facts and statistics related to the organization or the event, a media guide should be produced which contains information about the history and context of the event, team, club or league. The media guide will provide the media with essential background information they need to conduct their jobs and therefore lead to greater and better quality coverage, while it will also free up communications and publicity staff to generate targeted media coverage. The question of whether a sport organization should produce a media guide is typically answered by a simple cost–benefit analysis. For larger sports and organizations, a media guide is a useful way of gaining publicity, ensuring accuracy of information and providing the media with significant help. Thus, the benefit outweighs the cost. For smaller sports and organizations that do not attract significant media coverage the production of a media guide is a questionable enterprise. Often, the cost outweighs the benefit. In order to produce a media guide, the sport or organization must receive enough regular coverage to make it worthwhile. In other words, the time, energy and money spent on a media guide might better be directed at strategic opportunities or events, where media coverage is more likely.

The 2005 Rip Curl Pro Media Guide contained the following elements:

- A welcome from the Association of Surfing Professionals (ASP), the world governing body.
- A table of contents for the guide.
- An introduction to the Rip Curl Pro event.
- Competition format.
- Information on how the competition is judged.
- A schedule of events.
- Website and web casting information.
- Media contacts and general media information.
- The top 45 competitors and a list of previous winners.
- A history of the event's location.
- A series of 'fast facts' about the event.

Media guides are able to be provided in hard copy or electronic form, as are all the media communication tools examined in this chapter. The Professional Golfer's Association (PGA) of America's online media guide is a good example of the way in which a large professional organization responsible for a multitude of tournaments is able to compile its history, statistics and profiles into a manageable and informative resource for the media (www.pgamediaguide.com). Constructing an online media guide means that the PGA does not have to continually produce a hard copy media guide for each of the tournaments the organization is involved with, which would essentially reproduce much of the information. Case 2 in this chapter demonstrates the way in which UEFA (Union of European Football Associations) have also adopted an online media guide system, but instead of generic information provided by the PGA, UEFA provides a mix of generic and specific information tailored for each game.

Case 2   Online communications: UEFA's media information portal

UEFA is the peak governing body for football throughout Europe and second only to the Federation Internationale de Football Association (FIFA) in terms of power and influence in world football. UEFA's core mission is to promote, protect and develop European football at every level of the game. As part of its mission it organizes a series of competitions at various levels of football, including the UEFA European Championship, which is held every 4 years, and the European Champions League, an annual tournament that features the best clubs from each of the European leagues in a round robin and knockout competition to determine the premier club in Europe.

The European Champions League is a significant income stream for UEFA, with revenues generated through broadcast rights and sponsorships. The competition's format, which emphasizes a battle between the best in Europe and an exciting series of knockout games as the competition draws close to determining a winner, means that media interest is high. This media interest is not limited to Europe, as the Champions League has global appeal, with popular teams such as Real Madrid (Spain), AC Milan (Italy) and Liverpool FC (England) among the most successful clubs to have competed.

One way that UEFA manages its media communications is through its website (www.uefa.com), which provides a substantial amount of information for the media, in order to receive more, as well as better quality coverage for its competitions. This is a particularly good strategy given the global appeal of the European Champions League in particular. For each of the games in the European Champions League, UEFA provides a press kit, match preview and team lineups prior to the game, as well as a half-time report, full-time report and a summary of player statistics. All this information is able to be downloaded in PDF.

The 'match press kits' or media guides for the Champions League finals in 2006 were approximately 35 pages in length and followed a consistent format. Each included (using examples from the first leg of the Arsenal versus Juventus quarter final in parentheses):

- A summary of some interesting match facts (former Arsenal captain Patrick Vieira returned to Highbury as a player for Juventus).

- Match facts (Thierry Henry was joint third on the UEFA Champions League top scorers' list).
- Team facts (Arsenal were making their eighth successive attempt at winning the Champions League with Juventus making its sixth successive appearance at the group stage).
- Competition facts (record number of goals by one team in a match – eight – Monaco versus Deportivo in 2003, most goals in a season – twelve – by Ruud van Nistelrooij, Manchester United in 2002/2003, fastest goal in a match – 20.07 seconds – by Gilberto, Arsenal, 2002).
- Head coach profiles (Juventus coach Fabio Capello coached Milan to four Serie A titles in fives seasons between 1991 and 1996, as well as the 1994 UEFA Champions League).
- All-time statistics (Arsenal's all-time Champions League record consisted of nineteen games, eight wins, seven draws and four loses while Juventus had played thirty-two games for fourteen wins, six draws and twelve loses).
- Squad lists.
- Bookings list (Juventus player Pavel Nedved was suspended from the first leg of the quarter final after receiving two consecutive yellow cards in the first knockout round).
- Player statistics.
- Match officials.
- Referee (Swede Peter Fröjdfelt earned his FIFA international badge at the start of 2001 and was promoted to elite status in 2005).
- Domestic news (English and Arsenal defender Sol Campbell played in a reserve game victory after a 2-month layoff with an ankle injury).
- Domestic league details (Juventus was top of the Serie A table with 78 points, with 61 goals for and 20 goals against).
- General competition information (UEFA estimated that the 2005/2006 Champions League income would be €598 million, which would result in €453 million being distributed to the 32 participating clubs).
- UEFA information (UEFA agreed to a distribution scheme of 75% for the competing clubs and 25% for European football up to €530 million and an 82:18 ratio thereafter).
- Legend.

The UEFA 'match press kits' in particular are examples of the ways in which a sport organization can provide the media with enough information to assist them in providing comprehensive coverage of an organization, competition, match, club, player or coach. Using the information provided by UEFA in an accessible format, the media might reasonably broadcast a brief segment on a radio news programme that announces a forthcoming game at one end of the spectrum, or engage in a lengthy game preview and discussion as part of a speciality sport programme on pay or free-to-air television at the other.

Source: www.uefa.com

Video releases

A video release is essentially a media release in video format. A sport organization will produce a video, or in some cases an audio file, in which one of the employees of the organization will be recorded, then supply the video to television stations for broadcast (Fortunato, 2000). A video release will provide the media with broadcast quality content at no expense, however, the video release is usually used to communicate a particular point of view on an issue of sensitivity, rather than act as an advertisement. A video release is an expensive communication strategy, but does have the advantage of ensuring the sport organization's point of view is broadcast faithfully, in contrast to an interview or media conference statement that may be edited. Video releases should be used sparingly, however, because their credibility can be questionable among media professionals, as they are typically regarded as public relations spin rather than news (Stephens, 2005; White, 2005).

Follow-up

Each of the media communications introduced above can be improved by a simple action called the 'follow-up'. The next chapter deals in greater detail with media interactions, but it worth noting within the context of media communications that tools such as media releases, in particular, are more effective when they are supplemented by personal communication, which usually takes place via the telephone, and in some cases in-person. The 'follow-up' will typically establish whether the journalist or producer requires more information or requires interviews with key personnel to complete the article or broadcast segment.

Summary

This chapter has examined a variety of media communication tools. When used well, each of these communication tools has the ability to not only capture media attention, but to acquire media coverage for a sport club, league or association. The media release, media advisory and media guide are the key tools used by sport organizations in the daily media communications. The chapter also provided criteria and checklists to both assess and improve the quality of media communications produced by sport organizations. Review questions and exercises are listed below to assist with confirming your knowledge of the core concepts and principles introduced in this chapter.

Review questions and exercises

1. What is the purpose of media communications?
2. What are the key rules for writing a media release?
3. Acquire a media release from a semi-professional or professional sport organization. Evaluate the release using the rules outlined in this chapter. Can the release be improved? How?
4. Use the media release writing rules and guidelines to write a release on one of the following topics: the team has just signed a new major sponsor; the team has just signed a new star player; a celebrity will be opening the cultural festival which complements a major sport event; the team captain will be celebrating a milestone in the forthcoming game; a legend of the sport will be making a comeback at a forthcoming event after being in retirement for a year; or the forthcoming game, match or event has a special feature to attract more spectators.
5. After writing the media release, critically evaluate the chances of it resulting in media coverage, considering both structural and contextual issues.
6. Produce a fact sheet for a local sport event you are involved with or have attended.
7. Write a media advisory for a forthcoming sport event (such as a conference or season launch) and outline which athletes will be available for interviews (as well as when, where and for how long).
8. Identify the elements you would include in a media guide for a sport organization or sport event in your local area.
9. Identify the elements you would include in a media guide for a sport organization or sport event in a major city.
10. Identify the elements you would include in a media guide for a national sport organization or sport event.

10 Feeding the media: interactions

Overview

This chapter is the second of two chapters that examine the tools of the trade for professionals who manage the media, public relations or promotional activities of a sport organization. It builds on the previous chapter that examined written media communications by examining face-to-face media interactions. In particular, the chapter provides practical information on conducting interviews, media conferences and media events.

After completing this chapter the reader should be able to:

■ Apply a set of guidelines to prepare for and structure an interview for an employee of a sport organization.
■ Apply a set of guidelines to prepare for and conduct a media conference.
■ Apply a set of guidelines to prepare for and conduct a media event for a sport organization.

Introduction

The previous chapter examined a range of communication tools available to sport organizations. These communications, both in hard copy or electronic form, are designed to generate media coverage and in some cases are also intended to generate media interactions, which in turn lead to greater and better quality coverage for the organization. These media interactions might be as simple as a journalist contacting the media manager of a sport organization for more information, in response to a media release. Or, they might be as complex as a media conference or event to launch a new product or competition. This chapter examines the major types of media interactions that are likely to occur between sport and media organizations at a formal level, such as interviews, media conferences and media events. This chapter is not intended to specify how sport organization personnel should conduct informal interactions with journalists, editors and producers. These are often the result of a relationship built over time and also directly related to the personal qualities and preferences of the individual.

Coverage on network television stations is the most competitive of all the media environments. Newspapers, radio, magazines and the Internet all have more time and space to devote to news. This has three important implications. First, non-television media forms are able to provide more coverage to a single story, leading to potentially more in-depth features, which means that sport organization employees must be able to participate in lengthy interviews if required. Second, the time and space available to non-television media forms results in greater opportunities for smaller sports to gain media coverage. This means that even in smaller sports the members of a sport organization must be competent in the field of media interactions. Finally and most importantly, because television is also the most visual of the media forms, sport media management must ensure it delivers content that has visual appeal. For the purpose of managing media interactions, in practice this means sport organization employees appear competent in front of a camera and behind a microphone and media interactions are conducted in a professional environment.

Media conferences

Planned events are a way of attracting media coverage for a newsworthy story or event and the most common is the media conference (also referred to as a press or news conference). Media conferences are an effective way of disseminating essential information to a wide variety of media. Rather than distribute a media release and then field questions from a range of media organizations, it is often more effective to gather the media organizations at a single venue for a media conference. Journalists will also have access to a range of sport organization employees, which will in turn facilitate the media coverage of the event or issue.

As indicated in the previous chapter, media are typically alerted to the staging of a media conference via a media release or media advisory. This communication will notify the media of the following:

- Issue or event for which the media conference is being staged.
- Venue.
- Date and time.
- Sport organization personnel who will be present.
- Opportunities for interviews, questions, photographs, etc.

Prior to sending out a media advisory or release it is essential to consider three key elements: value, timing and site. A media manager needs to assess whether the issue or event has enough value to warrant a media conference. In this respect, the newsworthiness criteria discussed in Chapter 7 is a good starting point. For larger professional sport organizations, the amount of media interest is likely to be significant enough to regularly hold media conferences. Media conferences are a rarity for small sport organizations, as they are unlikely to attract enough media attention to warrant the time and resources that will be expended. A targeted media release and follow up contact is likely to be a more effective strategy. In this respect the same cost-benefit analysis that was referred to in the previous chapter regarding media guides should be applied.

Whatever the size of the organization, the media conference must be valuable to the media. As such, the sport organization must critically assess whether calling a media conference will be an effective use of the media's time and resources. Inviting the media to conferences in which the information is either trivial or could have been disseminated through a media release is a bad strategy. In the worst case, the resentment at being called to a media conference in which there is little or no valuable information might adversely affect their willingness to provide media coverage of future events. Thus, the question 'should a media conference be held' must be the first question any sport organization asks (Wilcox, Ault, Agee & Cameron, 2000).

Wilcox and Nolte (1997) have identified six scenarios where is it appropriate for an organization to call a media conference. First, an announcement of significant public interest warrants holding a media conference, such as the appointment of a new national team captain in a high-profile sport or the addition of a new team or franchise to a league. Second, when an issue arises of significant public concern, such as a new stadium having problems with spectators getting access to the ground in time for the start of popular games. Third, where there have been a significant number of media requests and it is important to provide access equity. For example, there might be speculation about the retirement of a key player, which is leading to media requests for interviews. In this case it might be easier and more time effective for all concerned to hold a media conference. Fourth, a new product, facility or service is being announced, such as the construction or upgrade of a sporting facility or the installation of new technology to assist referees and umpires. Fifth, when a person of importance visits, such as the head of the International Olympic Commission conducting a site visit, or a high-profile athlete participating in an international event. Sixth and finally, a complex issue where the

153

BISHOP BURTON COLLEGE

media are likely to need further information may require a media conference, such as the announcement of new anti-doping regulations.

A media manager must also consider the timing of the media conference. Similar to the evaluation criteria applied to media releases in the previous chapter, staging the media conference at the right time is an essential element of its success. In this respect success is measured by the amount of media coverage that results from the conference, which in turn is directly proportional to the number of media personnel who attend. A media conference may fail because the value or newsworthiness of the conference is considered low relative to other conferences, events or incidents that take place at the same time. No matter how well planned the conference is in terms of timing and positioning relative to the work demands of journalists and competing events and sports, a story may break that will result in the media conference being abandoned for a news item with greater immediacy, interest or impact. Wilcox et al. (2000) suggest that a media conference be scheduled at a time that accounts for the deadlines of various media outlets. If the media conference is scheduled at a time that allows print media, but not television to cover the story then the sport organization risks offending television journalists. Importantly, a media manager within a sport organization must have a good working knowledge of local media deadlines (Johnston, 2004).

Finally, the media manager must ensure that the venue or site is appropriate for the size of the conference and the expected number of media personnel attending. A standard media conference may be held at the club, team or league head office if there is a space big enough, or at an indoor venue that has the necessary facilities. For a non-standard media event the venue could be staged anywhere, although consideration will need to be given to the facilities required by the organization and the media, as well as contingencies (such as weather if the event is being staged outdoors). Consideration should also be given to the amount of time it will take for media to travel to and from the venue. A venue that is central and accessible to most media outlets is preferable (Wilcox et al., 2000).

If the conference value, timing and site have been arranged and media advisories or invitations distributed, the conference set-up must be attended to. The following is a guide to the key elements of media conference delivery:

- *Team or league logo*: It is important that the logo and name of the organization (team or league) is visible in any media coverage that results from the conference. For major professional sports it is often necessary that a sponsor's logo is also visible. Set or background dressings, such as banners or posters, should be designed so that logos, names and website addresses are visible in newspaper photographs and television broadcasts. A background banner should have many small logos, so that the entire logo or logos are visible when one or more people are sitting or standing in front of the banner. A large logo, which may look impressive to those attending the conference, will in all likelihood be partly obscured when the interviewee is filmed or photographed. It is important to remember that the conference backdrop is for media coverage, rather than the aesthetic pleasure of those attending the event.

■ *Models and props*: If the media conference is announcing a new facility, product or uniform then models and props may be a useful visual addition (Helitzer, 1999). Hence, if the media conference is announcing the development of a new stadium then a giant scale model of the facility is appropriate, whereas if the media conference is designed to launch the season and unveil a new uniform, then a fashion parade of the new uniforms may be a way of acquiring television coverage.

■ *The room*: In order to maximize media coverage, all media must have an unimpeded view of the media conference and its participants. Television cameras should be allocated space at the rear of the venue, on the sides of the room or on a specifically placed platform that gives them a clear shot of the stage and the speaker. Journalists will usually be seated in front of a panel table or podium, which means that television cameras can be located behind the journalists, assuming that the venue does not have tiered seating and the view of the speakers is not impeded. Whatever the size of the room and the audience, it is likely that the media will need to set up microphones in front of the speaker to ensure high audio quality. The time and space required for this should be allowed for in the overall conference plan.

■ *Panel table or podium*: A table for the spokesperson or panel should sit on a slightly raised platform to ensure a clear view for photographers and camera people. The speakers should not be sitting at the same level as the reporters, as they will need to be able to see the journalists three or four rows deep. Alternatively, a single podium may be appropriate if there are only two or three speakers who are able to approach the podium one after the other. A panel table is usually preferred as it enables the speakers to deliver prepared statements and the entire panel to field questions that follow. The table must also be covered to ensure that the legs of the panelists are not visible to the media.

■ *Identify the speakers*: If there is only one speaker who is well known to the journalists then a nameplate is not necessary. However, if the media conference is conducted by two or more people then it is useful to have nameplates in front of media conference speakers, and for the media manager to introduce the speakers to the media prior to the commencement of the conference.

It is usual that the media conference will begin with a welcome to the media and an outline of the conference format, which will be followed by one or more of the speakers reading a prepared statement. In media conferences that deal with a sensitive issue, which is either part of or likely to cause a crisis or scandal, the end of the prepared statement may be the end of the conference. In this case, the prepared statement will be used to clarify the issue, present factual information or to dispel rumours. In this case the media conference's purpose is to provide footage for television networks in particular. Most media conferences, however, will also include a question and answer period. In these instances it is typical that little or none of the prepared statement will be aired, as the question and answer period with journalists usually provides the best sound bites (White, 2005). However, it is usual that the media are provided a copy of the statement, in order to ensure accuracy. It may also be useful to provide the media with a fact sheet that includes names, titles and brief biographies of the speakers. If the statement has been prepared well in advance then it is useful to conduct a conference rehearsal, which will give the speakers an opportunity to familiarize themselves with the text of the statement and acclimatize to the venue.

As noted previously, the question and answer period is an important component of most media conferences. Although the question and answer period cannot be rehearsed as effectively as the reading of a prepared statement, it is useful for the media manager and speakers to anticipate difficult questions and prepare answers. At worst, a mock question and answer period may eliminate any awkward pauses by the speaker and make them appear more fluid. At best, it may prevent the speaker from revealing confidential information, becoming angry in response to a particular line of questioning or becoming flustered as a result of being taken by surprise. For more experienced media performers a written or verbal briefing that includes potential difficult questions may suffice.

In many professional sport leagues it is a requirement for coaches, managers or players to participate in a media conference soon after the conclusion of a match. These conferences are typically question and answer sessions that allow journalists to elicit quotes for publication in newspaper articles or to provide television footage with sound bites to accompany highlight packages. Often these conferences are available on club or league websites. These conferences are potentially positive and negative. A winning coach or manager is more willing to answer questions from journalists, while their losing counterpart is more likely to make disparaging remarks about the standard of officiating and be unwilling to engage in meaningful conversation with journalists. It is essential that these conferences are also rehearsed, in order that the performance of coaches and managers is maximized.

The media manager or conference moderator must make a decision to draw a media conference to a close. The conference may reach its natural conclusion when there are no more fresh questions, when the time limit has expired or when the speaker or speakers requires a break from media questioning. Importantly, a speaker should never walk out of a media conference in anger or as a way of demonstrating power. This is only likely to exacerbate the issue and provide the media with sensational footage for the evening news. In order to draw the media conference to a close the media manager can announce that there is time for one last question. At the conclusion of the answer to this question the media manager can thank the media for attending and providing details of whether individual interviews are able to be conducted and if so, where they will be located and how much time is available. If there are no interviews to be conducted then the media manager can make themselves available for further questions or requests.

Some reporters will call prior to the conference to arrange an interview with one of the people involved in the media conference prior to it commencing, in order to save time and get ahead of other broadcast and print competitors. Agreeing to the interview can ensure media coverage, particularly if there is a concern that the issue might not attract a large crowd. In this case agreeing to the interview is insurance against other media outlets not participating in the conference. The downside to this strategy is that a degree of control will be surrendered to the media, as the conference format, with a prepared statement followed by questions and answers, is controlled by the sport organization. In the interview situation the media will have more control, with the question and answer component likely to be favoured in place of a prepared statement. For an issue that is likely to attract significant media interest, agreeing to an interview prior to the conference is a risky strategy. First, other media outlets might perceive that there is a degree of bias or favouritism towards one media outlet. Second, if the interview is held prior to the conference and runs overtime, the interview could turn into a mini conference as other broadcast journalists and their camera people arrive and start filming (White, 2005). Finally, if the broadcast media get what they need in terms of sound bites prior to the conference, the conference may be delivered to the print media alone, for the broadcast media are unlikely to stay if the chance of capturing more valuable footage is minimal.

Media events

Media events are another way of generating coverage through media interactions. They may include a media conference, will often provide opportunities for interviews and typically have an unusual theme or visual element that will ensure additional media coverage. The theme or visual element might be as simple as two surfers swimming in a shark tank, as illustrated in the previous chapter, or a day of golf at a luxury course to promote a forthcoming competition. In 2005, almost exactly a year prior to the 2006 PGA championship, the Medinah Country Club (Illinois, USA) held a media day to introduce the media to its new course layout and discuss the championship. Although one year is a significant lead in, the PGA and the golf club realized they could gain some valuable advance publicity. The media event consisted of a media conference, one-on-one interviews, lunch and a round of golf on the new course. The organizers were clever enough to realize that a media conference in itself was unlikely to secure all available media. But, a round of golf for sport and golf journalists, reporters and editors at the club that hosted the 1999 PGA championship was likely to be a major drawcard. In his introductions, moderator Barry Cronin noted 'we're very pleased and honoured to have you here today for what we're calling our one-year-out media day. Media obviously play a very important role when it comes to getting the word out about a major championship' (PGA, 2006).

Media events differ in size and scope. As noted in the previous chapter, in the lead up to the 2006 FIFA World Cup, one of the media events involved key personalities and footballers driving football boot shaped dodgem (bumper) cars as part of a larger launch. Not all organizations have the resources or the intense media interest to ensure these events are successful. However, not all media events need to be large and complex. A successful event might simply consist of a state, regional or national team being presented with their uniforms in a public place, such as shopping mall. At the other end of the scale, the announcement of the host city for the Olympic Games has become such an important public media event that it is broadcast live and watched by millions of people. This is unlikely to be achieved by all but the largest international sport organizations. Whatever the event, it is important that it contains a visual element or a special feature to attract the media.

Another form of event is often referred to as a media party (Wilcox et al., 2000). This function or reception usually consists of breakfast, lunch or dinner and may also include the media being presented with gifts, although this practice is ethically and strategically dubious. For instance, if the media party is to announce the signing of a major electronic goods manufacturer as the major sponsor of a league, the media might be presented with MP3 players at the end of the night, but the sport organization should be aware that this will not ensure positive media coverage. The primary purpose of a media party is to allow representatives from the media to socialize with employees from the sport organization, although the explicit reason for the party might be to introduce the media to a development or issue of importance to the team, club or league. In the Australian Football League teams have organized media parties to discuss negative media coverage of a team or particular issue, or to discuss the strategic development of the league. Thus, a media party might be used as a promotional strategy, or as defensive strategy in which the media is gathered so that the organization can clarify their position on a contentious issue. At a base level the media may be prepared to attend a party in order to establish or develop contacts, which are essential to conducting their work, as demonstrated previously in Chapter 7.

Interviews

The interview is a key point of interaction between sport and the media and one of the key forms of communication between individuals within sport organizations and the general public. In radio and television broadcasts in particular, the public get to hear information direct from the sport organization, rather than moderated through a secondary source. Thus, the interview can be a powerful tool for sport organizations, but just as easily it can prove dangerous. The athlete skilled in media relations might be able to charm the media and the public in equal measures, but the athlete, coach, manager or administrator who is uncomfortable in the media spotlight has the potential to look aloof, stupid, clumsy, incoherent and bumbling.

Some interviews are spontaneous, while others are planned. In general, it is best if interviews with athletes, coaches and administrators are planned, in order to give the subject time to prepare. There will be some occasions where spontaneous interviews are conducted, such as on the field after a game, but even these interviews will have been arranged in advance by the broadcaster as part of an agreement with the league or team. Thus, it is very rare for a situation to arise where a representative from the sport organization is unprepared. If they are it is the fault of the media manager or the over zealousness of the media organization.

Not all interviews will produce the same outcome and not all interviews will produce news (White, 2005). Different interview styles will result in different outcomes. The types of questions a journalist will ask the chief executive officer or general manager of a club or team after the sacking of the head coach because of poor on-field performance will be very different to those asked of a 16-year-old star who has just won her first professional tennis tournament. Similarly, an interview with a magazine or newspaper reporter is likely to be longer and more in depth than a television or radio interview in which the questions are straightforward and designed to elicit a specific response. The implication of the variety of outlets, styles and possible outcomes is that a media manager must be able to prepare interviewees for a range of possible media interactions. The media manager should:

- If possible, select the type of media that is appropriate to conveying the message or executing the media plan.
- Be aware of the style of most media outlets and prominent journalists and educate interviewees accordingly.
- Rehearse interviewees with mock questions and answers for both routine and extraordinary situations.
- Encourage interviewees to avoid sport specific jargon or insider language in order to appeal to a broad spectrum of the public.
- Encourage interviewees to be enthusiastic as there is nothing worse than watching an athlete or coach who does not want to be interviewed and appears bored and/or tired.
- Instil an organizational culture in which media training (interview skills) is an accepted part of professional development.
- Review the interviews of athletes, coaches and administrators as a way of improving performance.
- Exploit those athletes that have natural media skills.
- Establish a set of general media interview guidelines.

Interview set-up is important for creating an environment in which the subject feels comfortable and the organization is able to represent itself in the best possible manner. In short, the media manager needs to consider the site, date, subject matter, amount of time required/available, props or visual aids required and uniform/dress for the interviewee. The date and the amount of time available are simple logistical issues to be dealt with, while the subject matter will determine what and how much preparation the interviewee should complete. The site, props, visual aids and uniform or dress code are all essential if the interview is being conducted for television broadcast, or if the interview is part of a newspaper or magazine article that will include photographs. The site and any props required can be handled by the media manager, while the image of the athlete or coach is a little more problematic. It is particularly important to have policies and procedures within the league or team that govern player dress codes. In many instances this will be covered as part of a collective

159

bargaining agreement. For example, in the National Basketball Association in the United States of America, 'players are required to wear business casual attire whenever they are engaged in team or league business', which means 'a long- or short-sleeved dress shirt (collared or turtleneck), and/or a sweater, dress slacks, khaki pants, or dress jeans and appropriate shoes and socks, including dress shoes, dress boots, or other presentable shoes, but not including sneakers, sandals, flip-flops, or work boots' (NBA, 2006).

Because of the amount of space available to them, newspaper and magazine journalists are likely to conduct more in-depth interviews, while radio and television journalists will necessarily make their interviews more targeted, specific and compressed because they have limited airtime. This difference will alter the way journalists approach their interviews and the types of questions they ask. Similarly, the type of answers and approach of the subject will need to be altered if the media coverage received is to be of good quality. If the athlete, coach or administrator being interviewed wants to get their message across, then the answers they give will need to be appropriate to the media outlet that will be printing or broadcasting the results of the interview. Short concise answers that will make good sound bites will be appropriate for television and radio, while longer more considered answers will be appropriate for newspaper and magazines, particularly if the latter are publishing a profile or feature article on a player or coach.

Prior to an interview, journalists will have researched the subject, in order to find out as much information about it or them as possible. In order to make the interviewer's job as easy as possible, the sport organization should provide a detailed fact sheet on the subject to be interviewed. It should not be assumed that this will be the only information that the media will consider. In fact, ease of access to the Internet and the amount of information available means that the media will be able to gather far more information than you are able to give them in one fact sheet, however detailed. Thus, the fact sheet in this instance is a way of providing a range of standard information about the subject, so that the journalist will be able to crosscheck their information and sources if necessary. As an example, it makes sense to list in the fact sheet provided prior to an interview with Barcelona's Ronaldinho that he was named the Spanish Liga Primera Player of the Season in 2004, FIFA World Player of the Year in 2004 and 2005, the inaugural FIFPro World Player of the Year in 2005, and in 2005 also won the Ballon d'Or (European Footballer of the Year). This type of information is freely available, lacks controversy, but is likely to be mentioned in any media coverage, particularly print media.

Interviewee checklist

The following checklist is a good starting point for providing interviewees with practical skills to negotiate their media interactions. It applies specifically to interviews, but could be broadened to provide athletes, coaches, managers and administrators with more general media skills training.

Interview context

- What is the topic of the interview? This might seem obvious, but being prepared is a key to producing a good media image in interview situations. Athletes, coaches, managers and administrators will perform best when they are most comfortable, which includes being briefed on the topic or subject.
- Is there an angle or perspective to the interview? The interviewee may be aware of the topic or subject matter, but it is essential that they also consider what angle the reporter might be taking, and what role they might be asked to play in constructing the story.

Interviewer

- Who is the interviewer/what is the media outlet? It is essential that interviewees are aware of who will be interviewing them, and what media outlet they work for. Both of these points will have a bearing on how the interviewee might prepare, and what they can expect. Furthermore, the interviewer might be familiar to the interviewee, which might relax them, or alternatively lead to them saying things they would not normally divulge.
- Does the interviewer have an established position on the discussion topic? This is an important question to consider if the topic or subject matter is sensitive, or the interview forms part of a broader debate that the reporter has been a part of, or was an instigator of.
- What is the interview style of the reporter or media personality? Being prepared for a particular style might often be just as important as the subject matter itself. In this respect the interviewee's image might be determined by how they are perceived to have handled the interviewer.

Purpose

- Who is the audience I want to reach by giving this interview? All interviewees must have an audience in mind. Identifying the audience will help to focus the interviewee's answers.
- Where do I fit in the overall story? This is important if the issue is sensitive and others are likely to be interviewed on the same topic. For example, a range of athletes might be interviewed on their response to new anti-doping regulations. In this case it is essential to consider what the views of others might be and how the interviewee's opinion might be presented.
- What is my primary theme for the interview? It is useful if each interview has a central theme running through it. Identifying this theme can help an interviewee answer difficult questions or continue to answer if they lose their train of thought or become flustered.
- Can I develop one concise sentence that captures the reason for doing the interview and the message I wish to convey? Clearly identifying a concise reason for conducting the interview will give the interviewee purpose. This

will help to focus responses to questions responses and influence the overall tone of the interview by allowing the interviewee to be more proactive.

■ What are the three major points that I wish to make? If the interviewee is able to convey three major points to the audience in a coherent manner then it is likely the interview will be successful. Identifying these points prior to the interview will improve the interviewee's responses and overall performance.

Maximizing performance

■ Have I said too much? It is important to remember that the average attention span of people listening to interviews is about 15–30 seconds. Therefore, simple, short and straightforward answers will avoid diluting the message. Identifying an audience, interview focus and key points will facilitate more concise and direct answers.

■ What are the three most obvious or difficult questions I might be asked? While obvious questions might be easy to identify, as well as answer, it is useful to rehearse a response, while more difficult questions are both harder to identify and answer. Anticipating these difficult questions will improve an interviewee's preparation and in doing so they are less likely to be surprised or caught off guard in an interview.

■ Do I have any appropriate anecdotes, analogies or examples to help reinforce my position or provide an interesting angle to the interview?

Off the record?

Media communications, by their very nature, are on the record. Media communications, through a media release for example, represent the official views of individuals and organizations, whereas media interactions are less clear. Because media interactions involve personal verbal communication, the potential for an individual to express views that are not representative of the organization is far greater. It is generally accepted that employees at all levels of a sport organization should restrict themselves to on the record media interactions. In other words, they should assume that anything they say could be reported by the media and modify their comments accordingly. Off the record communications and interactions, in which the employee divulges information that she or he would prefer not to see in print, should be avoided.

Summary

This chapter has examined three major forms of formal media interaction – the media conference, interview and media event. The chapter has provided guidelines to prepare for and conduct each of these three interactions. With practice, a media manager should be able to use these guidelines to conduct successful media interactions and provide basic training for employees within the organization in interview skills in particular. Review questions and exercises are listed below to assist with confirming your knowledge of the core concepts and principles introduced in this chapter.

Review questions and exercises

1. When should a major professional sport organization stage a media conference?
2. When should a minor sport organization stage a media conference?
3. What are the three key factors to consider prior to announcing a media conference?
4. Why is it important that the media conference background incorporate small logos?
5. When will a prepared statement be broadcast by media organizations?
6. Should a sport organization agree to media interviews prior to a media conference?
7. Should interviewees be rehearsed or is better to have them give 'natural' answers? Why?
8. What are the three most important items of the interviewee checklist? Why?
9. Stage a mock media conference, either live or recorded. Make sure that both the speakers and media are briefed on the issues in order to make the conference as realistic as possible.
10. Stage a mock interview (either a conversational interview, or a direct to camera interview). Make sure that both the interviewer and interviewee are briefed on the issues in order to make the interview as realistic as possible.

Case 1   Ryder Cup captaincy conference

The following transcript is from a media conference held at the 2005 Dubai Desert Classic at the Emirates Golf Course in Dubai to announce the appointment of Ian Woosnam as the 2006 captain of the European Ryder Cup team. Importantly, the transcript illustrates several features of media conference conduct, including an introduction and welcome by a moderator, an introduction of the panellists, introductory remarks by a senior member of the organization to put the issue in context and a statement by the athlete involved in the announcement. The first statement below is from the Moderator, Gordon Simpson.

Gordon Simpson: Welcome, ladies and gentlemen and good morning to the Emirates Golf Club and for a very special Ryder Cup press conference. Without any further ado, I will introduce the top table to you. On the far left we have Jamie Spence, who is the Chairman of The European Tour's Tournament Committee; on Jamie's right is Richard Hills, The Ryder Cup Director; in the middle there is a man who needs no introduction, but he will get one anyway on his 47th birthday a very happy one Ian, Ian Woosnam; George O'Grady next to Ian, the Executive Director of The European Tour; and on my immediate left we have Mohamed Buamim, who is the vice chairman of the Emirates Golf Club and the Dubai Desert Classic. And we would all like to say thank you to the Emirates Golf Club and to the Dubai Desert Classic for helping host this conference today.

I will now pass on to George who will make the introductory remarks.

George O'Grady: Ladies and gentlemen, welcome to the Dubai Desert Classic. I thank Mohamed, as Gordon has said, for allowing us to use the media centre today, for what is a very important, and, in fact, an unprecedented announcement, is the Ryder Cup Captaincy.

Ian Woosnam will be the captain and has accepted the committee's invitation to captain on the side on 2006, as has Nick Faldo for 2008. This is the first time the committee and this decision has been ratified by our Ryder Cup board, having asked two captains at this stage. I think when you have captains of the calibre of Ian Woosnam and Nick Faldo, it's quite easy to understand why. It was the unanimous vote of the committee last night, and those members of committee who are not here have given their view by telephone. Although they were not voting, they all voted the same way; they are all together in having two captains announced together.

Ian Woosnam: Thank you, George.

Gordon Simpson: Ian, you might just want to say a few words on what this means to you.

Ian Woosnam: Well, absolutely delighted on my 47th birthday to have a present like this is something I'll cherish for the rest of my life because I've been involved in many, many Ryder Cups, also as a vice captain. And to have the chance to captain your side, the European side, it's something that I'll cherish for the rest of my life.

And so I'd like to thank Jamie and the committee for voting for me and George and everybody who has been involved. I'm looking forward to the matches in 2006. I'll be doing my utmost to make sure I win The Ryder Cup for the third consecutive time and try and make history.

And also I would like to congratulate the committee on deciding to give Nick Faldo the captaincy in 2008. I know it was a difficult decision, but I think it's the right decision and I'm sure we've got Britain's best ever golfer being the captain in 2008, I'm sure he's going to do a fantastic job, as well. Thank you.

Case 2   Round one question and answer – Williams and Henman

The following are excerpts from a transcript of a question and answer session as part of a compulsory post-match media conference with former world number one Serena Williams after her first round victory in the 2006 Australian Open Tennis Tournament. The four questions resulted in different types of responses, with questions 2 and 4 receiving media coverage as part of television highlight packages. The answers to questions 1 and 3 were indecisive and did not provide sound bites that could be used. Answers to questions about starting a tournament or the next opponent could be rehearsed as questions that are likely to be asked at any tournament.

Question 1: Is that a good way to start the tournament?
Serena Williams: Uhm, yeah, I guess. I think so because I haven't played in a while. It was nice – it wasn't nice, but at least I know what – yeah, I lost my thought train.

Question 2: How do you go from playing as poorly as you were at the end of the second, beginning of the third, to playing just so well in the last few games, like you were totally in control?
Serena Williams: Well, I play better the longer the match goes on. I just was able to – you know, I wasn't hitting out. At one point I started blocking too many balls. I just decided that I needed to hit out.

Question 3: Do you know your next opponent, Camille Pin?
Serena Williams: Yes, I know her. I think I played her last year. Yeah, I think I played her last year in the first round – I think.

Question 4: After you won the first round at Wimbledon last year, after you won the first round at the US Open, after winning the first round here, how much better do you feel physically and mentally about your game?
Serena Williams: I feel amazing right now. I just feel like dancing. I can just hear this song, this Beyonce song 'Check on It.' I just feel like getting down, doing the eagle. I have a lot of energy right now, it's really hot. I'm feeling much better than I have at The Open – Wimbledon, too.

The following are excerpts from a transcript of a question and answer session as part of a compulsory post-match media conference with Great Britain's Tim Henman after a first round loss at the 2006 Australian Open Tennis Tournament. Henman's answers to the questions were indecisive, but his use of the phrase 'you know' was even more problematic. It punctuated his answers to the point that he was criticized for it in subsequent media coverage. This type of situation could be improved by encouraging the interviewee to provide more concise answers to the question and establishing a clear focus for interviews.

Question 1: Is that match practice, the fact that you haven't played that much because of your back?

Tim Henman: I think, yeah – I think it's, you know, mental aspect. The 5-1 game is fine. He held comfortably. But, you know, I played a poor game. Nothing happened on my serve at 5-2 in the fourth. You know, you probably put it down to matches. But it's no excuse. You can't just, you know, let a game go that quickly without anything happening in it.

Question 2: Have you rationalized the fact that the best might not be top 10 again? Can you be happy with that?

Tim Henman: Who knows. You know, if somebody – if somebody, you know, was going to say, 'No, you're not going to get back into the top 20,' or something, you know, I might not do it. You know, there's no one to tell you that. And I believe, you know, I can get back to, you know, playing some good tennis. You know, as I said, who knows what's going to happen. You know, would you have said I was going to make the semis of the French? Probably not. But that's sport for you. That's why, you know, I want to give myself that opportunity because I didn't have that opportunity last year with my lack of health.

11

Cash cows? The commodity of sport celebrity

Overview

This chapter examines sport stars and celebrities, core elements of the sport media nexus. In particular, it explores the nature of sport stardom and celebrity and uses the concept of circuits of promotion to explain its importance within sport media. The chapter also examines the role of external player management, as well the types of narratives that the sport media creates to make sport stars meaningful and entertaining.

After completing this chapter the reader should be able to:

- Describe the core features of a sport star or celebrity.
- Explain the role of a sport star or celebrity by referring to the concept of a circuit of promotion and the rise of player management.
- Explain the ways in which sport stars and celebrities are represented via narratives.
- Identify the key narratives used by the media in the construction of sport stardom and celebrity.
- Use the knowledge about the ways in which sport stars and celebrities are represented in the sport media to inform sport media management.

Introduction

If there once was a time when professional athletes could play their chosen sport, collect a pay cheque at the end of the day and retire happily to the family home without the intrusions of the rest of the world dominating both their public and private lives, then it is a distant memory. Professional athletes are now part of a celebrity culture, public property like the stars of the film and music industries. This stardom has been driven by the media and the increasing desire of audiences to know more about the personal side of sport. Professional athletes are now considered entertainers as much as they are sportsmen and women. In many sports million dollar salaries are testimony to the appeal of sport stars, their ability to attract audiences and their capacity to sell products and services. These salaries are not directly proportional to the quality of their play, but to their worth as national and global commodities.

Whether in individual or team sport, in organizations at all levels, athletes are a major factor in acquiring or losing media coverage. Athletes are the public faces of sport organizations, more so than any other commercial or non-profit enterprise. Furthermore, the ways in which the media represents these athletes can determine their popularity and that of the sport. At best, these athletes can deliver professional sport organizations decades of financial stability, increase the popularity of specific sports at national and global levels and encourage young people to become physically active. At worst, they can act as models for socially unacceptable behaviour and destroy a sport organization's credibility, financial worth, reputation and capacity to create a positive public image. An analysis of the ways in which the media uses sport celebrity and stardom to drive the nexus is essential in managing the profile of sport organizations.

What are sport stars?

Whannel (2002:51) argued that the 'comparison of image and reality, of represented star and real person, becomes problematic when all we are dealing with is layer upon layer of mediation'. Sport stars are a media creation and although a real person lies beneath the media coverage it is unlikely they will be discovered by the audiences that consume media sport. Rather, these audiences will have access to media constructions, to narratives that tell stories about how and why these people are important and interesting. In contemporary society, particular with the popularity of reality television programmes, it is possible for almost anyone, however briefly, to claim the mantle of celebrity. There have been isolated instances when sporting incompetence has led to people becoming sport celebrities, but sport stardom is predicated on sporting talent. This talent alone is not enough, however, for stars on the field might not become stars off it. Thus, sport stars exist at the intersection between sporting talent and celebrity appeal. As Whannel (2002:49) noted, 'stardom is a form of social production in which the professional ideologies and production practices of the media aim to win and hold our attention by linking sporting achievement and personality in ways which have resonances in popular common sense'.

Andrews and Jackson (2001) noted that sporting celebrity has several points of difference from celebrity in other cultural contexts. First, sporting celebrity is often represented as the result of talent, dedication or hard work, rather than inherited wealth or status. Second, the place of sport as a highly valued cultural practice means that the visibility of athletes is likely to be inherently high, which makes the transition to celebrity relatively easy. Third, athletes are themselves in playing sport, whereas celebrities from the film and music industries often adopt fictitious characters in their work. Andrews and Jackson (2001) argued that the dramatic immediacy of sport provides its celebrities with authenticity. Fourth and finally, on-field performance sustains sporting celebrity, which means that it can quickly diminish through poor results, injury or off-field indiscretions.

It is also important to note that sport stars and celebrities are invariably men. By their very nature sport stars are drawn from the most popular mediated sports, which are typically the football codes, major sport circuits and motor sport as discussed in Chapter 2. These sports very rarely feature women and when they do the media coverage is limited relative to male sport. At various times sport stars are drawn from major events such as the Olympic Games, where relatively obscure sports and athletes are brought to prominence by nationalistic fervour, extraordinary feats or colourful personalities. In these circumstances the media coverage of women's sport typically increases and in some countries exceeds the coverage of male athletes, but invariably the stardom is short lived or deferred until the next Olympics.

Circuits of promotion

In order to describe and explain the interconnections between professional sport, the media, advertisers and business, Whitson (1998) used the concept of 'circuits of promotion'. Sport stars and their marketing is a central feature of these circuits, which serve to create mutually beneficial corporate synergies. Whitson suggested that in circuits of promotion 'there are no obvious starting points and endpoints, but rather recursive and mutually reinforcing public texts that generate more visibility and more business for all concerned' (67). Furthermore, these texts rely on sport stars for their visibility, because they become the 'face' of corporate brands and sport organizations.

The relationship between Nike and former Chicago Bulls and Washington Wizards player Michael Jordan is a perfect example of a circuit of promotion at work (Whitson, 1998; Hoye, Smith, Westerbeek, Stewart & Nicholson, 2006). The Nike advertising campaigns that featured Jordan contributed to building the profile of both the company and the athlete, while Jordan's

169

success in winning six National Basketball Association (NBA) championships with the Bulls enhanced the corporate synergy between the two 'brands' and helped to increase the return on Nike's investment. Furthermore, the success of Jordan and the global advertising campaigns developed by Nike increased the cultural, social and commercial profile of the NBA in America. In turn, the global promotion and advertising by the NBA, that either did or did not feature Jordan, helped to promote both Jordan, as the League's most visible and recognizable player, and Nike, as a major player in basketball footwear and apparel, either by direct or indirect association. Lastly, any advertising undertaken by Jordan's other sponsors, such as Gatorade, served to promote Jordan, but also the NBA and Nike through their association with Jordan.

McDonald and Andrews (2001:20–21) suggested that Jordan's image continues to circulate around the world as part of a 'global culture increasingly dominated by the exchange of commodity signs'. In essence, through his basketball playing Jordan became a very successful basketball player, but through his sponsorship, advertising and marketing activities, Jordan became a brand with its own highly recognizable image. When Nike launched Jordan Inc., the head of the new business division claimed 'we have the most recognizable person in the world' and that 'his appeal transcends sports, gender, race and age' (cited in McDonald & Andrews, 2001:21).

Player management

The importance of sport stars in circuits of promotion has given rise to the phenomenon of player management, although it had relatively early beginnings. International Management Group (IMG), one of the world's leading player management companies, was formed in the 1960s. It now employs in excess of 2,000 staff in 70 offices in 30 countries (Hoye et al., 2006). IMG represents Tiger Woods, Ernie Els, Jennifer Capriati, John McEnroe, Michael Schumacher, Manchester United and the USA Olympic Committee among others.

Golfer Arnold Palmer, winner of the US Masters golf tournament in 1958, 1960, 1962 and 1964, the US Open in 1960 and the British Open in 1961 and 1962, was the first athlete in the world to be branded by Mark McCormack, the creator and head of IMG. Back in the 1960s the 'brand-name' principle by which Palmer and McCormack approached sport was the first attempt to transform the business activities of leading athletes. Sport and business were previously related, but the scale of their operation was unique (Boyle & Haynes, 2000). McCormack took the relationship of the agent further than before, and began to handle contract negotiations, proactively sought business opportunities, and planned the sale of the Palmer brand on a long-term basis, rather than previous attempts that might be characterized as ad hoc. McCormack set an important precedent, selling people as marketable commodities.

IMG's competitor Octagon represents and promotes athletes in 35 different sports across the world, including some of the most prominent sportsmen and women, such as tennis players Lleyton Hewitt and Amelie Mauresmo. It also represents American swimmer Michael Phelps, winner of the 400 m individual medley and 200 m butterfly at the 2004 Athens Olympic games, who Octagon claimed was a perfect case study in what successful sport marketing and management can provide for an athlete in the contemporary hyper-commercial sport environment (www.octagon.com). Octagon suggests that Phelps laid the foundation with his performances in the pool, but that Octagon enhanced the Phelps story with a targeted publicity campaign, which included appearances in *Time*, *People*, the *Wall Street Journal* and *USA Today*. The result was what Octagon claimed to be the creation of a connection between Phelps and corporate America, including the largest ever endorsement deal in swimming with Speedo and subsidiary deals with VISA, Omega and AT&T Wireless. In the 1960s Mark McCormack believed that an athlete's profile, and therefore their celebrity, could be built through sustained positive media exposure. It many respects it was a deceptively simple strategy, yet the Phelps case illustrates that the same principles apply in the contemporary sport media nexus.

The value of athletes in individual and team sport is a challenge and an opportunity for successful sport media management at the sport organization level. Many of the world's high profile athletes, as indicated above, are associated with global or national player management companies. These companies, as in the case of Phelps, are charged with the responsibility of building athlete profiles and creating circuits of promotion. In some cases, like Jordan and Nike, a major sponsor might be the primary instigator in the circuit. These external relationships can mean that the sport organization is able to capitalize on the publicity being generated by the third party and join the circuit of promotion. In this respect the sport organization is able to complement the media management activities, as well as create opportunities for other less well known athletes. On the other hand, external commercial relationships that severely limit the organization's ability to use the athlete in its own media management plan can present a significant challenge.

Sport star narratives

According to Whannel (1992), sportsmen and women have three functions for television, although his typology can be extended to all media forms. They are entertaining performers, personalities who attract and keep audiences and the bearers of sporting narratives. The first function is the most obvious, for the performance of athletes, particularly live and televised, is the basis for all mediated sport entertainment. As noted earlier in Chapter 6, personification is one of the ways in which the media makes news meaningful and in sport this process is particularly important in constructing audience interest. Teams are almost never depersonalized by the media. Rather, sport stars are cultivated to represent and embody the team, which is why the player trading in contemporary team sport can cause consternation among fans. The final function of sport stars as the bearers of narratives is a complex process in which sport stars and celebrities are constructed by the media.

Whannel (2002) has argued that there are four distinct vehicles through which sport star narratives are produced. First, newspaper news stories, which are usually accompanied by career resumes and tend to focus on highs and lows. Second, magazine profiles, in which the personal and private lives of stars are probed. These profiles increasingly form part of newspaper coverage, as soft news becomes more prominent and sport celebrity culture grows. Third, television previews and reviews of sporting events, in which the central questions of 'who will win', 'who won' and 'why' are made meaningful through the past achievements and performances of stars. Fourth and finally, sport star biographies and autobiographies that increasingly appear at the start of careers, rather than at the end as they used to.

The stories that frame the media coverage of sport stars and celebrities are often dichotomous. In other words, the audience is invited to see the sport star as one of two distinct opposites. The most prevalent of these narratives is the hero and the villain, although it should be noted that these two categories in particular are not often used to construct narratives of female athletes. The two cases in this chapter highlight the use of hero and villain narratives, although footballer David Beckham illustrated in (Case 1) and cricketer Shane Warne demonstrate that media narratives are not static and can be adopted or adapted by the media depending on the context.

Case 1   What a match: Posh and Becks

One is a superstar of the field and the other is a superstar of the stage. Together, they have become one of the world's most mediated celebrity couples, rivalled only by American films stars such as Brad Pitt and Angelina Jolie. David Beckham is perhaps the most famous footballer in the world, while his wife, Victoria (Adams), was formerly a member of the Spice Girls, a popular five member girl band of the 1990s. Throughout the last part of the twentieth century and into the twenty-first century Posh (Victoria's stage name was Posh Spice) and Becks, as they have been labelled by the media, have become subjects of intense media scrutiny.

The popularity of Posh and Becks is due to their coupling, as well as the result of multi-layered media narratives. Foremost among these is fairytale, a narrative constructed by the media which effectively represented the couple as a prince and princess or king and queen. Victoria Adams was a major celebrity in her own right prior to meeting Beckham, while he was a rising young star at Manchester United. Their relationship and subsequent marriage catapulted them to the forefront of public attention. Media reports 'focused on regal splendour, royal connections and comparisons with royalty', which were assisted by the expensive 1999 wedding being staged in a luxurious Irish castle (Whannel, 2001:144). According to Whannel (2001:143), the wedding was an example of a media vortex at work, whereby it becomes difficult for the media to discuss anything else – 'television presenters alluded to it, politicians made asides about it, radio phone-ins discussed it, and comedians made jokes about it'. The fairytale has been extended through the birth of three sons and an extravagant lifestyle befitting the rich and famous. As an example of the power of the narrative, throughout the course of the European Football Championships in 2000, 44% of articles published in English newspapers the *Sun* and *Mirror* were related to David's relationship with Victoria and unrelated to football (Clayton & Harris, 2004).

As a player for Manchester United, the most famous club in the world, Beckham has enjoyed the narrative construction of hero. In 1996 his goal from the halfway line against Wimbledon granted him media notoriety only a year after his debut in the Premier League. Soon after he made his first appearance for the English national team and his on-field exploits were lauded by the media. But, the hero turned villain in the 1998 World Cup after Beckham was sent off in a game against Argentina, in which England were eliminated after a penalty shootout. Beckham became a target of abuse in the media, with the *Daily Mirror* newspaper printing a Beckham dartboard as part of its coverage. Despite the abuse on the field and through the media Beckham managed to play a key role in leading Manchester United to the treble in 1999 (English Premier League, FA Cup and European Champions League), which Whannel (2001) argued demonstrated his maturity and provided a context for rehabilitation and forgiveness.

Sources: Whannel, 2001; Clayton & Harris, 2004.

Heroes and villains are created by media and sport organizations to sell products and services. Villains increase interest and awareness and have an important role in increasing newspaper circulation and television ratings. Boxer Mike Tyson became a sport star by winning the heavyweight championship of the world in his youth, but became a notorious villain via his actions inside and outside the ring. Biting the ear of an opponent and charges of sexual assault were two of many elements that led to the media construction of Tyson as a villain, which enabled him to be used as a figure of public curiosity, fascination and pity. This publicity, however, was not considered good for the sport, nor was Tyson a valuable sponsorship and promotion tool. Villains created by the media as a result of on-field incidents or performances are impossible for sport organizations to control. The management of off-field behaviour, however, is an increasingly important part of sport management and its media impacts are discussed in greater detail in the next chapter.

By contrast, heroes create publicity, as well as commercial opportunities beyond increased circulation or ratings. Michael Jordan and Tiger Woods are both examples of athletes who have been extraordinarily successful on the field of play, presented as heroes for mediated audiences. Off the field they have variously been presented as ideals for audience consumption. At various times Jordan was constructed by the media as the doting family man, an antidote to the sexual adventuring of many professional athletes, while Woods has been portrayed as America's son, a symbol, among other things, of America's ability to reconcile its multi-cultural and multi-racial society (Cole & Andrews, 2001).

173

Whannel (2002) suggested that the following are useful themes in analysing sport narratives in which sport stars are made and unmade by the media:

- emergence of a striking talent
- accomplishment of extraordinary feats
- public celebration
- displays of arrogance
- public doubts
- erratic behaviour
- public scandal
- failure
- hero redeemed by extraordinary performance
- forgiveness and
- waning power.

The emergence of striking talent is one of the key ways in which narratives of sport stars are constructed. According to Cole and Andrews (2001:73), stories that examine the origin of Tiger Woods often emphasize that 'the American public has long recognized Tiger Woods' exceptionalism'. The emergence of striking talent often blends in with a narrative about child prodigy, of which tennis player Jennifer Capriati is an exemplar. In this respect the amazing sporting feats of a child provide a valuable human interest story for the media. Video clips of Woods as a child have been used, argued Cole and Andrews, to create a sense of national intimacy with the Woods story and position the golfer as 'America's son'. Nike's 'Hello World' advertising campaign played on the narrative of the emergence of striking talent, the accomplishment of extraordinary feats and the child prodigy, as the following text was included with images of Woods as a young golfer (cited in Cole & Andrews, 2001:75):

> Hello World.
> I shot in the 70s when I was 8.
> I shot in the 60s when I was 12.
> I won the US Junior Amateur when I was 15.
> Hello World.
> I played in the Nissan Open when I was 16.
> Hello World.
> I won the US Amateur when I was 18.
> I played in the Masters when I was 19.
> I am the only man to win three consecutive US Amateur titles.
> Hello World.
> There are still courses in the US I am not allowed to play because of the color of my skin.
> Hello World.
> I've heard I am not ready for you.
> Are you ready for me?

The narrative of the emergence of striking talent is often merged or blurred with other narratives, depending on the particular historical context of the athlete and the way in which the media can best construct a human interest story for audience consumption. For example, the 'rags to riches' narrative is particularly strong in sport, as it has often been a vehicle through which people seek (and very few obtain) social advancement. The achievements of tennis players and sisters Venus and Serena Williams are often contextualized by their poor and at times dangerous upbringing. This narrative has in part been assisted by their father referring to them as the 'Cinderella's of the Ghetto' (Spencer, 2001). The rags to riches narrative and the wealth of contemporary professional sport also serves to reinforce the notion that with hard work anything is possible, despite the fact that only a handful of people become sport celebrities.

Public scandal, failure, erratic behaviour and public doubt are all media narratives that result in bad publicity, a theme that will be examined further in the following chapter. On-field incidents can create media narratives, such as footballer Eric Cantona's (Manchester United) infamous kung-fu kick on an abusive fan (Boyle & Haynes, 2000). Players can be rehabilitated from these incidents, however, as Cantona's involvement in a series of Nike advertisements during the 2006 FIFA World Cup illustrates. Off-field incidents and issues, such as drug and alcohol abuse and sexual misconduct, are often far more serious and can lead to long-term media narratives in which athletes are represented as being beyond help or rehabilitation. The case of cricketer Shane Warne, illustrated in Case 2, is a good example of continual bad behaviour which has created a 'bad boy' narrative, yet as with many team sports, on-field successes tend to create an equally strong oppositional narrative in which the player is able to achieve redemption through victory.

Case 2   Tendulkar and Warne: the yin and yang of global cricket

Throughout the 1990s and into the twenty-first century Indian Sachin Tendulkar and Australian Share Warne have been the premier batsman and bowler of international cricket. Their records speak volumes about their achievements on the field. Tendulkar has scored over 10,000 runs in test cricket, to be fourth on the all-time list, at an average of in excess of 56 runs per innings, while in limited overs cricket he has amassed over 14,000 runs at an average of more than 44. He has scored in excess of 70 hundreds at international level after making his debut as a 16 year old against traditional rival Pakistan, while nobody else has made more than 50. Shane Warne has taken in excess of 650 test wickets at an average of approximately 25, which ranks him as the best bowler in cricket history, while he has taken approximately 300 in international limited overs cricket at an average of less than 26. In 2000, Warne was named as one of *Wisden's* five cricketers of the century.

According to Warne's biographical profile on cricket's most popular website, cricinfo, 'his story is part fairytale, part pantomime, part hospital drama, part adult's-only romp, part glittering awards ceremony'. Warne's colourful career has been closely followed by the media, particularly the British tabloids, and his off-field antics have resulted in headlines that Australian and international cricket administrators would have preferred to avoid. Controversies to have beset Warne include being banned for 12-months for taking a banned substance, admitting to taking cash from an illegal bookmaker, involvement in a phone sex scandal involving a British nurse, smoking while being sponsored by a company dedicated to helping people to stop the habit and allegedly conducting extra marital affairs that led to the breakdown of his marriage in 2005. Negative media coverage of allegations in 2003 that Warne had sent 'salacious text messages' to a South African woman prompted Cricket Australia chief executive officer James Sutherland to suggest that issues such as these were detrimental to the image of the game (Brown, 2003).

By contrast, Tendulkar's off-field persona is more discrete, but he is no less visible. According to a profile in a special issue of *Time* magazine on Asia's heroes, Tendulkar was the first sport star to achieve real media prominence in India, which is partly explained by the commercialization of cricket during Tendulkar's career and the increasing amount of cricket broadcast on television in particular. Tendulkar is a global brand ambassador for Adidas and has been associated with numerous companies, including Fiat, who named a car after the cricketer (Palio Sachins).

Off the field Tendulkar and Warne's impact on global cricket has been to markedly increase the popularity of the game, yet their respective narratives illustrate the ways in which the media create heroes and villains for public consumption and enjoyment. The Australian public has vacillated between interpreting Warne as a hero because of his sporting prowess, and seeing him as a partly comic partly tragic figure who acts more like a boy than a man. At times Warne has been loved and adored, but at others, which became too frequent, he has been vilified by some elements of society and the media. By contrast, Tendulkar has been consistently adored by the Indian and world media. What remains to be seen is how both men will be remembered once they leave the game.

Source: Brown, 2003; http://www.time.com/time/asia/features/heroes/sachin.html

---

Finally, the sexualization of female athletes lies at the intersection between media narratives, the framing of female athletes in order to reproduce gender stereotypes and the use of the female body to market products and services. The case of Russian tennis player Anna Kournikova is an exemplar in this respect. Kournikova became a sport celebrity because of her looks, rather than her tennis ability. In fact, this dichotomy framed the media narrative of the latter stages of her career. Kournikova's popularity and global celebrity helped to rescue women's tennis from a trough of public interest in the mid 1990s and create a sport marketing success story. However, it also popularized a way of viewing women's tennis, in which beauty is revered as much as sporting talent. Russian Maria Sharapova, like Kournikova, has received much media attention, although she was overtly sexualized through media coverage prior to her eighteenth birthday. The influence of media narratives in which public interest is explained by reference to an athlete's beauty and sexual attractiveness is pervasive.

Implications for sport media management

The use of narratives in the construction and maintenance of sport stardom and celebrity has important implications for the practice of sport media management. First, the media coverage of athletes and teams involves telling stories, because media consumers are attracted to items of human interest or drama. Media coverage will increase and improve in quality if the media manager or organization identifies those individuals and organizational features that might contribute to good stories. Second, athletes with extraordinary talent should be identified and utilized in media planning, communications and interactions. Importantly, these talents are not relative to the rest of the world. In other words, an athlete can have an extraordinary talent at local club or high school level, relative to his or her peers. This will make the athlete interesting to the media. Third, media coverage will be improved if sport media managers can identify any characteristics that might make the athlete part of an interesting or appealing story. For example, using a variation of the rags to riches narrative, an organization might identify special personal histories or barriers that athletes have overcome to participate or excel in their chosen sport. Fourth, sport organizations that involve women must attempt to use positive narratives to attract media coverage. This is difficult given the bias towards male sport, but attempting to attract media coverage by emphasizing elements of a narrative in which athletes are sexualized contributes to stereotypes. Fifth and finally, sport media management must plan for bad publicity as part of negative narratives. This theme will be discussed in detail in the following chapter.

Limitations

Sports stars are a valuable resource, but it is also clear that they can become a liability, often unexpectedly and quickly. For example, in the lead up to the 2006 world Match Play championship in golf, Tiger Woods was drawn to play Trinidad born Canadian Stephen Ames, with Woods seeded first and Ames sixty-fourth in the sixty-four man draw. Asked about his chances of beating Woods, Ames noted to reporters that 'anything can happen', but then followed the comment with 'especially where he's hitting the ball'. The result was that Woods birdied the first six holes, won the first nine and recorded a nine up with eight to play victory in the first round, the greatest winning margin in the history of the tournament. After the victory Woods admitted that Ames' comments had provided him with the motivation to play well. In attempting to create awareness and interest in a sport or sport organization through its stars, it is important to be aware that athletes are people, not machines. They often make mistakes, both on and off the field of play.

177

More than any other element of sport media management, the management of sport stardom and the media presentation of athletes is a fickle process. As Andrews and Jackson (2001) noted, 'as with any cultural product, there is also no guarantee that celebrities will be consumed in the manner intended by those orchestrating the manufacturing processes'. The carefully crafted image of an athlete nurtured by a sport organization or a narrative constructed by the media might be abandoned by the audience in favour of alternate, if not contradictory readings. Any attempts to create sport stars and celebrities through the media must be moderated by an acknowledgement that audiences are not homogenous, but are composed of a people with a wide variety of values, beliefs and interests, not to mention disparate social, racial, ethnic, sexual, national and religious histories and identities.

Summary

This chapter has examined the role of sport stars and celebrities in the sport media nexus, in order to contextualize their importance for sport media management. In particular, the concept of sport stars, circuits of promotion, the role of player management and the construction of sport narratives were explored. Review questions and exercises are listed below to assist with confirming your knowledge of the core concepts and principles introduced in this chapter.

Review questions and exercises

1. What is a sport star?
2. Explain the place of sport stars in the sport media nexus by referring to a circuit of promotion?
3. Is the player management of athletes by external organizations a positive or negative for sport media management within sport organizations? Why?
4. What was the simple strategy applied by Mark McCormack that still applies in the contemporary sport media nexus?
5. Who are the ten biggest sport stars in the world?
6. Who are the ten biggest sport stars in your country?
7. What narratives have been used to construct the celebrity of the 20 stars of the previous two questions?
8. Which narratives are most prominent or frequent? Why?
9. Who are the most notable sport villains in the world or your country?
10. What themes have been used to construct their narratives?

12

Not all publicity is good: managing crises, scandals and reputations

Overview

This chapter examines crises and scandals. It highlights their impact on sport organizations, as well as the strategies available to sport media managers to manage the image and reputation of a sport organization or athlete during these events. In particular, this chapter investigates the most important stages of crisis and scandal media management and provides guidelines for beginning a crisis management process. The prevalence of crises and scandals within professional sport organizations, as well as the competitive nature of the media market, means that effective media management is essential to ensure the credibility and profitability of an organization or athlete are maintained.

After completing this chapter the reader should be able to:

- Describe what crises and scandals are in terms of their impact on a sport organization.
- Generalize about the impact of crises and scandals on sport organizations.

- Identify the types of crises that might beset a sport organization and in particular distinguish between sporadic and systemic crises.
- Establish a crisis media management process within a sport organization.
- Apply a set of crisis media management guidelines at a time of crisis or scandal within a sport organization.

Introduction

The saying 'any publicity is good publicity' assumes that creating any amount of public awareness is worth the consequences. In the case of sport, bad publicity can ruin careers and severely damage organizations. Artist Andy Warhol claimed that in the future everyone would be world famous for 15 minutes, and in a world saturated by media this means that bad publicity is likely to be the only publicity that some people receive. Professional sport organizations and their employees, however, are subjected to intense media and public interest, which means that the likelihood of receiving bad publicity is great. Bad publicity, which results from crises and scandals at one end of the spectrum to accidents and minor misdemeanours at the other, is to be avoided because of its potential negative impacts.

Importantly, managing crises, scandals and reputations is not about making sure procedures are in place to clean up the mess as quickly as possible (Pearson, Clair, Misra & Mitroff, 1997). Nor is it about implementing practices and tactics that will limit the amount of information available to the media, in order to protect employees that have been negligent or have transgressed boundaries governed by social values and norms. Rather, as Pearson et al. have noted, 'crisis management is a mindset and process that, on a daily basis, drives a company's decisions and actions' (p. 52). As such, this chapter is a starting point for the implementation of broader management processes that contribute to media management practices and organizational culture. Framing crisis and scandal management within the context of media management is useful because sport organizations are often able to recognize that their public profile makes them a natural media target when things go wrong.

Crises and scandals

Crises have 'become front-page material – a key word in the vocabulary of official and everyday speech' (Keane, 1984:10). From a cursory glance at the mass media it is clear that the term crisis is both used and abused freely. In both official and everyday speech, crisis is used to signify a broad range of traumatic happenings, from wars, acts of terrorism and political coups at one end of the spectrum, to sportsmen and women having sustained career threatening injuries, taken drugs or committed sexual indiscretions at the other.

As a result, there is much debate about what exactly a crisis is. The academic definition refers to a threat to a system or organization (Offe, 1984). The threat implies change and the change must be significant, to the point that the system or organization will undergo an irrevocable transformation. In the sporting context, examples based on this understanding of crisis might be two clubs merging, a club relocating to another city, province or state, or a league folding because of financial insolvency. In each of these instances a massive change in identity would result.

In the main, however, this academic definition does not reflect common usage, such as within the media coverage of sport. In this context the word crisis primarily refers to a problem that a club, league, association or individual is experiencing, albeit a serious one, which typically has the potential to cause a negative impact or at very least negative publicity. In short, a crisis in this respect is likely to transform the functional into the dysfunctional, often at a moment's notice.

Derived from the Greek *krisis*, in its most literal form the term crisis means decision. At its core, a crisis event is a decisive or critical turning point, a moment of rupture. If the everyday workings of an organization are perceived as continuous, relatively stable and normal, then crises are moments of discontinuity, in which the threat of change necessarily defines them as abnormal. By their very nature, crises are the antithesis of the status quo. Crises are often ambiguous (where the link between cause and effect can be unclear), have a low probability of occurring (but a high impact or consequence), require an immediate response, are often a surprise to the members of the organization and require a decision that will have positive or negative results (Pearson & Clair, 1998).

Like crises, scandals also threaten the status quo and relative stability of sport organizations. Rowe (2000) suggested that sport scandals are an integral feature of the contemporary media landscape that requires serious attention, rather than dismissed simply as the work of tabloid or gutter journalism (McKay, Hutchins & Mikosza, 2000). Both crises and scandals are the result of disruption, although a crisis is able to cause disruption without media coverage while a scandal's disruption by definition is created by media attention. In fact, it is more accurate to adopt the term media scandal, as the two are inextricably linked.

The terms crisis and scandal are often used as synonyms by the sport media, however it is useful to separate them. Crises typically relate to institutional, systemic and widespread dysfunction or an event or incident that occurs outside the control of a sport organization, such as an act of terrorism or a lighting strike. By contrast, scandals more often relate to individual instances of personal impropriety. The terms are confused by their usage, such as the way in which the media refer to a spate of injuries suffered by a team as a crisis. In this situation the term scandal is not appropriate because no impropriety has been committed. Yet, the severity of the situation does not warrant the description of crisis, particularly if media uses the same nomenclature for

181

a stadium collapse or similar calamity. Whatever the context, it is clear that scandals almost always relate to the actions of individuals and more often than not involve sex, money, power, corruption and incompetence.

Lull and Hinerman (1997) identified a range of scandal criteria. The first, that social norms are transgressed, is fundamental to the media scandal. Without this transgression, a scandal cannot occur. These transgressions are carried out by specific people and their actions reflect the extent of their desires and personal interests. Through the media scandal these individuals are identified and held accountable for actions that are demonstrated to be intentional and reckless. Scandals are widely circulated via the media, are constructed as a story for audience consumption and typically inspire widespread interest and discussion. The moral transgression is magnified in sport because of the difference between its romantic ideals and its commercialized and corruptible reality (Rowe, 2000). In turn, the public profile and intense interest in sport stars means that sport scandals are particularly attractive to the media and volatile for sport organizations. Sport news is already subject to significant audience consumption, which makes the sport scandal a complementary product. Importantly, in the case of major scandals and crises, the promotional and protective elements of the sport media nexus discussed in Chapter 7 are often abandoned.

Even the broad definitions of scandal and crisis referred to above can be obscured and complicated by media reporting. Ben Johnson testing positive to steroids at the 1988 Seoul Olympics and former South African cricket captain Hansie Cronje's involvement in match fixing have both been described in the media as scandals because of the moral boundaries that were transgressed. But, the actions of both men were symptomatic of a broader crisis that engulfed world sport and cricket respectively. Whether it is a crisis or scandal that generates negative publicity, each have the potential to adversely affect, and in some instances irrevocably destroy the reputations of individuals and organizations.

Crisis and scandal impact

In order to understand their impact, it is useful to classify crises into four distinct categories: internal; external; sporadic; and systemic. Internal crises are limited to the internal workings of the organization and have no impact on the general public. These crises require management, planning and effective and efficient internal processes, but very rarely require media management, because they are of little interest to the media or the public, are dealt with quickly or are of limited consequence beyond the organization.

On the other hand, external crises have an impact beyond the boundaries of the organization. External crises are defined by the interest of both the general public and the media and require significant media management because of the negative impact they can have on an organization. The distinction between internal and external crises is important because when a crisis becomes public, its impact, as well as the course the crisis might take, is partly out of the control of the beleaguered organization. An internal crisis, although it may involve stakeholders outside the organization, should be able to be managed satisfactorily through internal processes. External crises, like scandals, are controlled in part by the media. The media will report on crises, as well as create the context in which the general public is able to understand and interpret them.

Sporadic crises occur without warning, and are typically isolated and unique. An example of a sporadic crisis might be a light plane carrying tourists on a joy flight crashing into a baseball stadium or football field, injuring players and spectators as a result. The plane crash is in all likelihood a one-off event and will occur with little or no warning. Furthermore, although the team or league running the event at the stadium should have a crisis management or emergency response plan, a light plane crash is not likely to be high on the list of things that might go wrong. The sporadic crisis will hopefully only have to be dealt with once, if ever.

The systemic crisis is like an organizational disease. If the sporadic crisis is akin to a small child getting a broken arm from a freak accident that was no fault of their own, the systemic crisis is akin to a middle-aged man or woman being diagnosed with lung cancer as a result of a sustained nicotine habit. Unlike the sporadic crisis, which occurs suddenly and without warning, the systemic crisis has been growing and festering within, usually as a result of organizational inadequacy, such as corruption, illegal activity or manifestly inappropriate culture and procedures. The systemic crisis is the most dangerous for a sport organization, because not only is it difficult to remedy, but the media is likely to feed off the story, for weeks or months, and in the worst cases, for years (see Case 1). An example of a systemic crisis is a sport league

---

Case 1   Baseball and steroids

In 2002 Ken Caminiti, the 1996 Most Valuable Player in Major League Baseball's (MLB) National League, revealed in a *Sports Illustrated* article that he had used anabolic steroids and that half the players in MLB had also. This article was the beginning of the media coverage of a long-term crisis in American baseball and to a lesser degree American sport. The extent of the crisis was such that MLB was forced into instituting a drug policy, which in turn was critically examined in a 2005 American congressional hearing titled 'Restoring Faith in America's Pastime: Evaluating Major League Baseball's efforts to Eradicate Steroid Use'.

The congressional hearing, which was the result of a crisis of confidence in baseball and a fear that steroid use was becoming epidemic among adolescents in America, included testimony by star players such as Mark McGwire, Sammy Sosa and Jose Canseco. Earlier in 2005 Canseco's biog-raphy had been released, titled *Juiced: Wild Times, Rampant 'Roids, Smash Hits and How Baseball Got Big*, in which he attributed his success in baseball to steroids. Canseco also claimed that he had injected steroids with other players, among them McGwire, who broke baseball's single season home run record in 1998.

McGwire's record was in turn broken by Barry Bonds in 2001, who in 2006 moved to second on the all-time home run record list, an achievement met with much outrage among baseball supporters. Bonds was implicated in the Bay Area Laboratory Co-Operative (BALCO) drug scandal that threatened to engulf a significant number of American sports in 2003. Investigations into BALCO resulted in founder Victor Conte and trainer Greg Anderson (who had trained Bonds) pleading guilty to steroid distribution. It is alleged that BALCO developed and distributed the designer drug tetrahydrogestrinone (THG). Track and field athletes such as Tim Montgomery, CJ Hunter, Marion Jones and Dwain Chambers were implicated in the scandal because of associations with BALCO.

In response to criticisms that their drug policy was too lenient, MLB responded by establishing new penalties for drug taking. First-time offenders are suspended for 10 days, second-time offenders for 30 days, third-time offenders for 60 days and fourth-time offenders are suspended for 1 year. In contrast, the World Anti-Doping Agency code stipulates that a 2-year ban be imposed on an athlete who is found to have taken a prohibited substance, while a lifetime ban applies to an athlete who tests positive twice. It is still unclear whether MLB has recovered from the crisis or is still immersed in it. Since 2002 it appears that the League has either ignored the issue of performance enhancing drugs or put in place half measures, which have led to further scrutiny.

---

underpaying its players over an extended period of time, as a percentage of total revenue, therefore making it more profitable for the players to bet on as well as alter the result of games. Initially, when the story breaks in the media about one athlete and match fixing allegations the crisis might appear to be sporadic, a one-off event in which the player is represented as a 'bad seed'. However, further examination will reveal that corruption and match fixing is widespread. This chronic and long-term problem within the sport, as well as the crisis, is systemic.

Once these four crisis categories or types are combined, a matrix of the potential impact is revealed, as illustrated in Table 12.1. Crises that are sporadic and internal have the lowest impact in the media and with the general public, while crises that are systemic and external have the highest impact.

Table 12.1 Crisis Types and Impact

	Sporadic	*Systemic*
Internal	Low	Medium
External	Medium–High	High

Sport scandals are always external. Sport organizations invariably attempt to ensure the actions of their employees are for internal consumption and analysis only. In these instances moral transgressions may either be hidden in the hope they are never discovered or dealt with through an internal rehabilitation process. But, a moral transgression that is internal is not a scandal, for it must be reported by the media in order to generate widespread public interest. Single transgressions, by an individual or a group, can be considered sporadic within the crisis typology. Depending on the profile of the people involved and to what extent moral and social boundaries have been transgressed, the impact may be anywhere between medium and high. Multiple transgressions by an individual or group will mean that the scandal is becoming systemic and the impact will be high. This is particularly the case where a high-profile athlete repeatedly transgresses moral boundaries and in doing so becomes a regular feature of tabloid journalism in particular.

Despite its relatively humble beginnings, sport is no longer simple. It is typically not just a group of people getting together to engage in play, games or athletic contests on an ad hoc basis. Even in the amateur club environment, sport is governed by a set of regulations that cover a range of issues such as insurance, health and safety and member protection, to name only a few. In the professional context, sport is a complex activity that involves significant organization. In fact, as the activity becomes more commercial, the level of complexity increases and as the complexity increases, so too does the risk. Put simply, the bigger the organization or the event, the greater the chance and opportunity that things will go wrong. Similarly, the potential for individual moral transgressions increases as the organization becomes larger and more commercial. In essence, as professional sport organizations and their employees gain greater commercial and cultural influence, there is a greater likelihood that crises and scandals will occur and as the likelihood increases, so too does the potential impact.

The challenge for sport organizations is to develop and implement processes to limit the damage to the organization. Crisis management and crisis and scandal media management go hand in hand. Without effective and efficient crisis management, media management is difficult, if not a waste of time. Furthermore, media management at a time of crisis or scandal without any substantive attempts to address, change or remedy the situation is simply an attempt to disguise the problem and ensure the reputation of the organization is maintained, at whatever cost. In short, this is unethical and is to be avoided.

In a media saturated professional sport landscape, protecting a sport organization's reputation and image is becoming increasingly important. Sport organizations, like generic business organizations, need to do more than make a profit or have more wins than losses in order to be considered successful. In order to be successful, sport organizations must operate and behave in ways that conform to social norms and expectations (Galloway & Kwansah-Aidoo, 2005). In short, they must demonstrate that the values of the organization and general society are aligned. If the distance between the actions of the sport organization and the values of society is small then the crisis is likely to be small, if it can be considered a crisis at all. On the other hand, if the distance between actions and values is great, then the crisis is likely to be amplified, as

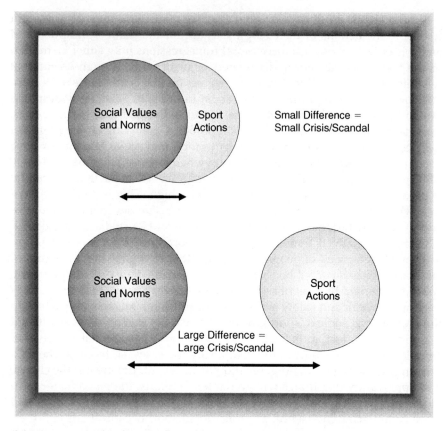

Figure 12.1 Social Values and Norms Compared to Sport Actions

illustrated in Figure 12.1. The degree to which actions and values are aligned in generic business organizations is not always clear, partly because the 'public face' of the business is its products, rather than its people. Sport faces distinct challenges because the 'public face' of its business is people, the athletes. This visibility, which is created partly by the nature of the enterprise and partly by the media's involvement, means that the degree of alignment is a constant issue. The visibility also means that small breaches of social and public trust by the sport organizations can result in significant short-term crises and scandals.

The case of sexual misconduct by athletes is an example of where the distance between the actions of the organization and the values and norms of society is great and the breach of social and public trust is significant. In these cases the media crisis that results has the capacity to damage the reputation of the athlete and the organization for years, if not for good. In 2004 both the Australian Rugby League and the Australian Football League were subjected to months of media reporting and speculation over two alleged rape cases involving the Canterbury Bulldogs and St Kilda Saints respectively. In the *Age*, one of Australia's major daily newspapers, it was reported that 'Gang rape allegations involving six members of a prominent Sydney Rugby League team have highlighted what many see as a pervasively anti-female

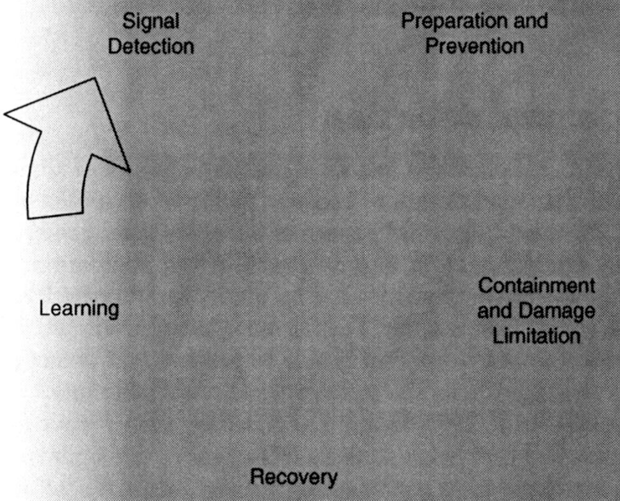

Signal
Detection

Preparation and
Prevention

Learning

Containment
and Damage
Limitation

Recovery

Figure 12.2 Crisis Management Phases

are useful for understanding the place of crisis media management, the way in which a crisis or scandal will develop and how it should be managed. The five phases are: signal detection; preparation and prevention; containment and damage limitation; recovery and learning. These five phases apply equally well to the management of scandals and throughout the following discussion the term crisis will be used to describe both crises and scandals.

Phase 1: signal detection

Although sport organizations focus a significant amount of attention on containment and damage limitation, because this is when media attention is at its greatest, the most important phases of the crisis management process are the first two, signal detection, and preparation and prevention. Importantly, in these two phases an organization has the ability to define itself and its actions as proactive, rather than reactive. Furthermore, the sport organization can create an organizational culture that is able to prevent and detect crises, rather than simply manage the media storm when it inevitably hits.

Pearson and Mitroff (1993) found that crises invariably leave a trail of early warning signs, but that organizations often ignore the signals. Early detection can ensure that a sport organization is aware of a crisis before the media, whereas late or no detection can result in a sport organization being forced to react to media reports and public condemnation. In other words, beginning a crisis management process means cultivating an awareness of the dangers and a system that is receptive to the signals. Pearson and Mitroff found the most successful organizations were those that established lines of communication within the organization that allowed and encouraged employees to report bad news. Furthermore, these organizations institutionalized the internal scrutiny of their operations to ensure that faults and problems were discovered. For some sport organizations, simply beginning a crisis management process may be sufficient to start a process whereby employees are more aware of potential dangers and are more alert to the signals.

Phase 2: preparation and prevention

Planning for a crisis should be an essential part of any sport organization's day-to-day business. Organizations in which the senior employees believe that the organization is bullet proof and that a crisis will never happen because their team, club or league is run better than its competitors are only tempting fate. Pearson et al. (1997:59) suggested that this type of thinking 'reinforces organizational vulnerability: early warning signals may go undetected or unreported; key internal contacts for resources may remain unaware of needs; critical alliances with external stakeholders may not be made; [and] learning after an incident or a near-miss may not be formalized or disseminated throughout the organization'. In essence, an organizational culture in which an 'it can't happen to us' attitude prevails is likely to cause crises, rather than prevent them. A healthier and more constructive perspective is to acknowledge that bad news is simply an unavoidable consequence of being in the sport business.

Beginning the crisis management planning process is often very difficult, and is met with resistance. Sport organizations are often resistant to change and have difficulty accepting that they might be susceptible to crises. It is essential to begin planning for the occurrence of crisis, but the question is where to start? A useful way to begin is by assessing how ready the organization is to deal with crises. A simple method is to ask the following questions of and within your organization:

- What crises present a risk to our organization and which ones are we susceptible to?
- What is the probability of these crises occurring based on the history of our organization, current personnel, organizational culture, external environment, etc.?
- What is the potential impact of each?
- Are we prepared to deal with each of the crises we have identified?

Asking these questions is an effective method of raising awareness within the organization about the need for crisis management, but it should be noted that they are merely a starting point, not an end in themselves. Furthermore, Pearson et al. (1997) suggested that this questioning should occur throughout the organization, because they found that the best prepared organizations have staff at all levels that know where to turn for help and have a clear sense of their own roles and responsibilities. Attempting to brainstorm the crises that your organization might be susceptible to should be a relatively easy process if the organization's employees agree to abandon the phrase 'that will never happen to us'. Table 12.2 provides some examples of crises and scandals that might occur, although this is by no means an exhaustive list.

Table 12.2 Sport Organization Crises and Scandals

Crisis/Scandal
Stadium Fire
Player/Coach/Administrator Death or Serious Injury (on-field)
Player/Coach/Administrator Death or Serious Injury (off-field)
Sexual Misconduct
Bomb Threat
Bomb Explosion
Terrorist Attack
Drug Taking (Performance)
Drug Taking (Recreational)
Match Fixing
Spectator Injury or Death
Facility Malfunction or Collapse
Drunk Driving
Public Fighting

One of the most important steps in this process is determining the probability of each of the crises occurring based on the history and culture of the organization, which might also be referred to as risk assessment. A common mistake of crisis planning is to develop plans for worst case scenarios and to be under prepared for crisis events that are more likely to happen (Fallin, 2005). An organization must do both, but also be prepared to prioritize. If the team's players have previously been charged and convicted of driving while drunk or have been charged and convicted of sexual misconduct and these incidents relate to organizational culture, then there is a higher probability that this type of crisis will occur again. Good crisis management planning should recognize and acknowledge that the prevalence of some of these issues indicates a systemic problem, rather than a series of sporadic crises. As such, there should be a crisis management plan in place, but perhaps more importantly, the crisis management process should alert the organization to more substantive problems such as a poor organizational culture or poor professional development and training for younger members of the team. If team players are constantly being caught driving while drunk, it is likely that the team has a culture in which excessive alcohol consumption is the norm, rather than the exception. If the organization constantly has to deal with media reports about their players and alcohol consumption then the more systemic problem needs to be addressed.

Likewise, if the facility that the team plays in is old or in need of repair, then the crisis management plan will need to reflect that there is a greater probability of a significant fault and a significant crisis occurring as a result. Similarly, to return to the original light plane crash scenario, the chances of a crisis occurring dramatically increase if the venue is near an airport or on a major flight path. Often the sheer organizational complexity of the sport and its inherent danger will mean that the crisis potential is high. Motor racing and horse racing are prime examples in this respect, where there is a significant chance of personal injury, for participants, spectators and officials alike.

The final steps in the initial planning process are to assess the potential impact of each of the crises that the organization is most susceptible to, and then assess how prepared the organization is to deal with these crises if they occurred. In assessing how prepared the organization is, it is useful to consider what the organization would do upon hearing the bad news. Is there a process in place to communicate the news to the media? Is there a process in place to communicate the news within the organization? Has a person or people been nominated as the organization's spokespeople at a time of crisis? If the answer is 'no' or 'we are not sure' then the organization is not prepared.

Pearson and Mitroff (1993) have noted that a goal of the prevention and preparation phase should not be to eliminate the possibility of all crises. In many professional sport organizations this is a difficult task made impossible by media attention and the prevalence of highly paid young men. Rather, a sport organization should set itself a goal of preventing most crises and scandals, while being prepared to handle those that go undetected or are beyond its control.

A key strategy that will contribute to effective crisis media management is the formulation of a crisis plan. Crisis management plans must be put in writing, but they need not be overly complex. Importantly, a crisis management plan must create protocols that instil confidence in the organization and provide direction at times when chaos may threaten to take over. A crisis management plan for a sport organization might consist of the following elements:

- A title page that contains the title, effective date and the signature of the organization's senior manager.
- A clear and direct policy statement that details how the organization will manage a crisis and its goals.
- A list of emergency telephone numbers for essential staff within the organization who will be contacted at a time of crisis.
- A criteria for activation that prioritizes crises and scandals into different levels depending on their severity and impact on the organization.
- A set of step-by-step procedures that correspond to the crises based on their level of severity.
- A section that describes appropriate media communication at a time of crisis.
- A set of appendices that may include items such as media release templates, speech guidelines and a media list.

Phase 3: containment and damage limitation

Sport organization employees face many challenges when a crisis breaks in the media, including the assessment of the crisis and communicating necessary information to stakeholders as quickly as possible. The following communication principles will aid the containment of the crisis or scandal (Patterson, 1993; Helitzer, 1999; Massey, 2001; Mackey, 2004; Ramsey, 2004; Stephens, Malone & Bailey, 2005):

- Do not ignore the problem, as any delay in your response will worsen the resulting crisis or scandal.
- Do not attempt to cover the problem up, as the cover up will become part of the crisis or scandal when the media finally uncover it. Revealing bad news is a way of establishing control, rather than relinquishing it.
- Gather all the facts as quickly as possible and try not to comment with only partial knowledge of the crisis or scandal.
- Appoint a spokesperson to act as the media liaison for the duration of the crisis. This may be the most senior manager, the media manager or the person most comfortable in front of the media.
- Establish a consistent message or story and communicate this with all stakeholders, including the media. It is important that the media do not use your mixed messages as a way of elongating the news story.
- Explain the steps the organization has or will be taking in order to rectify or manage the problem.
- Be accessible throughout the crisis or scandal, in order to build trust with the media and have the organization's point of view recorded.

- Be as truthful as possible throughout the crisis or scandal, as lying will destroy trust with the media and reduce the organization's overall credibility.

Phase 4: recovery

Another key challenge of effective crisis management is to return to business as usual as quickly as possible. With intense media and public interest this can often be a difficult task. Recovering from the crisis or scandal is partly about the way in which the organization communicates with the media, for a strong and consistent message will help to maintain credibility with a variety of stakeholders. Recovery is also dependent on the strategies that the organization puts in place to deal with the cause of the crisis or scandal. In Case 2 of this chapter, the International Olympic Committee (IOC) ignored systemic problems for a very long time, which caused the crisis and the resultant media interest. The strategies the IOC put in place enabled it to return to business and restore credibility, but this also took considerable time.

Case 2   Salt Lake City – Citius, Altius, Corruptus?

Michael Payne, former marketing director of the IOC, describes the 2002 Salt Lake City Winter Olympics as a 'catalyst for the most significant reform and change in recent Olympic history' (Payne, 2005). In terms of the performances of athletes, the Salt Lake City Games were as successful as preceding Games, with a record 78 events and gold medallists from 18 separate countries, but prior to the Games it was a completely different story as a widespread and damaging crisis engulfed the IOC. If the crisis that beset the 1972 Munich Olympics, where terrorists killed 11 Israeli athletes and coaches was sporadic, then the Salt Lake City crisis was systemic, the result of long-term institutional corruption.

In late 1998 a local Salt Lake City television station reported allegations of unethical behaviour by Salt Lake City bid committee members and an IOC delegate, which resulted in the IOC executive board establishing a special commission to investigate the allegations. Media coverage of the allegations and revelations, which lasted throughout 1999, damaged the reputation of Salt Lake City and the IOC irrevocably. Headlines such as 'Olympic vote buying scandal' were juxtaposed with 'Is the Olympic ideal destroyed?' The IOC commission discovered that IOC members were bribed for their votes and that the gifts offered by the Salt Lake City bid committee included cash, overseas trips, educational scholarships and medical treatments. The IOC's investigative commission widened its net to include other Olympic Games, such as those held in Nagano, Atlanta and Sydney and found similar instances of unethical dealings by members of bid committees and the IOC. The crucially decisive move that the IOC made during the Salt Lake City crisis was to establish the investigative commission, despite the fact that at the time it might have been interpreted as increasing media and public interest. From the moment allegations were levelled at the successful Salt Lake City bid committee the media was going to pursue the story vigorously. Any attempt to conceal the corruption would have resulted in even more negative publicity. Taking decisive action to expose further corruption seems counter intuitive, but in the long term indicated that the IOC was willing to fix a systemic problem.

In his speech to the 113th session of the IOC, president Jacques Rogge remarked that it was in Salt Lake City that the IOC first learned 'of a profound crisis which nearly destroyed the IOC' and that 'inappropriate structures and human weaknesses on both sides [the IOC and the bid committee] were the roots of [the] evil'. Rogge also noted in his speech that the IOC had reacted decisively to punish its members, set up a commission to investigate, altered its processes and reformed its structure to improve its transparency and democracy. The process by which a city can bid to host the Olympic Games is now totally different to the one that allowed Salt Lake City to win the rights.

Payne suggests that the Salt Lake City crisis was a clear breach of public trust, but that the positive side of the crisis was that it illustrated how much both the media and the general public cared about the Olympics and its values. Thus, in Payne's view the crisis and the institutional reform that followed might have clarified the meaning of the Olympics and 'unleashed the power of the Olympic brand' (Payne, 2005). In this respect it might be said that the IOC, although besieged by the world's media at the time, benefited from the crisis because it resulted in improved institutional processes and eradicated corrupt practices and people. It also strengthened the resolve of the organization to adhere to the fundamental principles within its own charter, which states that 'Olympism seeks to create a way of life based on the joy found in effort, the educational value of good example and respect for universal fundamental ethical principles'.

Sources: www.olympic.org; Payne (2005); www.bbc.co.uk; www.cnn.com

Phase 5: learning

A crisis is often a crucial moment in the development and evolution of an organization. As such, crisis can be used as an analytical category, a unique opportunity for making a diagnosis. In other words, a crisis can be conceptualized as an ideal moment to understand the system as a whole, rather than see it as an isolated event that has occurred outside the boundaries of the organization or system (Morin, 1976). Using the crisis to understand the organization as a whole enables the crisis to be used as a catalyst for improvement. As Augustine (1995:4) noted, 'almost every crisis contains within itself the seeds of success as well as the roots of failure'. Effective crisis and scandal media management is a process whereby a sport organization is able to demonstrate publicly that it is able to rehabilitate or sever the damaged and rotten roots, propagate the seeds and foster new growth. The five phases of crisis management are part of a loop, as illustrated in Figure 12.2, whereby the learning that occurs during a crisis event can be used to aid detection and improve prevention and preparation. For some sport organizations the phases of crisis management may begin with a crisis, which then leads to a broader evaluation of the organization's susceptibility and preparedness.

Summary

This chapter has demonstrated that crises and scandals are events and incidents that sport organizations must be prepared for. Furthermore, it has highlighted that crisis and scandal media management must be an essential part of an organization's long-term media planning, as well as its short-term media strategy. In other words, crisis and scandal media management is being prepared for something that may never happen, as well as responding decisively and effectively to something that has happened. How an organization prepares, responds and learns from crises and scandals is equally important. Without planning an organization leaves itself open to crisis events and scandals being controlled entirely by the media. With sound media management practices in place an organization can reasonably hope to achieve some degree of control and have its side of the story told through the media, which will in turn limit the damage to the organization. Review questions and exercises are listed below to assist with confirming your knowledge of the core concepts and principles introduced in this chapter.

Review questions and exercises

1. What is a crisis?
2. What is a scandal?
3. Why is crisis and scandal media management more important for sport organizations than most non-sport organizations?
4. What is the difference between sporadic and systemic crises?
5. What are the five phases of crisis management and in which phase is media management likely to occur?
6. Which phase of the crisis management process is the most important for sport organizations with limited resources (human or financial)?
7. Conduct some preliminary research on a professional sport organization and then prepare a list of crises and scandals to which the organization is susceptible.

8. Which of the crises and scandals you have identified is likely to be reported in the media? Which will have the biggest impact given the history of the organization?
9. Choose one of the crises or scandals you have identified and write a media release that communicates essential information to the media.
10. What can a sport organization learn by going through a crisis or scandal?

Sport Media Futures

13 Sport media futures: a brave new world?

Overview

This chapter examines possible sport media futures within the context of the sport media nexus presented in the previous 12 chapters. These possible futures are contextualized by reference to the key sport media nexus drivers identified at the beginning of the book: technology; commercialization; convergence; and globalization. The purpose of this chapter is to identify a range of likely developments in the sport media nexus and assess what skills and knowledge a sport media manager might require in these new environments.

After completing this chapter the reader should be able to:

- Identify possible sport media futures.
- Generalize about possible futures by referring to the key drivers of technology, commercialization, convergence and globalization.
- Reflect on the content of the previous 12 chapters in order to assess what skills and knowledge will be required in order to operate in possible sport media futures.

Introduction

Where to now? This question is both perennial and inevitable. The rapid developments in the sport media nexus and its increasing commercialization and globalization mean that it is natural and legitimate to wonder what the future might hold. In sport this future gazing is usually prompted by a desire to obtain a competitive advantage or chart a course of action to remedy inequality or disadvantage. If this chapter helps in achieving these ends then it will be a bonus, for its goals are more pragmatic. First, this chapter aims to stimulate reflection about the content of the previous 12 chapters by engaging in the challenge of creating possible sport media futures. Second, this chapter aims, through this reflection, to force an assessment of what skills and knowledge will be required to operate as a professional in these possible futures. Hence, this chapter examines possible sport media futures by referring to the key drivers of the sport media nexus, as well as specific themes such as ownership, broadcast rights and sport celebrity.

Nexus drivers

In order to contextualize the sport media nexus, the first chapter identified four key drivers: technology; commercialization; convergence; and globalization. It is likely that they will also drive possible sport media futures. The extent to which one theme or driver is dominant will determine whether these futures are brave new worlds, or exaggerated versions of the one discussed throughout this book.

Technology

The evolution of the sport media nexus has demonstrated the power and influence of technology development and change. The introduction and diffusion of television altered the relationship of sport and its consumers, which in turn was altered by the introduction of pay television, the Internet, mobile communications and digital television. The latter three media forms, however, are yet to mature and deliver sport media at anywhere near their capacity. As a converged medium, the Internet has the capacity to bundle multiple media together in combinations to suit consumers, while mobile technologies have the potential to detach sport media consumption from the home, the traditional site of sport media. Digital television meanwhile, threatens to change the ways in which people consume television and associated products and services. The impact of the Internet and digital television in possible sport media futures will be discussed in more detail in the following sections.

Commercialization

As demonstrated throughout the previous chapters, the sport media nexus is highly commercialized. Broadcast rights and associated sponsorships now provide a majority of total revenue for many major sport organizations. Sport and the media are engaged in a co-dependent relationship, in which the media supports the infrastructure of professional sport: players; coaches; trainers; administrative staff; facilities; equipment; events; and travel. As illustrated in Chapters 3–5, the commercial dimensions of the sport media nexus are a complex web of activities that involve major corporations, governments, world events and thousands of millions of dollars. Sport media futures will necessarily be predicated on how and how much sport and the media will invest in the nexus, but perhaps more importantly, how they will seek to achieve a return on their investment. In this respect new technologies will be a key driver of change.

Convergence

As discussed earlier in Chapter 1, convergence refers to four distinct trends in the media and sport industries. First, the merging of previously separate technologies; second, increasing cross media ownership; third, national and global domination of media conglomerates and a subsequent lack of media diversity; and fourth, the ownership of content (sport) and distribution (media) by one entity. It is likely that each of these forms of convergence will influence possible sport media futures, as they have influenced the past and the present. Technological convergence through the Internet and digital television and ownership within the sport media nexus both have the potential to create the brave new world referred to in the title of this chapter.

Globalization

The sport media nexus is more than 200 years old, yet it only began to develop rapidly and then mature throughout the last quarter of the twentieth century and the early part of the twenty-first. In this context it is difficult to predict possible sport media futures, because in relative terms it is such a recent phenomenon. Furthermore, this maturity and development has generally been isolated to the western developed world. It has been particularly evident in North America and Europe, where consumer cultures and comparatively high levels of disposal income have resulted in the sport media nexus becoming more intense and complex. As discussed in Chapter 2, the sport media nexus is in its infancy in many parts of the world and for a significant proportion of the world's population is represented by the mediation of the Olympic Games and the World Cup, if at all. For much of the developing world in Africa, China, India, South America and the Middle East, the power and value of sport media is an emerging concept.

The dichotomy of the developed and developing world has important implications for possible sport media futures. First, the starting point for possible sport media futures in the developed world is advanced relative to the rest of the world. Thus, some sport media futures might be brave new worlds for only a minority of the world's population, however important they might appear. Second, sport media futures in the developing world might consist of elements that have already occurred in the developed world. In this respect, radical sport media futures might not be as relevant as modest futures that reconceptualize previous developments in the nexus within different geographic and cultural contexts. Third and finally, possible sport media futures in the developed world will influence the developing world, as sport and media organizations seek to explore and exploit as yet untapped markets. The growth in the Chinese and Indian economies in particular makes it difficult to predict how fast change might occur.

Themed futures

The previous chapters in this book examined a number of aspects and features of the sport media nexus, each of which influence possible media futures. The following sections explore how these futures might be constituted.

Ownership, rights and regulations

Although the media and sport industries have both toyed with the idea of vertical integration, the ownership of sport and the media is an issue that will have a significant influence on possible futures. Indeed, it is so important that it has the capacity to create a brave new world of sport media.

Major media organizations have purchased and continue to purchase professional sport teams in an attempt to align the content and means of distribution, a concept that was at the core of BSkyB's attempted takeover of Manchester United in the late 1990s, World Series Cricket in the 1970s and rugby's Super League in the mid 1990s. The cost of acquiring broadcast rights to some of the world's premium sport properties is so high that purchasing sport teams and leagues may become a better long-term financial option for large media organizations. In many respects, this type of development would be a logical extension, given the substantial investment media organizations have made in various sport leagues and teams and the ways in which sport has modified its practices and traditions to suit the needs of media, sponsors and advertisers. Other types of media content, such as television drama, filmed drama, television news, current affairs or reality television are able to be produced and owned by the media organization or one of its affiliates. By contrast, sport has in general been a unique product that media organizations have had to pay an external organization for the rights to. Owning the content would streamline the production and distribution of sport media for media organizations.

In this future sport media scenario the role of sport managers and sport media managers would be subsumed within the broader management functions of the media organization. It is possible that many of the skills examined within this book would be far less relevant, as the media organization would simply filter the news of the sport organization through its various media outlets in television, radio, print media and the Internet. Furthermore, in this sport media future, media organizations would control access to its products to ensure exclusivity. If a consumer wanted information about a series of games played in the league, they would have no option but to watch the approved television news programme or buy the approved daily newspaper. In this future scenario it is clear that aligning the content with the means of distribution would increase consumer loyalty, however, it is also likely that the cost of accessing sport media would also rise.

As illustrated in the examination of the regulations that govern sport broadcasting and ownership in Chapter 5, it is likely that this future scenario would limit competition between media organizations and might not be in the interests of consumers. Current sport broadcasting regulations are strong in many countries because of the rationale that sport occupies a special place in our individual and collective cultural, social and national identities. It remains to be seen, however, whether the increasing commercialization of sport will erode the legitimacy of the argument that it should be treated differently. In other words, as broadcast rights fees, sponsorship revenue, player salaries and advertising revenue continue to rise, it may become increasingly difficult to view sport as anything other than a commercial product that should be regulated by the free market. The counter argument is that governments regulate the buying and selling of a range of non-sport commercial products. But, the growing cultural and political influence of sport organizations such as FIFA and the IOC might be sufficient to convince governments in the future to let sport organizations determine what is their best interests, as well as their consumers.

Media owned sport is a possible scenario that would alter the landscape considerably, but the lack of sufficient capital to make widespread purchases suggests that it might not constitute a brave new world, at least not in the foreseeable future. On the other hand, sport owned media has the capacity to create a paradigm shift, in which current practices and beliefs are irrevocably altered. This media future is dependent on technology development and sport organizations increasing their commercial and managerial sophistication. Sport owned media requires sport organizations to abandon the view that they organize live games and events, which are then sold to media organizations in favour of one in which they provide consumers with direct access to sport.

In the United States of America the National Football League (NFL) has its own television station to provide consumers with football content, as does Manchester United in the English Premier League, so in the future it is conceivable that sport organizations could own and operate their own media. However, the costs involved with establishing a television network or vertically integrated media organization are such that only the biggest sport organizations in the world could consider this option. More likely is that sport organizations will begin to utilize a media form that many of them already own and operate, which does not have significant infrastructure costs that are typical of traditional media: the Internet. As previously noted, most of the world's sport organizations have a website that consumers can access. For small non-profit community-based sport organizations, a website might simply act as a way of communicating with its members, whereas the website of a large professional sport organization may feature game highlights, web casts, interviews and interactive games.

Sport organization websites have the capacity to be interactive multi-media portals that service all the sport media needs of consumers. Through the websites of the future, consumers will be able to: watch live games; listen to audio commentary; print news on demand; download pod casts of interviews and analysis; bet on the results of games, goals, penalty kicks, conversions and foul shots; communicate with friends individually or in virtual communities; play interactive and fantasy games; buy tickets to matches and events; watch day, month and year old games on demand; and buy merchandise, not to mention access and purchase the products and services of sponsors and advertisers. In fact, many of these things are already possible, but quality and speed is limited largely by technology. When these technical barriers have dissipated, sport organizations will have the capacity to create their own radically different sport media landscapes.

In the current sport media nexus, large sport organizations obtain a significant proportion of their revenue through selling the broadcast rights to their games and events. In a sport media future in which these organizations owned and operated interactive multi-media portals, revenue would be generated through the sale of games, as well as the sale of advertising and sponsorship. The advantage media organizations have in the contemporary sport media nexus is that they are able to use sport programming to attract viewers to additional non-sport related content, thereby generating further advertising revenues. This suggests that sport owned and operated media would result in an overall decrease in revenue because sport organizations in the current context have limited capacity to sell additional products. However, the interactivity of the Internet may provide sport organizations with a significant advantage. Specifically, advertisers and sponsors might be willing to pay more for the opportunity to engage directly with potential consumers. In other words, the advertising revenue might increase as sport organizations move the consumer closer to the point of sale.

Figure 13.1 is a graphic representation of the possible sport media future in which sport organizations act as broadcasters through their websites. Unlike the figure presented earlier in Chapter 4 of this book, this figure does not include sport broadcasters that enter into exclusive contractual agreements with sport organizations for the rights to broadcast matches, games or events. In Figure 13.1 the sport organization is the broadcaster and derives revenue from selling its content to consumers, selling advertising space and time or selling sponsorships. As in Figure 4.1 presented earlier, in Figure 13.1 the sport organization still provides sport content to other media providers in the form of news, which further stimulates interest in the sport. In the future represented by Figure 13.1, the ability of sport organizations to secure revenue would be based on the audiences they could generate directly, rather than the audiences generated by a media organization.

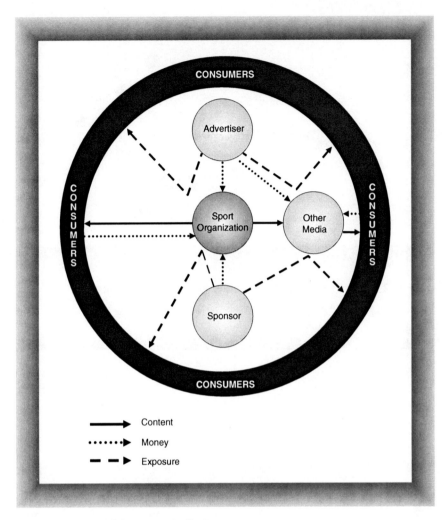

Figure 13.1 A Possible Sport Media Future

This sport media future necessarily implies that major sport organizations will grow in size and complexity, as they assume some of the roles and responsibilities previously undertaken by the broadcast partner. At a base level the responsibility for telecasting games, matches and events will be assumed by the sport organization, which will necessitate establishing additional infrastructure. Sport organizations will also need to develop additional capacities and knowledge to support activities such as sport gambling. As in the current broadcasting context, sport organizations will be subject to regulatory mechanisms in the conduct of these activities, but the ability of consumers to bet on sport action as it occurs has the potential to vastly increase revenues.

The potential challenges for sport organizations in this new sport media future are in part graphically represented in Figures 13.2 and 13.3. Figure 13.2 illustrates the current situation where the sport organization's relationship

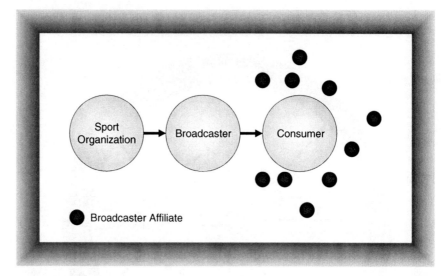

Figure 13.2 Sport Organization–Consumer Relationship (Moderated)

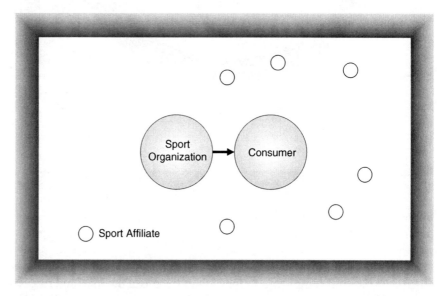

Figure 13.3 Sport Organization–Consumer Relationship (Mediated)

with consumers is often moderated by the broadcaster. Furthermore, the advantage the broadcaster has, particularly within organizations such as News Corporation, is that a significant number of affiliates are clustered around the consumer (as discussed in Chapter 3), creating interest in its media and sport media products. Figure 13.3 demonstrates that a sport organization's relationship with its consumers in which it provides the mediation is more direct, but the sport organization does not have the advantage of well defined and clustered affiliates. In Figure 13.3 the sport organization's affiliates are primarily media companies that provide coverage for their own financial gain. In this case the sport organization is not able to utilize the networks of a larger commercial organization. However, these limitations may only be evident in the contemporary sport media nexus and sport organizations that broadcast their own games, matches and events might stimulate interest in their product through affiliates that have commercial ties, such as sponsors and advertisers. Importantly, the transition from Figures 13.2 and 13.3 would not occur instantly, but would potentially evolve over one or two decades, which would give consumers time to adjust their sport media rituals and habits.

It is possible that in order to realize a sport owned media future, sport organizations might establish strategic partnerships outside the traditional major media players. For example, Google, the widely used search engine, was rated in 2006 as the largest media organization in the world based on estimated total worth of US $80,000 million, despite having annual sales of less than a tenth of Time Warner AOL. Non-traditional partnerships in which technology, software or Internet companies provide sport organizations with the technical capacity to create a new model of sport 'broadcasting' might well result in a brave new world.

New media

The possible sport media future in which sport organizations might control their own commercial destiny through the Internet relies on leagues and clubs developing the capacity and mindset to break away from current sport broadcasting models. There are significant barriers to this occurring. Many of the major media organizations presented in Chapter 3 have diverse and integrated media interests, of which the Internet is one component. Media organizations are increasingly investing in new technologies and exploring ways to generate profit from them. In this context media organizations might continue to purchase the rights to sport events, but use the Internet more often in the delivery of the mediated product. Many large organizations already sell the rights to their website to media or telecommunications companies, so this might also be regarded as a natural progression in which rights holders spread the sport product over more media forms and outlets.

Another significant barrier to the brave new world of sport owned media is the brave new world of digital television. Many of the features described above are increasingly available through this media form and are being exploited by media organizations. For example, like the Internet digital television also has the capacity to move the consumer closer to the point of sale than traditional analogue television. As Griffiths (2003:14) has noted, 'everything needed to make a purchase can be packaged together in the remote programme control', as a digital system 'can monitor who you are, check your credit card limit and allow you to buy'. However, the ability of viewers to watch television programmes whenever they choose to also means they have the capacity to avoid advertising, which partially negates some of its advantages. In this respect sport is likely to become an even more valuable property for media organizations, because more than any other form of content, sport is most valuable when it is live.

Global players and niche markets

There is very little evidence in the history of the sport media nexus to indicate that anything other than the major sport players will continue to dominate world sport and its mediation. Events such as the Olympic Games and the FIFA World Cup demonstrate the appeal of global events that unite people, albeit within the context of nationalistic competition. In this respect, football has a massive advantage over its competitors. Several factors discussed throughout this book lead to the conclusion that a selected number of global sports will dominate the future of sport media, while a range of lesser sports will occupy niche markets.

First, global media players require access to mass markets and mass audiences, in order to capitalize on their sport investments. Second, investing in too many premium sport properties reduces economies of scale within the media, thus reducing their profit margins. In other words, it is far easier to concentrate resources on one or two products, rather than 20. Third, sport media is produced within institutionalized routines that favour sport organizations that can provide the most efficient and convenient access to information, resources and personnel. This provides elite professional sport organizations with a considerable advantage, which is likely to continue to increase. Fourth and finally, minor sport organizations are increasingly able to capture niche markets that cross national boundaries. As highlighted in previous chapters, the web casts of the world surfing tour through the websites of sponsors are indicative of the possibilities of new technologies, but also of the value of highly committed fans and consumers.

Positive or negative coverage?

The chapters in this book that dealt with sport media production and crisis management presented different views of the sport media nexus and the role of the media in reporting the activities of sport organizations and athletes. On the one hand, media and sport organizations are engaged in a complicit, mutually dependent commercial relationship. In essence, a commercial symbiosis lies at the very core of the relationship that the two industries enjoy. On the other hand, the reporting of crisis and scandals demonstrates that a good (or bad) media story can fracture the relationship.

The question is which one of these scenarios will become more or less prevalent in the future? Will the commercial nexus deepen, or will the media and audience's need for sensationalism drive a wedge between sport and the media. These are difficult questions to answer because there are competing forces at work. The increasing value of premium sport rights means that the big media players will be increasingly disinclined to present sport in a negative light. Achieving a return on investment will be predicated on attracting the largest mass audience possible, which will be influenced by the actions and activities of teams and players. These media organizations are likely to ignore crises and scandals and place increasing pressure on sport organizations to adopt and enforce stricter behaviour clauses in collective bargaining agreements. The subsequent losses in personal freedom will invariably be offset by increases in salary as a result of increases in broadcast rights. In other words, through the value of their investment, media organizations will exert greater control over teams and athletes. Furthermore, the segmentation of these rights, such as in the case of the NFL or NASCAR in America, will mean that sometimes two or more of the major media players will have an interest in positive news, creating even more silence and pressure on sport organizations and their athletes.

The counter argument is that media outside exclusive broadcast rights agreements will not be bound by the same commercial code. In fact, for media outlets such as tabloid newspapers, the value of broadcast rights and premium sport properties in general will mean that crises and scandals have even greater cultural currency. In the future, media outlets that are not part of exclusive agreements may actively undermine the investments of rival organizations by emphasizing bad news, thereby increasing their own market share and profitability. However, if media diversity continues to decrease with the growth of companies such as News Corporation, very few media outlets will exist outside the reach and influence of the major media players profiled in Chapter 3. In this scenario, the major media players will control almost all media outlets except for a few rouge organizations that operate on the margins of the sport media nexus.

Sport celebrity

Mass markets have driven the sport media nexus since the establishment of the modern mass circulation newspaper at the end of the nineteenth century. Global events such as the Olympic Games and the FIFA World Cup are valuable media properties because of the depth and breadth of the audiences that access media coverage. Similarly, the most valuable sport media performers are those that are able to transcend national and cultural boundaries. In the future it is likely that media organizations will use sport celebrity to create and then exploit new markets.

The value of sport broadcasting rights, the vertical integration of global media organizations and the commercial interdependence of sport and the media creates the necessary climate for the construction of new sport stars to ensure a return on investment. The case of Chinese basketball player Yao Ming has demonstrated the power of sport celebrity in opening new markets, as has the rise of Indian Formula One racing driver Narain Karthikeyan. In this sport media future, sport and media organizations might conspire to use more players from Asia and the Middle East. In turn, these athletes might have compelling narratives created to ensure audience interest. These athletes might not be as successful on the field of play, but they would be more than make up for it through broadcast and associated marketing revenue.

209

Summary

This chapter has explored sport media futures based on the sport media nexus examined throughout the preceding chapters. In particular, technological developments, sport and media ownership, broadcast rights and regulation and sport media production have been discussed. Review questions and exercises are listed below to assist with confirming your knowledge of the core concepts and principles introduced in this chapter.

Review questions and exercises

1. What will be the most important driver of change in the future of sport media? Why?
2. What will be the least important driver of change in the future of sport media? Why?
3. Who will own sport media in the future?
4. What will the sport media nexus look like in 2015, 2030, 2050?
5. What are the implications for sport media management in the possible futures examined in this chapter and in the answers to question 4? What are the skills that will be required by sport media managers in these futures? Are they different or similar to those discussed throughout the book?

References

American Project for Excellence in Journalism (APEJ) (2006) www.journalism.org.

Andrews, D. & Jackson, S. (2001) Introduction: Sport Celebrities, Public Culture and Private Experience. In *Sport Stars: The Cultural Politics of Sporting Celebrity* (Andrews, D. & Jackson, S., eds). London: Routledge.

Augustine, N. (1995) Managing the Crisis You Tried to Prevent. In *Harvard Business Review on Crisis Management*. Boston, MA: Harvard Business School Press.

Australian Broadcasting Authority (2001) *Investigation into Events on the Anti-Siphoning List*. Sydney: Australian Broadcasting Authority.

Barnett, S. (1990) *Games and Sets: The Changing Face of Sport on Television*. London: BFI Publishing.

Barnett, S. (1995) Sport. In *Television: An International History* (Smith, A., ed.). Oxford: Oxford University Press.

Barrett, D. (2005) Cash the Key to Broadcast Rights. *Foxsports*, December 30.

Barthes, R. (1977) *Image Music Text* [translated by Stephen Heath]. London: Fontana Press.

Becker, K. (1992) Photojournalism and the Tabloid Press. In *Journalism and Popular Culture* (Dahlgren, P. & Sparks, C., eds). London: Sage.

Bell, A. (1991) *The Language of News Media*. Oxford: Blackwell.

Bertelsmann (2004) Annual Report.

Bignell, J. (1997) *Media Semiotics: An Introduction*. Manchester: Manchester University Press.

Billings, A. & Eastman, S. (2003) Framing Identities: Gender, Ethnic, and National Parity in Network Announcing of the 2002 Winter Olympics. *Journal of Communication*, **53** (4), 569–586.

Bishop, R. (2003) Missing in Action: Feature Coverage of Women's Sports in *Sports Illustrated*. *Journal of Sport and Social Issues*, **27** (2), 184–194.

Bivins, T. (1995) *Handbook for Public Relations Writing*. Illinois: NTC Business Books.

Blain, N., Boyle, R. & O'Donnell, H. (1993) *Sport and National Identity in the European Media*. Leicester: Leicester University Press.

Boyd, T. (1997) Anatomy of a Murder: O.J. and the Imperative of Sports in Cultural Studies. In *Out of Bounds: Sports, Media and the Politics of Identity* (Baker, A. & Boyd, T., eds). Bloomington, IN: Indiana University Press.

Boyle, R. & Haynes, R. (2000) *Power Play: Sport, the Media and Popular Culture*. Sydney: Longman.

Briggs, A. & Burke, P. (2005) *A Social History of the Media: From Gutenberg to the Internet*. Cambridge: Polity.

Brown, A. (2003). Scandal 'Hurting the Game'. *Sydney Morning Herald*, August 13.

Cave, M. & Crandall, R. (2001) Sports Rights and the Broadcast Industry. *The Economic Journal*, **111**, F4–F26.

Chandler, J. (1988) *Television and National Sport: The United States and Britain*. Urbana, IL: University of Illinois Press.

Clayton, B. & Harris, J. (2004) Footballers' Wives: The Role of the Soccer Player's Partner in the Construction of Idealized Masculinity. *Soccer and Society*, **5** (3), 317–335.

Coakley, J. (2003) *Sports in Society: Issues and Controversies*. Maidenhead: McGraw-Hill Education.

Cole, C. & Andrews, D. (2001) America's New Son: Tiger Woods and America's Multiculturalism. In *Sport Stars: The Cultural Politics of Sporting Celebrity* (Andrews, D. & Jackson, S., eds). London: Routledge.

Comcast (2004) Annual Report.

Competition Commission (1999) *British Sky Broadcasting Group Plc and Manchester United Plc: A Report on the Proposed Merger*.

Consoli, J. (2005) XM Scores Exclusive NHL Deal. *Mediaweek*, September 12.

Cooke, A. (1994) *The Economics of Leisure and Sport*. London: Routledge.

Cowie, C. & Williams, M. (1997) The Economics of Sports Rights. *Telecommunications Policy*, **21** (7), 619–634.

Cricket Australia (2005) From Backyard to Baggy Green 2005–2009 [Strategic Plan].

Dahlgren, P. (1992) Introduction. In *Journalism and Popular Culture* (Dahlgren, P. & Sparks, C., eds). London: Sage.

Davis, L. & Harris, O. (1998) Race and Ethnicity in US Sports Media. In *MediaSport* (Wenner, L., ed.). London: Routledge.

Denton, P. (2000) *How to Write and Pitch Your Press Release*. New South Wales: Prentice Hall.

Duncan, M. & Messner, M. (1998) The Media Image of Sport and Gender. In *MediaSport* (Wenner, L., ed.). London: Routledge.

Duncan, M. & Messner, M. (2005) *Gender in Televised Sports News and Highlight Programs, 1989–2004*. Los Angeles, CA: Amateur Athletic Foundation of Los Angeles.

Eco, U. (1986) Sports Chatter. In *Faith in Fakes: Essays* (Eco, U., translated from the Italian by Weaver, W.). London: Secker and Warburg.

Ericson, R., Baranek, P. & Chan, J. (1991) *Representing Order: Crime, Law, and Justice in the News Media*. Toronto, Ont.: University of Toronto Press.

Fallin, S. (2005) The Five Most Common Mistakes in Crisis Planning – and How to Avoid Them. *Tactics*, February, 11–12.

Ferguson, A. (1999) Sport: The New Media Power. *Business Review Weekly*, July 23.

FIFA (2004) Annual Financial Report.

FIFA (2006) www.fifa.com.

Fortunato, J. (2000) Public Relations Strategies for Creating Mass Media Content: A Case Study of the National Basketball Association. *Public Relations Review*, **26** (4), 481–497.

Foster, G., Greyser, S. & Walsh, B. (2006) *The Business of Sports: Text and Cases on Strategy and Management*. London: Thomson South-Western.

Future Systems (2001) *Unique Building: Lord's Media Centre*. London: Wiley-Academy.

Galloway, C. & Kwansah-Aidoo, K. (2005) Getting to Grips with Issues Management and Crisis Communication. In *Public Relations Issues and Crisis Management* (Galloway, C. & Kwansah-Aidoo, K., eds). Melbourne: Thomson Social Science Press.

Galtung, J. & Ruge, M. (1988) Structuring and Selecting News. In *The Manufacture of News: Social Problems, Deviance and the Mass Media* (Cohen, S. & Young, J., eds). London: Constable [revised edition].

Gans, H. (1980) *Deciding What's News: A Study of CBS Evening News, NBC Nightly News, Newsweek, and Time*. New York: Vintage Books.

Gardiner, S. & Gibson, A. (2004) Sport Scandals and Sponsorship. *Sport Business International*, July 1.

Garrison, B. & Salwen, M. (1989) Newspaper Sports Journalists: A Profile of the 'Profession'. *Journal of Sport and Social Issues*, **13** (2), 57–68.

General Electric (2004) Annual Report.

Gitlin, T. (1980) *The Whole World is Watching: Mass Media in the Making and Unmaking of the New Left*. Berkeley, CA: University of California Press.

Goodbody, J. (2006) Nothing Odd About Drop in Viewing Figures. *The Times*, January 2.

Gough, P. (2005) NASCAR's Motor Running. *Hollywood Reporter*, December 8.

Griffiths, A. (2003) *Digital Television Strategies*. New York: Palgrave Macmillan.

Grigg, A. (2006) Seven Wins AFL with $780 m bid. *Australian Financial Review*, January 6.

Gripsrud, J. (1992) The Aesthetics and Politics of Melodrama. In *Journalism and Popular Culture* (Dahlgren, P. & Sparks, C., eds). London: Sage.

Gupta, R. (2005) It's Not Just Cricket. *Sport Business International*, April 1.

Guttmann, A. (1978) *From Ritual to Record: The Nature of Modern Sport*. New York: Columbia University Press.

Hall, S. (1973) The Determinations of News Photographs. In *The Manufacture of News: Social Problems, Deviance and the Mass Media* (Cohen, S. & Young, J., eds). London: Constable.

Hall, S., Critcher, C., Jefferson, T., Clarke, J. & Roberts, B. (1978) *Policing the Crisis: Mugging, the State, and Law and Order*. London: The Macmillan Press.

Hardin, M. (2005) Survey Finds Boosterism, Freebies Remain Problem for Newspaper Sports Department. *Newspaper Research Journal*, **26** (1), 66–72.

Hartley, J. (1982) *Understanding News*. London: Routledge.

Harvey, A. (2004) *The Beginnings of a Commercial Sporting Culture in Britain, 1793–1850*. Aldershot, England: Ashgate.

Helitzer, M. (1999) *The Dream Job: Sports Publicity, Promotion and Marketing*. Ohio: University Sports Press.

Henningham, J. (1995) A Profile of Australian Sports Journalists. *The ACHPER Healthy Lifestyles Journal*, Spring, 13–17.

Herbert, J. (2000) *Journalism in the Digital Age: Theory and Practice for Broadcast, Print and On-Line Media*. Oxford: Focal Press.

Higgins, J. (2005) TV Touch Down: Can Networks Make Money on Record NFL Deal? *Broadcasting and Cable*, April 25.

Hinerman, S. (1997). (Don't) Leave Me Alone: Tabloid Narrative and the Michael Jackson Child-Abuse Scandal. In *Media Scandals* (Lull, J. & Hinerman, S., eds). New York: Columbia University Press.

Hoehn, T. & Lancefield, D. (2003) Broadcasting and Sport. *Oxford Review of Economic Policy*, **19** (4), 552–568.

Hoye, R., Smith, A., Westerbeek, H., Stewart, B. & Nicholson, M. (2006) *Sport Management: Principles and Application*. London: Elsevier Butterworth-Heinemann.

Hughes, H. (1981) *News and the Human Interest Story*. London: Transaction Books [reprint of the 1940 University of Chicago Press edition].

Hunter, P. (2005) NASCAR Popularity Running in High Gear. *The Toronto Star*, February 20.

Jhally, S. (1984) The Spectacle of Accumulation: Material and Cultural Factors in the Evolution of the Sports/Media Complex. *Insurgent Sociologist*, **12** (3), 41–57.

Jhally, S. (1989) Cultural Studies and the Sports/Media Complex. In *Media, Sports, and Society* (Wenner, L., ed.). London: Sage.

Johnston, J. (2004) Media Relations. In *Public Relations: Theory and Practice* (Johnston, J. & Zawawi, C., eds). Crows Nest, NSW: Allen & Unwin.

Keane, J. (1984) *Public Life and Late Capitalism: Toward a Socialist Theory of Democracy*. Cambridge: Cambridge University Press.

Kinkema, K. & Harris, J. (1998) MediaSport Studies: Key Research and Emerging Issues. In *MediaSport* (Wenner, L., ed.). London: Routledge.

Klatell, D. & Marcus, N. (1988) *Sports for Sale: Television, Money and the Fans*. Oxford: Oxford University Press.

Knight, G. (1989) The Reality Effects of Tabloid Television News. In *Communication for and Against Democracy* (Raboy, M. & Bruck, P., eds). Montreal, Que.: Black Rose Books.

Koppett, L. (1981) *Sports Illusion, Sports Reality: A Reporter's View of Sports, Journalism and Society*. Boston: Houghton Mifflin Company.

Law, A., Harvey, J. & Kemp, S. (2002) The Global Sport Mass Media Oligopoly. *International Review for the Sociology of Sport*, **37** (3–4), 279–302.

Lowes, M. (1997) Sports Page: A Case Study in the Manufacture of Sports News for the Daily Press. *Sociology of Sport Journal*, **14** (2), 143–159.

Lowes, M. (1999) *Inside the Sports Pages: Work Routines, Professional Ideologies, and the Manufacture of Sports News*. Toronto, Ont.: University of Toronto Press.

Lull, J. & Hinerman, S. (1997) The Search for Scandal. In *Media Scandals* (Lull, J. & Hinerman, S., eds). New York: Columbia University Press.

Mackey, S. (2004) Crisis and Issues Management. In *Public Relations: Theory and Practice* (Johnston, J. & Zawawi, C., eds). Crows Nest, NSW: Allen & Unwin.

Magnay, J. (2004) Rugby Rocked by Fresh Rape Claims. *Age*, February 29.

Maguire, J. (1993) Globalization, Sport Development, and the Media/Sport Production Complex. *Sport Science Review*, **2** (1), 29–47.

Maguire, J. (1999) The Global Media–Sport Complex. In *Global Sport: Identities, Societies, Civilizations* (Maguire, J., ed.). Malden, MA: Polity Press.

Maguire, J., Pulton, E. & Possamai, C. (1999) Weltkrieg III? Media Coverage of England Versus Germany in Euro 96. *Journal of Sport and Social Issues*, **23** (4), 439–454.

Manoff, R. (1986) Writing the News (by Telling the 'Story'). In *Reading the News* (Manoff, R. & Schudson, M., eds). New York: Pantheon Books.

Massey, J. (2001) Managing Organizational Legitimacy: Communication Strategies for Organizations in Crisis. *Journal of Business Communication*, **38** (2), 153–183.

McChesney, R. (1989) Media Made Sport: A History of Sports Coverage in the United States. In *Media, Sports and Society* (Wenner, L., ed.). Newbury Park, CA: Sage.

McCoy, J. (1997) Radio Sports Broadcasting in the United States, Britain and Australia, 1920–1956 and Its Influence on the Olympic Games. *Journal of Olympic History*, Spring, 20–25.

McDonald, M. & Andrews, D. (2001) Michael Jordan: Corporate Sport and Postmodern Celebrityhood. In *Sport Stars: The Cultural Politics of Sporting Celebrity* (Andrews, D. & Jackson, S., eds). London: Routledge.

McKay, J. & Rowe, D. (1987) Ideology, the Media, and Australian Sport. *Sociology of Sport Journal*, **4**, 258–273.

McKay, J., Hutchins, B. & Mikosza, J. (2000) 'Shame and Scandal in the Family': Australian Media Narratives of the IOC/SOCOG Scandal Matrix. *Fifth International Symposium for Olympic Research*.

Messner, M. & Montez de Oca, J. (2005) The Male Consumer as Loser: Beer and Liquor Ads in Mega Sports Media Events. *Signs: Journal of Women and Culture in Society*, **30** (3), 1879–1909.

Messner, M., Duncan, M. & Cooky, C. (2003) Silence, Sports Bras and Wrestling Porn: Women in Televised Sports News and Highlight Shows. *Journal of Sport and Social Issues*, **27** (1), 38–51.

Michael, E. (2006) *Public Policy: The Competitive Framework*. South Melbourne, Vic.: Oxford University Press.

Morin, E. (1976) Pour une crisologie. *Communications*, **25**, 149–163.

NBA (2006) www.nba.com.

New, B. & Le Grand, J. (1999) Monopoly in Sports Broadcasting. *Policy Studies*, **20** (1), 23–36.

Newhagen, J. & Levy, M. (1998) The Future of Journalism in a Distributed Communication Architecture. In *The Electronic Grapevine: Rumor, Reputation,* and *Reporting in the On-Line Environment* (Borden, D. & Harvey, K., eds). Mahwah, NJ: Erlbaum Associates.

News Corporation (1999) Annual Report.

News Corporation (2005) Annual Report.

Offe, C. (1984) 'Crises of Crisis Management': Elements of a Political Crisis Theory. In *Contradictions of the Welfare State* (Keane, J., ed.). Cambridge, MA: MIT Press.

Olympic (2006) www.olympic.org.

Oriard, M. (1993) *Reading Football*. Chapel Hill: University of North Carolina.

Patterson, B. (1993) Crises Impact on Reputation Management. *Public Relations Journal*, November, 47–48.

Payne, M. (2005) As Time Goes By … *Sport Business International*, March 1.

Pearson, C. & Clair, J. (1998) Reframing Crisis Management. *Academy of Management Review*, **23** (1), 59–76.

Pearson, C. & Mitroff, I. (1993) From Crisis Prone to Crisis Prepared: A Framework for Crisis Management. *Academy of Management Executive*, **7** (1), 48–59.

Pearson, C., Clair, J., Misra, S. & Mitroff, I. (1997) Managing the Unthinkable. *Organizational Dynamics*, Autumn, 51–64.

PGA (2006) www.pga.com.

Phillips, M. (1996) *An Illusory Image: A Report on the Media Coverage and Portrayal of Women's Sport in Australia*. Canberra: Australian Sports Commission.

Productivity Commission (2000) *Broadcasting Inquiry Report*. Canberra: Commonwealth of Australia.

Rader, B. (1984) *In Its Own Image: How Television Has Transformed Sports*. New York: Free Press.

Ramsey, R. (2004) Responding to a Crisis. *Supervision*, **65** (10), 6–7.

Real, M. (1975) Super Bowl: Mythic Spectacle. *Journal of Communication*, **25** (1), 31–43.

Real, M. (1998) MediaSport: Technology and the Commodification of Postmodern Sport. In *MediaSport* (Wenner, L., ed.). London: Routledge.

Reynolds, M. (2005) NASCAR TV Deals Done. *Multichannel News*, December 7.

Rovell, D. (2002) Spirit of ABA Deal Lives on for Silna Brothers. *ESPN.com*, January 22.

Rowe, D. (1992) Modes of Sports Writing. In *Journalism and Popular Culture* (Dahlgren, P. & Sparks, C., eds). London: Sage.

Rowe, D. (1999) *Sport, Culture and the Media: The Unruly Trinity*. Buckingham, Philadelphia: Open University Press.

Rowe, D. (2000) Let the Media Games Begin. *Australian Quarterly: Journal of Contemporary Analysis*, June–July, 21–23.

Rowe, D. & Stevenson, D. (1995) Negotiations and Mediations. *Media Information Australia*, **75**, 67–79.

Rumphorst, W. (2001) *Sports Broadcasting Rights and EC Competition Law*. Switzerland: European Broadcasting Union.

Salwen, M. & Garrison, B. (1998) Finding their Place in Journalism: Newspaper Sports Journalists' Professional 'Problems'. *Journal of Sport and Social Issues*, **22** (1), 88–102.

Sandy, R., Sloane, P. & Rosentraub, M. (2004) *The Economics of Sport: An International Perspective*. New York: Palgrave Macmillan.

Schudson, M. (1978) *Discovering the News: A Social History of American Newspapers*. New York: Basic Books.

Schudson, M. (1995) *The Power of News*. Cambridge, MA: Harvard University Press.

Shoemaker, P., Danielian, L. & Brendlinger, N. (1991) Deviant Acts, Risky Business and US Interests: The Newsworthiness of World Events. *Journalism Quarterly*, **68** (4), 781–795.

Sigal, L. (1986) Who? Sources Make the News. In *Reading the News* (Manoff, R. & Schudson, M., eds). New York: Pantheon Books.

Slater, J. (1998) Changing Partners: The Relationship Between the Mass Media and the Olympic Games. *Fourth International Symposium for Olympic Research*.

Smith, D. (2005) A Hit or Miss. *Sport Business International*, February 1.

Spencer, N. (2001) From 'Child's Play' to 'Party Crasher': Venus Williams, Racism and Professional Women's Tennis. In *Sport Stars: The Cultural Politics of Sporting Celebrity* (Andrews, D. & Jackson, S., eds). London: Routledge.

Stapleton, R. (2005) Australian TV Football Rights Battle Royal in Prospect. *Sport Business International*, April 1.

Stephens, M. (2005) *Broadcast News*. Belmont, CA: Wadsworth.

Stephens, K., Malone, P. & Bailey, C. (2005) Communicating with Stakeholders During a Crisis. *Journal of Business Communication*, **42** (4), 390–419.

Stewart, B. (1995) 'I Heard It on the Radio, I Saw It on the Television': The Commercial and Cultural Development of Australian First Class Cricket: 1946–1985. Unpublished Doctoral Thesis, La Trobe University, Melbourne, Australia.

Stewart, B., Nicholson, M., Smith, A. & Westerbeek, H. (2004) *Australian Sport: Better by Design? The Evolution of Australian Sport Policy*. London: Routledge.

Theberge, N. & Cronk, A. (1986) Work Routines in Newspaper Sports Departments and the Coverage of Women's Sports. *Sociology of Sport Journal*, **3**, 195–203.

Time Warner AOL (2004) Annual Report.

Toft, T. (2003) Football: Joint Selling of Media Rights. *European Commission Competition Policy Newsletter*, **3** (Autumn), 47–52.

Tonazzi, A. (2003) Competition Policy and the Commercialization of Sport Broadcasting Rights: The Decision of the Italian Competition Authority. *International Journal of the Economics of Business*, **10** (1), 17–34.

Trujillo, N. & Ekdom, L. (1985) Sportswriting and American Cultural Values: The 1984 Chicago Cubs. *Critical Studies in Mass Communication*, **2**, 262–281.

Tuchman, G. (1978) *Making News: A Study in the Construction of Reality*. New York: The Free Press.

Turner & Cunningham (2002) *The Media and Communications in Australia*. Crows Nest, NSW: Allen & Unwin.

Tymson, C. & Lazar, P. (2002) *The New Australian and New Zealand Public Relations Manual*. Chatswood: Tymson Communications.

UEFA (2006) www.uefa.com.

Verdier, M. (1996) The IOC and the Press. *Olympic Review*, **25** (9), 66–67.

Vivendi Universal (2004) Annual Report.

Walt Disney Company (2005) Annual Report.

Weaver, D. & Wilhoit, C. (1986) *The American Journalist: A Portrait of US Newspeople and Their Work*. Bloomington, IN: Indiana University Press.

Wenner, L. (ed.) (1998) *MediaSport*. London: Routledge.

Wenner, L. (1998) Playing the MediaSport Game. In *MediaSport* (Wenner, L., ed.). London: Routledge.

Wenner, L. (2004) Recovering (From) Janet Jackson's Breast: Ethics and the Nexus of Media, Sports, and Management. *Journal of Sport Management*, **18**, 315–334.

Whannel, G. (1992) *Fields in Vision: Television Sport and Cultural Transformation*. London: Routledge.

Whannel, G. (2000) Sport and the Media. In *Handbook of Sport Studies* (Coakley, J. & Dunning, E., eds). London: Sage.

Whannel, G. (2001) Punishment, Redemption and Celebration in the Popular Press: The Case of David Beckham. In *Sport Stars: The Cultural Politics of Sporting Celebrity* (Andrews, D. & Jackson, S., eds). London: Routledge.

Whannel, G. (2002) *Media Sport Stars: Masculinities and Moralities*. London: Routledge.

White, T. (2005) *Broadcast News Writing, Reporting, and Producing*, 4th edn. London: Elsevier.

Whitson, D. (1998) Circuits of Promotion: Media, Marketing and the Globalization of Sport. In *MediaSport* (Wenner, L., ed.). London: Routledge.

Wilcox, D. & Nolte, L. (1997) *Public Relations Writing and Media Techniques*. New York: Longman.

Wilcox, D., Ault, P., Agee, W. & Cameron, G. (2000) *Public Relations: Strategies and Tactics*. New York: Longman.

Ziffer, D. (2006) Packer at Peace with His Father and Hoping He's Watching as the Tributes Flow. *Age*, February 16.

Index

219

Lightning Source UK Ltd.
Milton Keynes UK
02 November 2010

162300UK00001B/126/P